P9-CLY-714

AFRICAN VISIONARIES

Translated into English by
MARY ESTHER KROPP DAKUBU
&
EVA MARIA ASANTE

Edited by
Agnes Ofosua Vandyck,

Molly Nyagura & Rosemary Brooks

Original German version edited by
M. MOUSTAPHA DIALLO

Sub-Saharan Publishers

First Published in Ghana 2019
by Sub-Saharan Publishers P.O.Box 358
Legon-Accra
Ghana
Email: saharanp@africaonline.com.gh

© of this English edition SUB-SAHARAN PUBLISHERS 2019

ISBN 978-9988-8829-9-0

Copyright Notice
No part of this publication may be reproduced, stored in a retrieval system
or transmitted in any form or by any means electronic, mechanical,
photocopying, recording or otherwise, without the prior written permission
of the publishers.

DEDICATION
To the loving memory of
Emeritta Professor Mary-Esther Kropp-Dakubu

Original German edition;
VISIONÄRE AFRIKAS. DER KONTINEN in ungewöhnlichen Portraits
© Peter Hammer Verlag GmbH, Wuppertal 2014

FROM SUB-SAHARAN PUBLISHERS

We have bought the English language rights to children's books in other languages but never an adult one. The first adult book in German we have had translated was EWE STEIMME by Jocob Spieth; a very serious piece of work and we came out with flying colours; the Goethe Institut and the German Embassy in Accra were delighted with the work and they financially supported it.

The translation of VISIONÄRE AFRIKAS has been quite a challenging experience. Firstly, the original translator, Mary-Esther Kropp-Dakubu, (may she rest in peace), passed away unexpectedly, after translating about half of the work. Getting someone to complete the translation became a headache. Eventually we contacted Eva Maria Asante, a German language teacher at the Goethe Institut to complete the translation.

Then we had to find editors to edit the translation. That too was a drag; in fact we feared Peter Hammer Verlag might even withdraw the rights because it was expected that the English version would come out two years after the purchase of the rights. Well, it has taken four years! Editing diverse papers, originally written in a myriad of languages, but translated into German, and now into English, is no mean task.

Our sincere thanks to Agnes Ofosua Vandyck of Ghana and Molly Nyagura of Zimbabwe, for doing meticulous editing; and to Rosemary Brooks of Oxford, for her help in checking the final proofs. The portraits described in the collection are varied and extremely interesting.

Now the book is available in English and thus to a wider audience.

Akoss Ofori-Mensah
MANAGING DIRECTOR.

FOREWORD

'If the hare only listens to what the hyena is saying, it will never know what the buffalo is really like.'

By means of such proverbs, African people like to underscore the value of a personal narrative or the influence of someone's perspective on the perception of another person. This advice is nowhere else more justified than in the case of Africa. Even today, this continent is seen in Europe from a viewpoint which is very much subject to stereotypes and prejudices. It is reduced to wars, diseases and catastrophes. Even today, in the 21st century, African women and African men only very rarely get the chance to speak in Europe. This book should change this. About forty female and male authors from Africa came together to try and show an authentic picture of their continent, of its diversity and vitality. This can definitely be best achieved by taking a close look at the people. Therefore, every author portrayed a personality from the African past or present, who is important for himself or herself. They are personalities, who are, or were, engaged in shaping their community, their village or their country according to their own ideas.

This book would not have been possible without the modern communication media. With the help of the internet, we were able to present our ideas to many African authors from different countries in Africa but also from Europe, the USA and Canada. Many have encouraged us to continue with our plans, sent us suggestions spontaneously and participated. Often, they had problems with weak and slow internet connections, so that it was not always easy to transmit data and to meet deadlines. But finally, 42 portraits were collected, and I would like to take this opportunity to express my greatest thanks to all the authors who participated.

Who is portrayed? It is inevitable that the selection is subjective, because it is based on the suggestions of the authors. We do not intend to claim that the book is complete; it would be rather sobering, if every personality in question could find space in one book. Not all people portrayed are famous personalities. But something else is much more decisive: all the people the book tells us about did not want or do not want to accept their fates. They had and have a vision of a better life for themselves and their fellow human beings. The vitality of Africa comes to light in the forty-two portraits from twenty-three countries, which range from Yennenga, who founded the Mossi Kingdom   to our contemporary era. These are true stories about women and men, who tell us about dignity in human life ; about the complexity, the dreams and the disillusions; about victories and defeats; about the long-lasting struggle for autonomy and the longing for the political unity of all Africans. They also tell us about the close relations between Africa and Europe, which have been shaping the daily lives of Africans for centuries already. One can read about Africans who were abducted to Europe and who achieved something remarkable over there, as well as about musicians, writers, visual artists, resistance fighters, politicians, feminists, civil rights campaigners, progressive thinkers and inventors, who changed the history of present day Africa.

The African women and men who are portrayed in this book, wanted to realise their dreams in their lives. It started with the dream of the provision of clean water but did not end with the dream of a just society. All of them used all of their abilities and their energy to make their dreams come true. May their dreams and their engagement be an inspiration for us.

M. Moustapha Diallo

ACKNOWLEDGEMENTS

Finally, after a long time of preparation, the book is ready: *The Visionaries of Africa – The Continent in Extraordinary Portraits*! Forty African authors wrote forty-two portraits about African women and men they consider important. In the end, it came to more than three hundred pages. Such an undertaking cannot be accomplished without the cooperation of numerous persons and institutions. This book would have hardly been published without their unselfish support. To all of them, I say a heartfelt thank you.

Foremost, I would like to thank the Peter Hammer publishing house with its publishing director Monika Bilstein, who included *The Visionaries of Africa* as a matter of course in the programme for African literature. And I would like to express my gratitude to the Peter Hammer Association for Literature and Dialogue (registered association), who assisted with the creation of the book with help and advice. Hermann Schulz generously allowed me to profit from his years of experience in book-making. Gudrun Honke offered her years of experience in editing African literatures to the portraits. Many thanks to the two of you for this!

Not least, such an undertaking also requires financial support. The Peter Hammer Association for Literature and Dialogue, Wuppertal; the North-Rhine Westphalian Foundation for Environment and Development, Bonn; the Municipal Savings Bank in Wuppertal and the Circle of Friends Bagamoyo, (registered association), Bockum, deserve particular thanks here.

I would like to thank, posthumously, Ms. Helga Paasche, who has died at a ripe age in 2011. Shortly before her death, she had provided money to support our book project. Her motivation was closely linked to the unusual life story of her father. Before the First World War, Hans Paasche had criticised colonialism and the disparagement of African nations, both orally and in writing. In doing so, he had been one of the few persons who stood up against the rulers and against widespread racism.

Hans Paasche was born in 1881 in Rostock and went to German East Africa in the year 1904. This had probably happened at the instigation of his father, who was a naval officer. There, he became a horrified eyewitness of the Maji-Maji-War (1905-1907) against twenty African nations, who fought against the brutal German colonial rule. His efforts to mediate between the front lines certainly had to fail, but he expressed his personal revulsion for the violence and suppression in the colonies and towards the destruction of the natural treasures in Africa. In many articles, Hans Paasche made public what he experienced and saw. In 1912/1913 he published the biweekly journal *The Vanguard,* a fictitious travel report, written by himself. It consisted of nine individual letters and bore the title *The Expedition of the African Lukanga Mukara into the Heart of Germany.* This text, which was so explicitly antiracism and anticolonialism was only published as a book in 1921, but it already had a widespread effect on the eve of the First World War, in the youth movement and later it became a bestseller. In October 1913 on the eve of the meeting of the Free German Youth on the Hohen Meißner near Kassel, Hans Paasche was one of the keynote speakers, because he had become well known, due to such and other pacifist writings.

Despite his pacifist attitude, at the beginning of the First World War, he voluntarily signed up to join the army as a patriot. But in 1916, he was dishonourably discharged from the army. His father admitted him to a psychiatric clinic to protect him. In 1918, he was freed by revolutionary seamen. For a short time, he became a member of the Executive Council of the workers' and soldiers' councils in Berlin that had the function of a provisional popular representation. Furthermore, he was very active as a publicist critical of the times.

In May 1920, Hans Paasche was shot by volunteer corps soldiers. The perpetrators have never been brought to justice. As a child, Helga Paasche had to witness the extra-judicial murder of her father. It became her mission in life to keep the memory of his thinking and his actions alive.

Wuppertal, March 2014
M. Moustapha Diallo

BIBLIOGRAHPY

THE TRANSLATORS ARE:

Barbara Bäumer: Patrick Awuah, Jimmy B, Steve Biko, Miria R.K. Matembe (from English to German);

Anja Bengelstorff: Kinjikitile Ngwale, Kwame Nkrumah (from English to German);

Elke Diallo; Mariama Bâ, Cheikh Ahmadou Bamba, Amílcar Cabral, Valdiodio N'Diaye, Thomas Sankara, Babemba Traoré, Youssouf Ouro Guézéré Tschadchédré, Yennenga (from French to German);

M. Moustapha Diallo; John Baloyi, Sofia Kawawa, Samuel Maharero and Hendrik Witbooi, Ken Saro-Wiwa, Weldedingl (from English to German); Djérassem Le Bemadjiel, Olaudah Equiano, Fela Anik lapo-Kuti, Samory Touré, Aminata Traoré (from French to Geman);

Bettina Kutzer: Charles Chanthunya, Angeline S. Kamba, Wangari Maathai, Nehanda, Alick Nkhata, Margaret Ogola, Oliver Tambo, Miriam Tlali (from English to German);

Oona Leganovic: Abraham Petrowitsch Hannibal (from English to German);

Gudrun and **Otto Honke:** Sultan Ibrahim Njoya (from French to German).

THE LIST OF CONTRIBUTORS

Rokhaya **Diallo** was born in 1978 in Paris, her parents are from Senegal and Gambia. She founded the women's organisation, *Les indivisibles* She is an activist at Attac and fights with her spoken and written words on TV and radio, in newspapers and books against racism and for women's rights.

Samson **Kambalu**, was born in 1975 in Malawi. He now lives and works as a writer and visual artist in London. In 2010, the German translation of his autobiographical novel *Jive Talker* was published. Kambalu's art was exhibited worldwide in museums and art galleries. The most famous piece is his *Holy Ball*, a football wrapped in biblical texts, which hops from one continent to another.

Helon **Habila**, was born in 1967 in Nigeria, he studied literature and worked as a journalist in Lagos. He taught Creative Writing in Fairfax, USA and lives at present as DAAD scholarship holder in Berlin. His short stories and novels have won multiple awards. *Oil on Water*, a crime novel about environmental pollution, was published in 2012 in German.

Ayni **Camara** was born in Senegal. She is a lawyer, a musician and focuses on the history of modern African music. She lives in Dakar.

Patrice **Djoufack** was born in Cameroon. He studied German language and literature at the University of Yaounde and teaches German. At present, he is a lecturer at the University of Hanover. In 2010, he completed his postdoctoral thesis: *Dislocation, Hybrid Language and Identity Formation*.

Solomon **Tsehaye** was born in 1956 in Eritrea. He went to school in Addis Ababa until the military coup in 1974. From 1977 to 1991 he was a soldier and a 'barefoot doctor' in the liberation struggle of Eritrea. He is a poet, writer, researcher and the author of the Eritrean national anthem and a master in the orally transmitted poetic tradition of Eritrea. At present, he is working in the Ministry of Education.

M. Moustapha **Diallo** was born in Senegal. He studied German language and literature in Dakar, Austria, Germany and France, and wrote his thesis about Ingeborg Bachmann. He works as a teacher in Paderborn and Münster in Germany. Since 2011, he is a freelance publicist and translator and has interest in publications about inter-culturalism, Afro-German relations and Africa in German literature.

Bananuka Jocelyn **Ekochu** was born in Uganda, lives in Kampala and works as a financial manager. She has written *Shock Waves across the Ocean* (2004) and published short stories. At present, she is writing her second novel.

Azzo,was born in 1967 in Senegal, and studied German language and literature, history and geography. He was committed to the anti-apartheid movement in South Africa and Namibia. He lives in the USA.

Patrice **Nganang** was born in 1970 in Yaounde, Cameroon. He wrote his doctoral thesis at the University of Frankfurt/M. about Soyinka and Brecht. Since 2000, he has been living in the USA, teaches literary science at the Stony Brook University of N.Y. Two of his novels have been translated into German: *Dog Times* (2003), for which he was awarded the *Grand Prix de l'Afrique Noire*, and *The Shadow of the Sultan* (2012).

Virginia **Phiri**, born in 1954 in Mzilikazi Township, Bulawayo (Zimbabwe). Since her childhood, she has been a literature fan. She is a skilled accountant, an expert for orchids and has published novels and non-fiction books. She is a founding member of the *Zimbabwe Women Writers*, and board member of *Zimbabwe International Book Fair*.

Mike **Khuria** was born in Kenya. He studied pedagogy and literature in Nairobi and Leeds. He is the director of the Centre for Quality Management at the University of Nairobi and published amongst others: *Talking Gender; Conversations with Kenyan Women Writers* (2003).

Ellen **Banda-Aaku**, was born in 1965 in Great Britain. She grew up in Lusaka (Zambia). She studied management in Lusaka and London as well as Creative Writing at the University of Cape Town, South Africa. Her children's books and her short stories have won multiple awards. In 2014, her first novel: *Patchwork* was published in German. She received the *Penguin Prize for African Writing* for it. She lives in London.

Chirikure **Chirikure** was born in 1962 in Zimbabwe. He writes prose, poems and children's books in Shona and English and appears on stage with his poems set to music.

Véronique **Tadjo** was born in 1955 in Paris and has French-Ivorian parents. She grew up in Ivory Coast. She is a poet, writer and painter. Her works include: *Nelson Mandela* (2012); *Behind us the rain* (2002); *The Shadow of God* (2001). She lives in Johannesburg.

Helen **Kijo-Bisimba** was born in 1954 in Moshi, Tanzania and lives in Dar es Salaam. She works as an educator and lawyer in numerous humanitarian organisations and human rights projects. She is for many years now committed to the promotion of women's and children's rights.

Ouaga-Ballé **Danaï** was born in 1963 in Sarh, Chad. He studied literature in Abidjan (Ivory Coast) and teaches at present at the Pedagogic University in Libreville (Gabon). He has published numerous plays and novels.

Sami **Tchak**, actually called *Sadamba Tcha-Koura,* was born in 1960 in Bowounda, Togo. In 1993, he wrote his PhD in sociology at the Sorbonne. He stayed in Central America and Cuba for research purposes and is the author of numerous novels and essays. He lives in Paris. In 2004, his novel *Fuck Life* was published in German.

Mamle **Kabu**, was born in 1968. She has Ghanaian-German parents. She studied in Cambridge, UK, and has been living in Ghana since 1992,where she spent her childhood. She writes novels and poems. Her short story *The End of Skill* was nominated for the Caine Prize.

Vonani **Bila** was born in the year 1972 in Elim/Shirley village in the Limpopo-province (South-Africa), where he lives today. He is a poet, musician, writer and organiser of cultural events, as well as the founder of the Timbila village of writers. He heads the Timbila-poetry project in Limpopo.

Brian **James** was born in 1983 in Lagos, Nigeria. His parents are from Sierra Leone. He studied communication science. As a writer, scriptwriter and documentary filmmaker,he has received numerous awards. At present, he is living in Freetown, Sierra Leone with his family.

Karfa Sira **Diallo** was born in 1971 in Thiaroye, Senegal. He was a law student in Bordeaux in 1996. He is a writer, and a local politician. He supports the maintenance of a memorial site to the slave trade in Bordeaux; and organizes guided city tours about this topic.

Urbain **N'Dakon** was born in 1964 in Ivory Coast. He studied German language and literature, psychology and marketing in Abidjan. In 1999 he wrote his doctoral thesis about Max von der Grün. From 2004– 2011 he worked as scientific co-ordinator of the International Doctoral Programme of the University of Bayreuth. Since 2004, he has been the Research Administration Officer for quality development and management in Fulda.

Issayas **Tesfamariam** was born in 1956 in Addis Ababa (Ethiopia). His parents are from Eritrea. He is a writer and a film maker and teaches Amharic at the University of Stanford, California.

Joe **Dramiga**, is of Ugandan origin, born in 1972 and raised in Cologne. He studied Neurogenetics and has a PhD from Cologne and London. At present, he is working as a science journalist and online editor. He writes poems and is committed to the fight against racism.

Monique **Ilboudo**, was born in 1959 in Burkina Faso. She is a writer and lawyer. She became Minister for the Promotion of Human Rights from 2002-2010. Since 2011, she is Ambassador of Burkina Faso to Copenhagen. She has published novels and short stories.

Tendai **Huchu**,was born in 1982 in Bindura, Zimbabwe; works as an expert in podiatry in Edinburgh, after he had given up his studies in mining technology, he did some odd-jobs. His first novel *The Hairdresser of Harare* (2010) is about homosexuality, which is a taboo subject in Africa.

Abednego **Keshomshahara** was born in 1969 in Bukoba, Tanzania. He works as a lecturer in theology at the University Makumira and coordinates the constitution of a University College in the region of Kagera, Tanzania. He had earlier on worked as a parish priest and director of the Evangelical Academy, in Ruhija., Tanzania.

Msafiri **Mbilu** was born in 1968. He studied theology in Tanzania, Norway and at the theological college in Wuppertal. At present, he is working as lecturer in Greek language and the New Testament at the University of Makumira, Tanzania.

Cheikh **Bâ** was born and raised in Senegal. He lives there and works as a history teacher, and mainly focuses on the resistance to the colonisation of West Africa.

Djibril Diallo **Falémé**, was born in 1959 in Senegal. He is a writer, teacher of modern literature and a school principal in Dakar. He has published novels, poems, plays.

Amina **N'Diaye-Leclerc** was born in 1952 in Kaolack, Senegal. Her parents are from France and Senegal. She studied Spanish language and literature in Toulouse, France and has been working since 1991 as a film producer and film director. She also started painting in 2000. She lives in Toulouse.

Bernard **Akoi-Jackson** was born in the year 1979 in Ghana. He is an installation artist and a writer who deals with hybrid postcolonial African identities. His works are exhibited in numerous European countries. He lives and works in Tema (Ghana).

Joséphine T. **Mulumba** was born in Lubumbashi (Congo-Kinshasa). She obtained her PhD at the University of Bayreuth. She is doing research on different aspects of African literature and teaches at the University of Munich.

Tandis comes from Guinea-Bissau and grew up in Senegal. She lives in Dakar where she works as a teacher.

Florentin Saha **Kamta** was born in 1979 in Balepo, Cameroon. He studied German language, literature and educational sciences in Yaounde and in Hanover. Since 2009, he has been teaching at the University of Paderborn. His PhD is on identity policies in Afro-German literature.

Kagiso Lesego **Molope** was born in 1976 in South Africa. She studied English language and literature and literary theory at the University of Cape Town. She has published three novels, including *The Mending Season* (2009). She lives in Canada.

Andile **M-Africa** was born in 1966 in the Township of Ginsberg near King William's Town, South Africa, where Steve Biko also grew up. He holds a Master's degree in Creative Writing and keeps the memory of Steve Bantu Biko alive in his publications.

Luli **Callinicos** was born in Johannesburg, South Africa and has Greek roots. She is a historian. Since 1970, she has concentrated on her journalistic work against the apartheid regime. She lives in Johannesburg. Her publications are about South Africa's social history, including Nelson Mandela and Oliver Tambo.

Moussa **Diallo** was born in 1973 in Senegal. He studied marketing and management. He teaches at a Technical College in Dakar and works as advisor in the fields of marketing and management. He writes poems, song texts, and short stories. He collects and translates fairy tales from Senegal and Guinea-Bissau.

Table of Contents

AMINATA DRAMANE TRAORÉ (Mali)

THE END OF DOMINATION

BY ROKHAYA DIALLO

Not long ago, French television was awakened from its deep slumber by an unusual phenomenon: an African woman took the stage in numerous political talks and joined in broadcast discussions. Unlike African intellectuals who quickly assume unobtrusive European masks in front of the camera, this woman confidently came forward dressed in gorgeous African clothes and did not hold a page before her. Without ceremony and with verbal skill, she advocated an unconventional point of view that threw her co-discussants completely off balance, for they were not used to crossing swords with somebody who brought up weapons different from those customary for one in their position. The ideas expressed by this proud woman exploded the clichés about Africa, as the continent of oppression and misery. Her name was Aminata Dramane Traoré.

Her story began in 1947, in Bamako, the capital of Mali. She grew up in a family of ten children. Her mother was a housewife but at the same time earned money by dyeing cloth. Her father was a clerk in the post office. A "completely normal family", they say. From her mother she inherited a passion for textiles. In a family in which girls were not sent to school, she became the first to go to school. Like many children at this time, little Aminata only wanted to go because her best friend went to school. For the little girl, that meant a long walk, every day for six years.

Even on the first day she was struck by the fact that the school was divided in two. On one side were the "natives" and the "mulattoes" from a hostel who were taught by African teachers. On the other side, were the white girls. The separation of the two worlds was as brutal as it was official. During the break a mental wall prevented the children from playing together. Aminata Traoré often recalled this "the distant world of the whites". From afar she observed the representatives of the other world and registered their "drink bottles full of cold red or green syrup". It was impossible not to perceive the difference with painful yearning. Against this abyss that developed in earliest childhood in the mentality of African people, she would direct her struggle.

Aminata did so well in school that she skipped a class. After the school-leaving exam she studied Psychology and Social Sciences at the University of Dakar, which now carries the name of the greatest African intellectual, Sheikh Anta Diop. However, in the storm of student revolt that broke out in May 1968, even in Senegal, the government sent the students home, so Aminata Traoré continued her studies in Frankfurt.

She was then in the world of those other pupils from primary school, and the questions of the two worlds pressed upon her still more intensively. Why the difference between Europe and Africa? Is it insurmountable? What effect does this inequality have on the thinking of Africans? She analysed this in her doctoral thesis, in which she investigated the "Development of identity among African youth".

After gaining her doctorate, she went to the Ivory Coast, her husband's homeland, where the economy was booming to the extent that people talked about the "Ivorian miracle". "In those days, one would certainly not think that it would be better to stay in Europe", she explains today. As one of the few female African scholars of that time she taught at the Institute for Ethnosociology. After her divorce she continued her career in the Ivory Coast. In the newly constituted Ministry for Women – the first in Africa – she became the project director for twenty-seven years! but was continually obstructed in her energetic efforts for the advancement of women. Incredulously, she had to recognise that important decisions were made by female experts who understood little or nothing about the realities of African countries. They all came from the industrialised countries. There it was again; this wall between north and south; between former colonial powers and dependent states. To stand up vigorously for the destruction of this omnipresent imbalance was a challenge for Aminata Traoré.

Purposefully, she put together contacts with representative women of her generation in Africa. In 1977, together with the Senegalese feminist, Marie-Angélique Savané, she founded the Union of African Women for Research and Development, one of the first organisations of African women scientists. For its first programme, the union set a clear goal: the topic was "The Decolonisation of Research on Women", which denounced the domination of African women by "female experts" from the dominant countries of the north. Through numerous initiatives this network became a central agency for the representation of the interests of women in Africa.

In 1988, by then forty one years old, she became the leader of one of the projects created by the United Nations Development Programme (UNDP) for the advancement of women and for the improvement of water supply in Africa. In this way she came into contact with women from other parts of the world. They strengthened her in her commitment to the independence of African women and societies, among them especially, the Indian, Lyra Srinivasan, who had developed a successful pedagogical strategy to deal with illiteracy among Indian women. Through the international context of her activities Aminata Traoré achieved a deeper insight into the connections between the world economy and the problems of Africa.

In the face of the economic crises and mistakes by the so-called developed countries, the World Bank and the International Monetary Fund had decreed Structural Adjustment Programmes (SAP) for adversely affected countries as the condition for credit. As Aminata Traoré could confirm from her professional experience, the experts of both of these international organisations, placed earnings from the "developing countries" above the requirements of the actual populations. Even worse, they insisted on measures that were obviously wrong, as could be seen for example in the water supply project. For, according to the rules of the SAP, African governments had to curtail all "non-profitable outlays", those were the resources for public services, which included water supply. The water supply promptly collapsed, and programmes had to be introduced to eliminate the problem, in fact, with credit from the same countries that were demanding structural adjustment. The same thing happened with education and health and also in the economic sector. Thus the African countries were forced into a nonsensical economic policy that plunged them into a vicious circle of destruction of infrastructure, forced privatisation, distress and borrowing. It was not surprising, then, that the social expenditures of several countries constituted four per cent of the budget, and the liquidation of debt, thirty-six per cent.

To play her part toward counteracting the results of these world economic abuses, in 1992 Aminata Traoré returned to Mali and became an active advisor to the United Nations Population Fund. She set standards with a series of projects that she planned.

Against the neglect of parts of the city that due to cuts in the context of SAP no longer had garbage collection, she hit upon an unusual measure. Against all the traditional division of roles, she persuaded sixteen young women who had not been able to find any employment after their education, to take an unheard of step: for the first time Malian women sat at the steering wheel of a lorry and drove from house to house to collect garbage! With that she had not only eliminated the problem of lack of garbage removal, but also found a way towards the accomplishment of her real mission. The UN Fund then appointed her to lead sensitisation on the delicate theme of female circumcision. Through co-operation with the sixteen women she won the trust of her target group and was no longer perceived as a know-it-all stranger from the city.

At the same time she set about the cleaning of her section of the city, in which pavements and gutters had been abandoned to decay. Other parts of the city followed the example with the support of Non-Governmental Organisations from Luxembourg and Canada. In a short time the inhabitants paved an expanse of more than three hundred thousand square metres.

Following the principle of self-help and independent development, she opened the restaurant "San Toro", in which everything came from Africa, and the Hotel Djenné for alternative tourism. The Amadou Hampâté Bâ Centre, which she co-founded, was also innovative as a culture devoted to the development and transmission of traditional know-how and cultural self-confidence. Aminata Traoré became a recognised figure throughout the country.

In 1997 after some delay, she took over the Ministry for Culture and Tourism. Three years later she resigned from her office because she realised that her appointment only served to silence a potential critic, for she received no means for implementing her projects. A year before, in 1999, she had published *L'étau* (The Vice). The book became a classic of the critical approach to globalisation and has been on the curriculum of several universities. Using the example of Mali, she showed how African countries are the football of neoliberal politics and how their local economies are systematically destroyed. She unmasked the "double standard" of the rich countries. While the African states had to withdraw economic support, the export economies in Europe and the USA received subventions, thus agricultural products from the rich countries could be offered for only a third of the price of local products in Africa. "They have only globalised hopelessness, anguish and hunger," wrote Aminata Traoré. With equal sharpness, she criticised the African elites who passively watched the selling off of their countries and spread the false belief that an incompetent state could be democratic. Thus she spoke of the "betrayal by the élites", which provoked a strong reaction, an "unparalleled lynching by the media" as the author says.

Through the book, the attention of the international public was drawn to this intellectual who confronted the powerful and attacked the ruling system with insider knowledge. The activists in the movement for criticism of globalisation were especially attentive and invited her to the first World Social Forum in Brazil at Porto Alegre. With the Egyptian Samir Amin, the Senegalese Demba Moussa and Taouffik Ben Abdallah, she belonged to the "Four Musketeers" who represented the African continent at this historical meeting of the movement for the criticism of globalisation, and later founded the African Social Forum. Under the title "Intellectual Assault", Aminata Traoré gave a talk in Porto Alegre that made her a figurehead of the movement.

That Aminata Traoré meanwhile has become an icon of the opposition to neo-liberal world politics, is due on the one hand to the clear language with which she brought to light the problems of the current world order. Thus she reminded, after the attack of 11th September 2001, "In Africa, every day is a September 11". On the other hand, she distinguished herself by a brand of aggressiveness that the professional politicians little knew how to oppose. At the World Summit in South Africa in 2002 she heard with some amazement how the French President Jacques Chirac – in contradiction to his policies – presented himself in his speech as an advocate for Africa. After the speech she went to him, "Mr. President, I have heard you make extremely friendly remarks on the affairs of African countries. Would you be prepared to initiate a revision of the relations between France and Africa?"

To this unexpected proposal, her interlocutor reacted as any politician would always react in such situations, "I'm sorry madame, just now I have no time."

Aminata Traoré was not to be put off so easily. She addressed the President again, this time with an *Open Letter to the President of France with reference to the Ivory Coast and Africa in general*, in which with remarkable precision, she demonstrated the connection between the dominance of the rich countries and the situation in African states.

Her next altercation was with Chirac's successor Sarkozy. In 2007 Sarkozy gave a speech in Dakar that is etched in the memory of Africans. In his arrogant manner, the freshly anointed President of the "Great Nation" went straight to the lectern. After he had informed the assembly in the colonial manner that colonial rule was not to blame for the problems of Africa, he spoke sanctimoniously about "the bloody wars that Africans conduct among themselves", "genocide", "dictators", "fanaticism", "corruption", "misuse of office", "extravagant waste" and "destruction of the environment". He didn't leave out a single cliché. That France vigorously supported the dictators, actively opposed critical politicians and used every means to get its hands on the profitable sectors of the economy of these countries, he forgot to mention. But the old song about the "continent of catastrophe" was only an opening phrase for a lecture about the "simple soul of the African". Apparently, illuminated by the African sun, the President became expansive and switched to cultural philosophy. Let us hear what Sarkozy proclaimed to his hosts:

"The drama of Africa resides in the fact that the African has not yet entered fully into history. The African peasant, who has lived with the seasons for thousands of years, whose ideal life is harmony with nature, knows only the eternal cycle of time that is stamped with the eternal repetition of the same deeds and the same words... In this notion of the world, where everything always begins from the beginning, there is no place for human adventure, for the idea of progress... The African never rages against the future. He never arrives at the idea of breaking out of repetition, to invent a future for himself."

In the great hall of the university, named after the one who had demonstrated the Black African origin of the Egyptian civilisation, the startled audience waited for the point, for something like, "With such fantasies was Africa distinguished in the 18th century" but it was nothing of the sort. This abstruse passage was no rhetorical figure, but seriously intended, as those present realised when the lecturer called upon them "to enter into history", and he emphasised that he said this 'as a friend of Africa "Open your eyes, youth of Africa and do not, as your ancestors so often did, regard global civilisation as a threat to your identity, but as something that also belongs to you". The crowd was speechless.

It is worthy of note that the main points of Sarkozy's tirade about the "African incapable of development" were modified citations from Hegel's racist defamation of the inhabitants of Africa, which apparently was not previously known to the honourable President. For this lecture Sarkozy received such a thrashing – from Africa and also from France – that he found it necessary to admit mistakes. In his later trips to Africa he hazarded no further flights of culture-historical imagination.

The most prominent reaction to this *Dakar Lecture* was Aminata Traoré's book *L'Afrique Humiliée* (Africa Humiliated). In this she analyses Sarkozy's arrogance, which expressed the attitude of the dominant countries. She condemned the long-standing exploitation of Africa, and the irresponsibility of Europe that had deteriorated into an all-out war against refugees, a war in which African countries became the handymen of the EU and "do the dirty work", as revealed by the shooting of refugees by Moroccan police in the year 2005. The author also described the contempt meted out to those who sought a future in Europe because their countries were choked in the stranglehold of neo-liberal policies.

In 2012 Aminata Traoré published another book, *L'Afrique Mutilée* (Mutilated Africa). In this book she gave a decisive response to the "cliché-ridden and degrading discourse about our situation in Africa", especially about African women, who are thought of as "mutilated and perpetually pregnant", and for this superficial, one-sided perception, she held the "neo-liberal mutilation" responsible as the worst evil. Finally, she examined the example of the crisis in Mali, in which she impressively presented the consequences of forced austerity measures, namely loss of direction and the destabilisation in the north of the country.

At fifty-six she fought on an additional front against the expansion of genetic engineering that threatened the existence of the cotton producers in Mali. To the question, what drove her and motivated her apparently hopeless struggles against all-powerful organisations, she replied, "I cannot passively observe how the world is destroyed." With her books, lectures, even with an appearance in the film *Bamako*, a political documentary, she expressed her conviction that another world is possible, a message that she conveys not least with her colourful *boubous*, the African symbol of self-assertion in a world in which the neoliberal steam-roller threatens to demolish everything.

Aminata Dramane Traoré:	*L'étau*. Arles 1999;
" " "	*L'Afrique humiliée*. Paris 2008;
" " "	*L'Afrique mutilée*. Bamako 2012.

CHARLES CHANTHUNYA (Malawi)

DEVELOPMENT THROUGH EXTRAVAGANCE

BY SAMSON KAMBALU

The summer vacation always began at sunset, with a long bus trip through the night to my mother's home village, Chingoni in the Ntcheu district of Malawi. I hated this trip. Every time, the bus was packed so full that I thought I would suffocate, like in a Noah's Ark, with every possible kind of animal in it: chickens, goats, guinea pigs, pigs, even a big cow with long threatening horns like the devil, complete strangers sweating and evil-smelling, and sacks full of maize, beans and peas. I spent a quarter of the trip standing, my hand pressed flat under the solid thigh of a snoring fat man who had been lucky enough to acquire a seat; his round face in sleep was careworn, but from time to time he broke into something like a smile. For another quarter of the trip I sat on my mother's lap and since I was already a big boy, I was jolted back and forth from the feel of her arms wrapped soothingly around my waist and her warm breath on my neck. Nothing could be seen through the window: the agonised sound of the diesel engine – snoring, snorting, galloping and bumping – made me believe that the driver had chosen the most out of the way route to Chingoni; through wild valleys inhabited by rabid hyenas, through wild canyons and over the steepest hills where "bushmen" and dodos still lived.

During the last half of the journey I wondered how it was apparently only me who had to go to the toilet in the night. The moon seemed to be laughing at me from behind the silver clouds. The bus driver kept the gas pedal pressed down for hours without a let-up; it had escaped him that people and animals too have to, at some point. It was fine for the animals – the cock under my seat freely relieved himself and ruined my new shoes. As soon as I got to Chingoni I would go to the toilet. This consisted of a hole in the ground, with a tin roof that made an unearthly howl when the wind blew through it ... But no, not this time. The bottomless pit was now a proper ceramic and warm toilet seat. I accomplished my business and looked around for toilet paper; there was a new aluminium holder, glistening in the morning sun that peeped through the tin roof, but there was no roll of paper. Instead, there was the usual pile of corn cobs on the floor, so I used this. When I turned around to flush it, the toilet only squeaked miserably and I remembered that it wasn't actually a real toilet. Then the name of Dr. Charles Chanthunya flashed through my head. Had the great man already been in the village this summer? I forgot the toilet and went to my grandparents' house to find out. A new Grundig boiler, a two-burner electric plate, Grandmother's hair-dryer ... at the same time there was no electricity in the entire village! My mother said it would soon come. The IMF and the World Bank were working on it. In the living room stood a new short wave radio with a red light shining in it. However, the radio could not work because in all of Malawi, there was no FM broadcasting. On FM the machine gave a rather interesting hissing noise. It sounded like a spitting cobra, and I stood there for quite a while turning the dangerous poison on and off. It said *Sony* on the radio.

The next day was a Sunday, and my grandmother, the choir leader in the parish, was late for mass because she was always turning herself about in her new print attire in front of the mirror, received with friendly greetings from Dr. Charles Chanthunya. The priest shut us out . He had had enough of congregation members who arrived according to African time and therefore too late. My grandmother held her own mass in front of the church, the African patterns on her new outfit glittering and sparkling as she recited her rosary. I suspected that human rights activists had been in the village; grandmother's speech was eloquent and pithy, without the usual digressions. Other villagers, who had similarly arrived too late collected around her, sang a few hymns with her, made the sign of the cross and then went home, content that no hostile church officer stood between them and purgatory.

In the afternoon my grandmother went to a Gumba-Gumba beer party that a neighbour further up the street was organising, and there too we followed her glowing wax print. Uncle Humphrey bought beer for everyone at the party. He managed the family's money and Dr. Charles Chanthunya had briefly been in the village. At nightfall the priest and my grandmother shared a calabash of *matsire* – they had buried their difference of opinion in laughter and good cheer. The priest was happy, for meanwhile he had also noticed that Dr. Charles Chanthunya had been there, and better times were ahead.

In the weeks that followed we visited Dr Chanthunya's mother, Anifa, my grandmother's sister, in Mpira. It was farther over the hill. We traversed the entire distance on foot at night to avoid the heat of the day and used an oil lamp that Dr. Chanthunya had brought. Anifa too was dressed from head to toe in a new cloth and a new automobile, a Peugeot 504, was parked in front of her premises. It belonged to Dr. Charles Chanthunya. We stopped at the shop on the corner of Anifa's house to drink warm Coca-Cola and noticed that strange glasses full of every possible sweet in colours of the rainbow stood on the counter. Just as I wanted to try a handful of every kind, it was time. Dr. Charles Chanthunya was waiting for us at Anifa's, the pockets of his grey suit full of money, of that I was sure. Every time he moved in his chair his trouser pockets rattled like a cocktail shaker.

Dr. Charles Lemson Chanthunya was a businessman, a Professor of Economics and Chancellor of Blantyre International University in Malawi, a university that he himself had founded. After studying in different places around the world for years, now he seemed to have found his place. In 2011 he had suddenly appeared in his grey suit, with a shiny black briefcase under his arm, at Niagara University College of Business Administration in New York and desired to speak to the Dean of the College, Dr. Tenpao Lee. When Dr. Lee's secretary asked of his mission he responded that he had come to find out how to run a university. When the secretary would not admit him to the Dean without an appointment, Dr. Chanthanya opened his briefcase and spread out in front of her some statistics about the situation of education in Malawi: eighty-three per cent of the approximately fourteen million inhabitants of Malawi lived below subsistence level. The rate of illiteracy in the country was alarmingly high; it was around thirty-four per cent. Only 3.5 per cent of those who went to a high school in Malawi could attend a university. Therefore he had decided to establish a university. He had come all the way from Africa to New York to inform himself on how one could begin such a thing, and he wanted to take Niagara University as a model. The secretary was not entirely clear what was going on but she changed her mind and let Dr. Chanthanya through. Dr. Tenpao Lee was quickly convinced of the idea of a new university of business administration south of the Sahara, in the heart of Africa. The Dean paid a visit to Malawi and spent a month on the campus of Blantyre International University. He passed on his knowledge in the area of Supply Chain Management, developed and reviewed teaching programmes, concerned himself with the education of teachers and carried out continuing education seminars for Dr. Chanthunya's recently employed assistants. A year later, Blantyre International University was a fully accredited academic institution, which taught Malawians how modern industry and political economy functioned.

As a young man Dr. Chanthunya attended the exclusive Zomba Catholic Secondary School run by the Marist Brothers, the earliest sign of his unusual intelligence. One needed top marks to get to "Round Two", as the state schools financed with government money were commonly called. There Chanthunya won a scholarship for a course in economics at the University of Glasgow in Scotland and finally, he did his doctorate at the University of Wales. Until 1994 Dr. Chanthunya was active as a leading currency expert for the most important regional trade block in Africa, south of the Sahara, the Preferential Trade Area for Eastern and Southern African States (PTA), now Common Market for Eastern and Southern African States (COMESA). During this time he also worked as a visiting professor in political science at the Southern African Institute for Policy Studies in Harare, Zimbabwe. After his return to Malawi he became a business leader at CLC Consulting Services and worked as a management consultant. This was something Dr. Chanthunya had always been engaged in, obviously he quickly became very rich from it. Now he lived in Chigumula, a stylish suburb of Blantyre, the business capital of Malawi, in a spacious white residence from the colonial era with a big green empty swimming pool that he never filled with water.

Dr. Chanthunya lived in Zambia when I was growing up. During the summer holidays he always appeared in Chingoni in the Ntchue District and shared some of his wealth with his relatives, in the form of the most varied objects from the modern world; digital radios, mountain bikes, expensive lengths of printed cloth, self-heating tea cups, thermos flasks, silver spoons, shoes too big and too small, even a pair of jet skis; things that mainly served decorative ends rather than practical. In this country that is what often happens with wealth; it was no capitalist approach, such as he propagated professionally. The man is no Protestant but a Catholic, yet his personal economic practices went deeper than that. They were Malawian and Ngoni. Dr. Chanthunya grew up with an alternative economic model, a model of a state economy based on the destruction of wealth and extravagance, such as can be observed at the traditional markets in Malawi, as well as in the daily exchange of "gifts", quite the opposite of the economy of accumulation and profits, which he then taught at Blantyre International University.

In the traditional economy of Dr. Chanthunya's childhood, capital accumulation was actually obscene; goods were not to be assembled to make a profit, but to be energetically redistributed. Among his people, the Ngoni, the one who gained the greatest reputation was not the one who had accumulated the most and made the greatest profit, but the one who had most to share. Therefore the residents of Chingoni worked hard in the field and hoarded up their meat, vegetables and grain for the dry period, a time that was not so much devoted to work, apart from the manufacture of hand crafts and tools, as to the performance of various traditional ceremonies. The people drank *matsire* from midday to evening and danced the war dance, *ngoma*, while they exchanged chickens, cows, mushrooms, maize, beads and skins as "gifts". Those who had the most to share gained the highest regard and the greatest respect. People pointed their finger at those who hoarded and censured them, together with those who had nothing to share, the lazy, the parasites.

My father was a Presbyterian from the Dowa district. He hardly ever opened his briefcase, which he managed very carefully. He was respected, but was never loved like Dr. Chanthunya in Chingoni. Through his marriage with my mother, a Catholic, he made up for it, for like her cousin Dr. Charles Chanthunya, money ran through her fingers like water, and she continually distributed presents. She was also much beloved in the villages. After her husband's death she gave up working as a teacher and she and her daughters set themselves up to convert my father's life-long

13

hard-earned savings into fashionable prints and shoes that filled a room from one wall to the other, as well as exuberant donations to the church, such as a modern satellite dish with which South African channels could be received, as soon as the Chinese put up the mast in Lumbadzi. As far as I know, the work on the international television antenna in Lumbadzi has lasted up to today. My father died in 1995. Three years after her husband's death my mother was financially finished. At the time she lived in Lilongwe, and moved to a house without window panes in Area Forty-Six, where her admirers from the villages constantly besieged her. She began to visit her eight children, (who at that time, for the most part, had modest jobs) to accept "gifts" from them that she would secretly take home to her big empty house in the Forty-Sixth to share out further. We found her unrestrained generosity irresistible, and we all competed as to who could give the most to our mother, this, in effect, goddess of giving. When I left Malawi for further studies in England, I was still employed as a teaching assistant at Chancellor College of the University of Malawi so I had my wages transferred to her bottomless bank account in Old Town. Until her death in 2002 this remained one of her dependable sources of money. She was fifty-seven years old when she passed on. However, this article is about her cousin, Dr. Charles Chanthunya, professor, founder and chancellor of Blantyre International University.

What I most admire about Dr. Charles Chanthunya is that, despite his profound understanding of the functioning of this new, strange economy of constant hoarding and acquisition of wealth called capitalism, he also apparently recognised certain merits in the traditional static economy of Chingoni, which he deemed advisable not to give up completely. In all appearances in his work as an economist, professor and businessman, he is more a pragmatist than a radical; to be a manager for him is only one way of being resourceful. The inhabitant of Chingoni went to the fields for harvest and gleanings so that during the dry season he would have something extra; Dr. Chanthunya went into business and earned a whole truckload of money, which he dissipated whenever he came to his home village.

With his unusual intelligence and his great foresight, Dr. Charles Chanthunya certainly saw coming all the paroxysms of capitalism in recent times: financial collapse, environmental catastrophes, the shameful social inequality, dispossession, AIDS epidemic .... While he was studying economics, according to Adam Smith, in Glasgow and

Wales, Dr. Chanthunya certainly understood what Martin Luther did not understand about the building of the monumental cathedral of St. Peter's in Rome: that the world acts in excess, and that social and economic problems are not the result of dearth but of abundance. As a Catholic, Dr. Chanthunya would have recollected that the difficulty in the Garden of Eden did not flow from a dearth but from sumptuousness; what to do with the excess of abundance and time, if one had eaten one's fill of the fruits. In Africa, the people use the excess for orgies of extravagance, for rich ceremonies and overflowing drink offerings and sacrifices for the spirits of their ancestors. Through this universal squandering, a parody of the generosity of the sun and stars above us, life and spirit are to be renewed by natural means. The whole society would flourish and grow, uniformly and organically.

The dogma of capital accumulation, that there is a shortage of resources and wealth must therefore be retained and carefully managed, had already started to affect the universal community of extravagance in Chingoni. At some time in the early 1990s, Dr. Chanthunya had to move his aged mother from Mpira to another district because the government planned to build an enormous water reservoir above the village. Anifa did not like it, and she and many other inhabitants from her village, who had lived in Mpira for centuries, died soon after their removal from *msamuko*, as the Malawians say, as a result of being "exiled."

Dr. Charles Chanthunya always defined himself as a businessman, but it is worth considering more closely what he understands by business. He is an African businessman, and we are very proud of him.

KEN SARO-WIWA (Nigeria)

FOR THE OGONI AND AGAINST SHELL

BY HELON HABILA

There are many designations for Ken Saro-Wiwa; many are justified, others are not. He is called a Nigerian patriot, Ogoni nationalist, the father of African environmentalism, a writer, poet, essayist, playwright, publisher, television producer and ... he is called a murderer, and as such on the 10th of November 1995, with eight other accused, he was condemned to death by hanging, and was hanged.

Kenule Beeson Saro-Wiwa, born on 10th October, 1941 in the city of Bori in the Niger Delta, belonged to the Ogoni tribe. His father was a chief and a practising Anglican. Ken attended the government college in Umuahia, where other famous Nigerians like the writer Chinua Achebe also went to school. After finishing school he received a scholarship to study English at the University of Ibadan; then he worked as an assistant at the University of Lagos. His goal, as he describes it in one of his books, was to become a teacher. That was his greatest dream, but it would never materialise, although one could argue whether as a writer and civil rights advocate, he did not become a more significant teacher than he could ever have imagined.

Destiny always makes itself felt in the life of an individual, and it collided with Ken Saro-Wiwa in the form of the civil war of 1967, when the Biafra region of Nigeria tried to secede. By the beginning of the civil war he had made his way to Lagos, and the central government appointed him civil administrator of Bonny, a big oil exporting port in the Niger Delta, which had been won back from Biafra. Bonny lay in the Rivers State, to which Ogoni land belonged. Thus as a young man of twenty-five, he occupied an important post which let him experience at first-hand how the oil interests were corrupting and destroying an entire society. The struggle against them became his life's work.

In *On a Darkling Plain* (1989), one of the most penetrating books about the suffering of the Ogoni in the civil war, Saro-Wiwa describes the war from 1967 to 1970 as a time of disorder. The Biafran war had split the Ogoni: one part sympathised with the separatists, while others, like Saro-Wiwa, advocated remaining within the Nigerian federation because in their opinion, alliance with Biafra only meant exchanging one dependency for another. This division and the chaos, he portrayed in his novel *Sozaboy: A Novel in Rotten English*. This experimental novel, that famously begins with the line "Although, everybody in Dukana was happy at first" and ends with the words "Believe me yours sincerely" tells the story of a naïve and gullible but sympathetic young man, Sozaboy, in a town called Dukana. Sozaboy goes into the army and is sent to the front. When he entered the army he wanted to be a hero, so that when he came home again one day the most beautiful woman in the village would throw herself at him, the irresistible lover. The book is a *Bildungsroman*; in the course of *Sozaboy*'s development one recognises the growing up and the loss of innocence not only of the Ogoni but of all Nigeria. Saro-Wiwa shows that in this war there are no heroes and no clear fronts. The soldiers fight on both sides at the same time, change uniform arbitrarily and do everything just to stay alive, and when Sozaboy goes back to Dukana, he finds his home town, to which he so badly wanted to return as a hero, in ruins.

Perhaps the most interesting thing about *Sozaboy* is not the way in which the war is represented in all its meaninglessness, but the language. The book is written in Pidgin English, or, as Saro-Wiwa calls it, in *rotten English*. This is the first African novel to set about the bravura task of making Pidgin viable for a literary text. The language can best be compared with the "broken" English that Amos Tutuola used in his books like *The Palm Wine Drinkard* of 1952, but while Tutuola adhered

17

much more strongly to the oral tradition, Saro-Wiwa's literary precedent is more modern, and for us today, perhaps more interesting.

Accordingly, the novel, from its language to its form and its content, shows the madness, the chaos and finally the evil that is war. Born of the Biafran war, the history of the new Nigeria is probably the most complex and intricate in all of Africa. With currently more than 179 million inhabitants, Nigeria is the most heavily populated country of the continent, with more than three hundred different ethnicities. Most of these are regarded and treated as minorities by the three biggest ethnic groups, Hausa, Igbo and Yoruba. The Ogoni belong to one of the smallest minorities.

The presence of vast amounts of petroleum and natural gas in their territory has reduced the Ogoni to pawns in the game of the oil concerns. The Nigerian government was generally complicit where the environmentally destructive, dangerous to health, even criminal activities of the oil concerns in Ogoni land were concerned. The pipelines, often rusty and leaky, ran through town centres and family properties and over fields. These pipelines frequently exploded and caused many deaths. The people had to look on helplessly as their streams and farmlands became polluted and useless for fishing and cultivation, the two occupations that up till then their livelihoods had depended on. In similar fashion, the story of the Ogoni was repeated in hundreds of other Nigerian communities.

After the civil war that had split the population of Nigeria, for Saro-Wiwa it became a kind of obsession to unite the people, to turn back again to the pre-colonial splendour of the past. Who appointed him leader? Nobody. But he felt that in times like these, times of crises, it was the duty of every patriot to step forward and do what he or she could to show the people the way. The civil war, he found, opened up one such occasion. For his people, captive within a larger national context, it pushed open a window of opportunities for action.

Naturally, he was not the first Ogoni who wanted to improve the life circumstances of his people. He built on the legacy of the Ogoni hero Timothy Birabi, who was viewed by many as the founder of modern Ogoni society. Birabi, the first Ogoni with an academic education, devoted his life to building schools and preached self-reliance and self-help. Saro-Wiwa said that his motive was the burning desire to stand up for the Ogoni cause. He wrote, "My interest in the Ogoni grew from a deep rooted conviction that began from primary school, grew and was consolidated during further schooling and became my duty during the Nigerian civil war 1967-70 and during my period in office, 1968-73, as member of the Executive Council of the Rivers State".

To get a picture of the Ogoni situation, he travelled in all directions, through and around a hundred Ogoni villages, learned to know the inhabitants and became an eye witness of the devastation that the war had left behind. He arrived at the recognition that the Ogoni had to reconcile with each other and unite, and that this could best be achieved through the development of a central leadership structure. The Ogoni had belonged to the larger federal state of Eastern Nigeria but were now assigned to the new, smaller federal state, the Rivers State, yet they still remained a relatively small population under the tutelage of larger ethnic groups. In addition, as long as they did not understand that they must raise their voices and demand their rights, they could never improve their condition. Therefore, Saro-Wiwa founded the Ogoni Development Association to mobilise the people and he drew up a kind of manifesto that named the goals of the association: "Rivers State was founded and a new Nigeria born. But we ought not to forget that there will be no progress for a people if it does not take control of its own fate, no matter in what system of government, ... We must begin immediately to prepare ourselves with passion for the difficult and turbulent times that lie ahead...".

He could not have been more prophetic. The future would be difficult and turbulent for the Ogoni, and especially for Ken Saro-Wiwa himself. One must realise that Saro-Wiwa was an exceptionally ambitious young man, and at this time, perhaps too young to take on such a difficult task as the leadership of the Ogoni people. So it was inevitable that he made a series of mistakes, most of them unintended, and thereby offended many people, who saw in him a young upstart who presumed to take on the role of a leader of the Ogoni and heir to the great Birabi. He made enemies internally as well as outside; many of them had grown up and gone to school with him. Conflicts in the executive council of the Rivers State, too much activism, too much pressure from interest groups and his refusal to join them, led to his dismissal in 1973. He was accused of being involved in the Ogoni movement and being an advocate for their autonomy.

However, he learned quickly, and the older he became the cleverer his strategy became. He was clever enough to recognise that he would not be taken seriously by the majority if he did not achieve something in the world, and so he decided to withdraw from politics, at least for a while. In the 1980s he devoted himself most of the time exclusively to writing and his businesses. He founded his own publishing company, Saros Stars Publishing Company, that published out all his books. In less than two decades he probably became the most productive author in Africa. At present most of his books are no longer in print, but some, including *Sozaboy*, are still available. From essays to children's books, folk tales and novels to plays - he wrote everything.

On his fiftieth birthday he determined, for instance, to publish in his company "no less than eight books, seven of them mine". But at no point did he forget his true goal: the struggle of the Ogoni. Meanwhile, he understood himself no longer as an advocate only of the Ogoni, but also of all disadvantaged peoples. If he published a book he transformed the publicity campaign, usually a big thing in Nigeria, into a political campaign calling for solidarity with the Ogoni. During the same period he wrote a hard-hitting political column, "Similia", in Nigeria's most important daily paper, the *Daily Times*. He used the column as a platform to talk about exploitation by the oil concerns, the distress of the ethnic minorities in Nigeria and the destruction of the environment. "Week after week, I made sure that the name Ogoni appeared before the eyes of the reader. It was a television technique, designed to leave the name indelibly in their minds".

Besides writing books he also produced the television sitcom *Basi and Company*, that propelled him to fame both internally and abroad in circles far beyond his readership. The series, which showed the superficiality and extravagant materialism of Nigerian society in a satirical manner, was described by the Indian writer Vivek Narayan as a mixture of *Waiting for Godot* and the American sitcom *Sanford and Son*. It ran from 1985 until 1990 and was watched at times by more than thirty million viewers.

With every TV episode and every newspaper column, Saro-Wiwa's fame grew, and he became all the more bound to his duty. In the book, *On a Darkling Plain,* mentioned above, he called attention to the idea of a federal Nigeria and the form and manner in which the realisation of this form of state had been frustrated by the military dictators. The duty of the African writer, he felt, lay in struggling against injustice and in sharpening the people's consciousness of the oppression under which they still existed: "...the writer must be *l'homme engagé*: the intellectual man of action. He must take part in mass demonstrations. He must establish direct contact with the people and resort to the strength of African literature, oratory in the tongue".

One of the best examples of such "engaged" writing is his short story, *Africa Kills Her Sun*, a satirical tale about a thief, Bana, who is condemned to death for armed robbery. The story is written in the form of a letter. Bana writes a farewell letter to his former girlfriend named Zole, from which the reader discovers how he became a thief: one day it became clear to him that he lived in a society in which only fraud and corruption were rewarded, while the honest man was always the loser. And since the honest man doesn't succeed against the swindler, Bana will become like the rest of the society. He became a thief but of course it went wrong. Why, he asked, do Ministers and Presidents plunder the national treasury without being punished, while he, a small-time thief who committed burglaries hand in hand with the police, stands before the firing squad? Why was he mocked when he comprehensively confessed to his offences and not once asked for clemency? He and his friends know their fate, they know they have earned it. With the recognition of their crimes they show that they are morally superior to the politicians who steal daily and never admit it. Bana writes to Zole, "We went into our career because we didn't see any basic difference between what we were doing and what most others are doing throughout the land today. In every facet of our lives – in politics, in commerce and in the professions – robbery is the base line". Bana is sorry for Zole, who must still suffer under these conditions.

The metaphor of imprisonment and arrest permeates Saro-Wiwa's work. He saw the Ogoni as prisoners in their own land; prisoners of Shell and the government; prisoners of the presence of vast amounts of oil, which absolutely should have been a source of wealth for them, but led them to ruin. In his book *Prisoners of Jebs* (1988) he took the metaphor of imprisonment still further. Vivek Narayan thinks that this is the key to an understanding of the work of Saro-Wiwa, whose *oeuvre* "develops a system". Narayan writes, "The fascinating thing about *Prisoners of Jebs* is that it is simultaneously dystopia and utopia. 'In the year of our Lord nineteen hundred and eighty-five,' Saro-Wiwa tells us, 'the Organisation of African Unity' decided in its accustomed wisdom to set up an elite prison on the Dark Continent' ". The Nigerians take this on and build the prison, an artificial island off the coast of Bar Beach ...On one hand, this prison is autocratically ruled by an ambitious director who eventually tries to declare it a republic, a contractor and likely self-invented chief, Chief Popa (the Pogopapa of Papapogo) and an arbitrary chief justice who happens to be, very literally, a kangaroo. On the other hand, this prison, like many of Africa's prisons at the time, incarcerates many of its finest minds and talents: 'the beautiful singing bird' that is obviously a stand-in for Fela Kuti, 'the erudite and chimerical Professor with magical and divinatory powers' who begins as a stand-in for Wole Soyinka..."

Prisoners of Jebs belongs to a trilogy, with *Pita Dumbrok's Prison* and *Return to Jebs*. In Saro-Wiwa's last work, *A Month and a Day*, his posthumously published memoir of prison, the metaphor of prison acquires an oppressive reality.

His literary creation, his journalistic activity and his publishing work he neglected in 1987, when he was invited by a new dictator, General Babangida, to co-operate with the constituent assembly that was to prepare for Nigeria's return to democracy. Soon he noticed, as did the rest of the country much later, that Babangida's intentions were not honest. He announced his resignation.

From the beginning of the 1990s he again devoted himself entirely to the struggle of the Ogoni. He was always travelling, and at international events struggled to direct the attention of the world to the Ogoni. Of course the great powers, joined together in the global economic system, shared responsibility for the ravages that Saro-Wiwa struggled against, yet among the western governments he found no audience for his concerns. Disappointed, he had to admit that "In the final analysis, no one is interested in the problems of Nigeria, of Africa."

If there was a solution it would have to be found at home, in Africa. On his travels he also met representatives of Non-Governmental Organisations who were engaged in the struggle against environmental destruction and social prejudice around the world. They imparted to him the recognition that his struggle for the self-determination of the Ogoni would not be won if the environmental catastrophe was not included. From this he drew the conclusion, "The expression 'Ogoni Land' has no meaning; the word 'Ogoni' alone says it all. The people are the land, they are inseparably bound to it, and if the land dies all the people die too; and that is what the oil concerns are actually doing, with the help of the government – genocide, extermination of a people".

It appeared to him that the best way to bring this message directly to the people was the **Movement for the Survival of the Ogoni People** (MOSOP), a civil rights organisation that he had co-founded and whose spokesman he was. In *A Month and a Day* he told of how the MOSOP became so big that the oil concerns could no longer ignore it and perceived it as a threat. A high point for MOSOP was the protest march of 4th January 1993. In the run-up to it, Saro-Wiwa had written a book, *Genocide in Nigeria: The Ogoni Tragedy*, that explained the reasons for the demonstration and where it would lead. Its goals were the autonomy of Ogoni, the cleaning up of the areas damaged by the oil industry and the sharing of the population in the income from the oil industry. In November 1992 the MOSOP members travelled throughout Ogoni land to summon the masses to participate in the planned demonstration. Especially, the youth – which in Nigeria means people aged under forty – were ready to finally do something about their dead-end situation. In selected villages, Saro-Wiwa gave speeches proposing a resolution, in which it was stated: "We call upon Shell, Chevron and the Nigerian National Petroleum Company, the three oil concerns, active in Ogoni, to pay damages of four billion US dollars for environmental destruction as well as six billion dollars for unpaid rents and fees for mining rights, and this within thirty days, otherwise we will conclude that you have decided to leave the country."

It was a daring, if not actually a dangerous move, since for a long time not all leaders of the Ogoni supported MOSOP and its plans. President Babangida had raised the ban on political activities, and the Ogoni elite, with their eyes on lucrative posts in the administration, had in any case no use for politically explosive action. Be that as it may, the protest march took place, and its success far exceeded Saro-Wiwa's expectations. Observers from local as well as international organisations and journalists from the whole world reported the event. On the day of the march Saro-Wiwa and members of MOSOP moved from village to village, from Gokana to Bori, to Baen and Tangh, and spoke to mass meetings. He gave his speech in Khana, the local language, and explained that Shell was *persona non grata* in Ogoni land, and "challenged the company, it would have to kill all the men, women and children of the Ogoni before it could extract more oil from the Ogoni area".

It was a strong speech, and naturally Shell took notice of it, as did the next Nigerian dictator, General Sani Abacha. From then on, Saro-Wiwa was a marked man. On 3rd April 1993 he was arrested by the security forces for the first time. He had just returned from England, where he had buried his fourteen-year-old son Tedum, who had died at Eton. Tired and heart-broken, he still found the strength to accept an invitation to give a lecture to students in Warri. At the entrance to the auditorium twenty armed policemen, who escorted him out of the city and back to Rivers State, awaited him. On 18th April 1993, he was again arrested for no reason. His house and office were ransacked and many important documents confiscated. He was arrested again on 21st June 1993 and held for a month in prisons in Lagos, Port Harcourt and Enugu. Then on 21st May 1994, the murders happened: amid disturbances during a rally, four Ogoni chiefs, known opponents of MOSOP, were killed. The next day Ken Saro-Wiwa and eight other representatives of MOSOP were arrested, "and since then I found myself in shackles in a secret military camp outside Port Harcourt, where I am held in isolation and exposed to physical and psychological torture", reported Saro-Wiwa from prison.

Over a year later, under the eyes of the entire world, Ken Saro-Wiwa and the eight other condemned were hanged on the orders of General Abacha, and many think that Shell also bore responsibility for it. International protests, the conferring of the Alternative Nobel Prize and the nomination for the Nobel Prize had been of no use. In the foreword to *A Month and a Day* (1995), Wole Soyinka, holder of the Nobel Prize for Literature, wrote, "These were brutal, gruesome killings, absolutely inexcusable. That the murders were committed by young Ogoni activists, members of MOSOP ... who were loyally devoted to their leader Ken Saro-Wiwa, that he neglected to condemn these murders in the sharpest terms, on that basis, Ken could be morally blamed to a certain degree. But to convict him of complicity, whether direct or indirect, was an act of cynical opportunism".

In a show trial, based on false witness, he was convicted of incitement and instigation and hanged, but history has absolved him, and he has become a role model. He showed the world that the oil companies shrink from nothing if it is a matter of profit. He made the world conscious that environmental damage such as happened in Ogoni land is an international phenomenon. Our environment is in danger everywhere, and nothing will change this as long as people do not stand up and say, Enough! – even if, like Ken Saro-Wiwa, they must risk their lives for it.

In a letter Saro-Wiwa assured his friend, the British writer William

Boyd, "There is no doubt that my ideas will prevail with time, but I must bear the pain of the moment ... To me the most important thing is that I have used my talents as a writer to enable the people of Ogoni to stand against their tormentors ... With my writing I have brought it about ... I believe I have won the moral victory".

Bibliography

By Ken Saro-Wiwa:

*Sozaboy,*Port Harcourt, Nigeria: Saros International Publishers (1985) republished as *Sozaboy : a novel in rotten English*, Burnt Mill, Harlow, Essex, England and New York, USA: Longman (1994).

A Month and a Day: A Detention Diary, Penguin (1995).

Genocide in Nigeria: The Ogoni Tragedy, Saros Nigeria (1992).

Similia: essays on anomic Nigeria. London: Saros International Publishers (1991)

Pita Dumbrok's Prison, Saros International Publishers (1991).

On a Darkling Plain: An Account of the Nigerian Civil War. Epsom: Saros. (1989).

Basi and Company: Four Television Plays. Port Harcourt: Saros International Publishers (1988).

Prisoners of Jebs, Saros International Publishers (1988).

FELA ANIKULAPO-KUTI (Nigeria)

THE MOST DANGEROUS MUSICIAN IN THE WORLD

BY AYNI CAMARA

One afternoon in the year 1949 the leading lights of the Abeokuta Women's Union – the former Abeokuta Ladies Club – sat together and carved out a fearsome plan. For ten years they had been agitating against the king of Egba, who had become their enemy. As the local ruler, he had the thankless task of carrying out the decisions of the British colonial administration. After the arbitrary taxes for the Second World War, the colonial masters had imposed a special tax on women. "There is least danger from the women, especially the market women," they must have thought. At last, in the course of colonisation, they would be pushed out of their traditionally powerful position and in the worst case, the local chief was there as lightning conductor.

With biting newspaper articles, pamphlets and impressive protest marches, the women of Abeokuta had fought the local executive. Now they were getting ready for the next move. "He will strip us down to our shirts. Then we'll give him our last shirt!" said the valiant chairperson. When they passed on the news of their unthinkable plan to the 20,000 members of the organisation, the message leaked out and reached the king's chamberlain. As if stung by a tarantula, the old man jumped up and stormed barefoot into the royal chamber. With great effort and wide staring eyes, he informed the shocked monarch of the threatening disaster,

"Majesty! The Abeokuta Women's Union are preparing to march on the palace to ... The women have something atrocious in mind... They want to come to the palace and ... undress and throw their clothes in front of the gate!"

For a moment the king thought it was just a bad joke, for such a sacrilege was beyond his powers of imagination, but he saw the horror in the staring eyes of his trustworthy chamberlain, and he knew that the matter was serious. From the name of the leader he also knew that she was indubitably capable of such a mad idea. A few years before she had made herself the talk of the town when she had abused the head of the British colonial administration before the assembled team as "prick" and "bastard". Not coincidentally, in 1947 she had acquired the name "Lioness of Lisabi". It was clear to the king that the shocking scene would cast a shadow over his reign for all time. He must prevent this threatening shame by all means and against the known resolve of his opponent, there was only one way, he announced his abdication.

On that day there stirred in the eleven-year-old Fela Ransome-Kuti the desire to stand up against grievances just as determinedly, and to teach fear to the mighty. The women's triumph over the chief not only filled him with pride but also gave direction to the course of his life, for the women's leader was his mother, Funmilayo Ransome-Kuti. As a small child, the young Fela accompanied the activist to demonstrations and thus was very early confronted with the various facets of repression endured by the majority of the Nigerian people. Besides the anti-colonial movement in which she was active with her husband, his mother worked for equal rights, international co-operation between women's organisations and for pacifism. Educated in England as a teacher, she founded a school that would prepare the younger generation for its tasks in a free Nigeria after the end of the colonial period. Her multiple efforts for change earned her the name "Mother of Africa". For her son she was the embodiment of steadfastness that would imprint itself on his life.

When Fela was sent to London in 1958 to study medicine, like his elder and later, his younger brother, his stubbornness became evident for the first time. The twenty-year-old decided against a respectable medical career in favour of his passion, music. He had inherited his musical gift from his father, the Reverend Israel Oludotun Ransome-Kuti and at the age of sixteen, he was already playing in a band. After his studies at Trinity College in London, where he founded his first band, he dared the next step when he resolved to compete against the dominant American style, towards which the African music scene was oriented, with something new; a music that would give expression to his own tradition. In 1967, with a mixture of jazz and African elements, he achieved a new music that he baptised Afro-beat. At a time when teenagers spent half their lives under colonial rule, the introduction of African sounds was more than a musical renewal. It was a cultural awakening.

In 1969 Fela decided to abolish the one-way traffic in musical influences and take his music to the USA. There too his obstinacy was astonishing: against the unwritten rules of the profession, he held fast to his principle of not playing recorded pieces in concerts. "Not only is it not creative, it also works against any further development," he explained. Because of this he had little commercial success. His uncompromising behaviour led to an early end of the tour. After he had fired an organiser, he had problems with the immigration officials: they had received anonymous information that the group had no work permits. The ten-month tour of the USA nevertheless counted as the birth of Afro-beat, for with this step, Fela brought African music to the international stage. Soon after that, other groups such as Osibisa from Ghana and Xalam from Senegal followed.

The American trip also marked a shift in musical and political attitudes. Besides the greats of the music scene like Miles Davis, James Brown, Sly Stone and Tony Allen, who became a central figure in the band, Fela met leaders of the Civil Rights movement such as Angela Davis, Sandra Smith of the Black Panther Party, Stokely Carmichael alias Kwame Touré, author of the famous book *Black Power*, and thus experienced at close proximity the African American struggle against racist domination. This experience proved decisive for his political consciousness. After the trip to the USA, he changed the name of the band Koola Lobitos to Nigeria 70, and decided to make his music the "voice of the voiceless". It was the beginning of a unique confrontation, for in Nigeria ruled a military dictatorship that reacted sharply to dissent.

In his songs Fela discussed the abuses in African societies and the oppression of Blacks in other parts of the world. His appearances in his own discotheque became regular rallies for democracy, human rights and social justice. To make his radical rejection of the military government clear, he founded a commune and declared it the Free Republic of Kalakuta. For this, the magazine *Rolling Stone* named him "the most dangerous musician in the world". What the ruling junta dismissed as an artist's harmless show quickly developed into a form of opposition that had to be taken seriously. The commune that grew to include more than three hundred inhabitants, not only allowed free expression, but also offered free medical care. The Free Republic of Kalakuta became the centre of opposition against the system. More and more raids were carried out to get rid of this source of disorder.

To these harassments and attempts at intimidation, Fela responded with the song 'Zombie', which let loose a colossal disruptive force. In the song he criticised the role of the security forces in an authoritarian regime, in which he characterised them as mindless henchmen who were let loose on the people like zombies to spread fear and horror. At a concert in neighbouring Ghana, the song caused such an uproar that Fela was asked to leave. In Nigeria the mighty had gotten into a lather. Foaming with rage, the President sent for his Minister of the Interior, so a sentry reported:

"This Fela is creating ever more unrest," he said, in an ominously quiet voice. "What are you thinking of doing about it?"

"This is a difficult case, General ... ah ... President," responded the Minister in a small voice. "He is very popular, and he can't be intimidated. Even the..."

"I don't want to hear any excuses from you, but a solution!" the President said angrily, making the table shake with his right fist. "I expect you to solve this problem once and for all! Otherwise I will have to look for a more competent minister."

In a still harsher voice, the Minister repeated the dressing down to the appropriate commander. Five minutes later, the head of the striking force winced when his boss informed him by telephone, of the presidential outburst. In an even harsher tone, the head of the striking force also gave the order for mobilisation which reached the end of the chain of command.

On 18th February, 1977, toward midnight, a unit of a thousand soldiers moved out, to smoke out the nest of opposition to the president. With unrestrained brutality, the uniformed mob fell upon the instruments and the unarmed inhabitants. After the destruction, the soldiers set the whole premises on fire. The uncontrolled horde did not even spare the musician's aged mother: the eighty-six-year-old was thrown out of the window of her room in the upper story; she later died of the injuries therefrom. Fela suffered a cracked skull and barely survived the murderous attack. The next day the powers-that-be let it be known through the media that an "unknown soldier" was responsible for the attack.

Fela responded to this crime with an act that in the strength of its assertion remains unrivalled: by secret means he got to the Presidential Palace and placed a coffin in front of the gate. For this public accusation he was beaten up by the guard. After these experiences the musician rebel sharpened his tone. Besides the songs 'Unknown Soldier' and 'Coffin for the Head of State', that broadcast his indictment, he directly attacked the President and his Vice in the song 'International Thief-Thief'. Just as bluntly he threatened to take the President to court. Eventually the charismatic musician had the masses behind him. When the military president found it necessary to organise a democratic election in 1979, Fela founded a party named Movement of the People. His candidature was rejected.

In the desperate manoeuvering by the military dictatorship that concluded the short democratic phase, the rebellious musician was faced with arrest. He received a prison sentence of only five years, but after twenty months, he was released by the new regime. Now he conducted his frontal attacks against the heads of state of other countries. On the cover of the record 'Beasts of No Nation', that denounced the plundering of the wealth of African countries and lack of action against the racist apartheid regime in South Africa, the Congolese dictator Mobutu, the English Prime Minister Margaret Thatcher, the US President Ronald Reagan and the South African President Piete Botha were perceived as blood-sucking monsters hovering over the chaos of the disoriented masses. Thus Fela openly raised accusations against the deposition and murder of African politicians like Kwame Nkrumah and Thomas Sankara.

That his accusations against the politics of the west were not mere general reproaches was shown above all by the behaviour of the brutal military dictator, Sani Abacha. Apart from the absurd murder charge against Fela and four members of his group, and the life sentence to which Fela's brother Beko, a prominent representative of Nigerian civil society, was condemned, the dictator shocked the world with the imposition of the death sentence against the Ogoni Nine – the Nigerian writer Ken Saro-Wiwa and eight other activists, who led the struggle of the Ogoni people against the massive destruction of their environment by the oil production activities of the Shell company.

Fela raised his criticisms not least also against the citizens of Nigeria, especially the privileged classes. Just as in 'Sorrow, Tears and Blood' he named the individual's anguish as the basis of social inaction, so he opposed the intellectual submission that prevented a new orientation for African societies. This was the case with the song 'Colonial Mentality', in which he highlighted the inadequate cultural self-assertion following political independence, and in 'Coffin for Head of State', he denounced the religiously motivated division in society:

I waka many business anywhere in Africa
North and South them get them policies
One Christian and the other one Muslim
Anywhere the Muslims them they reign
Na Senior Alhaji na him be Director
Anywhere the Christians them they reign
Na the best friend to Bishop na him be Director
It is a known fact that for many thousand years
We Africans we had our own tradition
These moneymaking organizations
Them come put we Africans in total confusion...

In the spirit of his reflections on his own culture, already as he was growing up, he had distanced himself from his Christian identity – with parsons for father and grandfather – and turned to traditional African religion. For the same reason, he did replace the non-African family name Ransome with Anikulapo, meaning "he who carries death in his pocket". His mother also adopted this name change.

The struggle for cultural self-assertion explains the seemingly contradictory Pidgin English, in which his songs were mainly created. In fact, it was one of his few compromises: limitation to his mother tongue Yoruba would not only have excluded the other population groups of Nigeria, but also the people of other African countries. Access to a bigger public was all the more important as Fela involved himself in the unification of Africa, for in such a state, he saw the only possibility for independent renewal. In the new union, Blacks from other parts of the world should also find a home. This vision of an African renaissance explained the last name change that Fela proposed for his band in 1980: with 'Egypt 80' he recalled the flowering of African civilisations at the time of the Pharaohs and brought to cultural consciousness what Africa historically had suffered comparatively even more under hundreds of years of foreign rule. Because of this, he was called the spiritual son of Kwame Nkrumah, the Pan-African visionary and of the radical civil rights organiser, Malcolm X.

The name of Fela however was also involved in an insoluble controversy. In 1978 he married twenty-seven singers from his group in one day, which produced an impression of an eccentric macho type and was the origin of accusations of sexist behaviour. Many explain this provokingly sensational behaviour by the legal status that the women thus acquired. That the first anniversary of the fall of Kalakuta was chosen for this extraordinary action suggested a political significance, and his great respect for his mother who spoke against hatred of women. Nevertheless, the mass wedding remained problematic.

With his nearly forty albums and his uncompromising response to the various forms of oppression, Fela today still exercises an inspiring effect. In Africa and beyond, he is remembered above all, as the pioneer of modern African music and ideal activist. The great recognition that he enjoyed was shown at his death in August 1997, when an estimated more than a million people accompanied him on his last journey.

Bibliography:
Carlos Moore, *Fela Kuti, this bitch of a life. Die autorisierte Biografie* (The authorised biography). Berlin 2011;
Michael Veal: *Fela: The Life and Times of an African Musical Icon.* Philadelphia 2000;
Rolf Brockmann and Gerd Hötter: *Szene Lagos. Reise in eine afrikanische Kulturmetropole* (Lagos Scenes: Travel to an African cultural metropolis). Munich 1994.

AHMADOU KOUROUMA, (Ivory Coast)

WITH A SHARP PEN AGAINST DICTATORS

BY PATRICE DJOUFACK

On 6th September 1943 at around 11 pm., a sixteen-year-old arrived in the Abidjan railway station. He was to continue his schooling in this strange city. Apparently, he had arrived on the wrong train: according to the rules of the colonial power, Blacks were forbidden to be out after 9 pm. As he stepped out of the station building he was imperiously stopped by a white policeman. At that moment a white pastor, who had evidently seen the impending conflict, approached. He defused the situation with a couple of words and took the bewildered youth home with him. On the way he explained to him what the policeman had wanted to do with him. Until then, the boy had only been aware that African languages were strictly forbidden in the school yard; all the more radically would he later absolutely reject French in favour of African Expression.

The next morning he learned a second rule of city living. On his exploratory tour through Abidjan, he met someone he knew, an Afro-French classmate who had also been admitted into the school in Bingerville, a neighbourhood near Abidjan. He went with him to the CFAO department store. Suddenly the young Kourouma felt somebody grab him by the ear and pull it vigorously. Thus did the black shop assistant haul him over to the area meant for Africans. The proud young man of the Malinke people would never forget this humiliation.

Chapter 5

The experience of degradation was embedded in the conspicuous contradictions of the city: on the one hand the abundance in the White quarters, and on the other hand the poverty of the Blacks, whose labour above all made possible the flourishing business of the Europeans in coffee and cocoa. For the young Ahmadou, who came from Boundiali in the north of Ivory Coast, which at that time belonged to French West Africa, and was descended from a Muslim trading family, the experience made a lasting impression on him. In his literary work he would always come back to how the powerful steal from the powerless.

In school, Ahmadou developed a great passion for newspapers. Since he had no money with which to buy them, he regularly ransacked the trash bins of the French district commander for them and spent hours reading. From the newspapers he learned much about the political situation in the colonies and in France, the so-called "motherland". Spellbound, he followed the news of the month-long strike of West African railway workers, who demanded the same rights as their colleagues in France and in 1947 forced the colonial administration to its knees. The legendary victory of African workers over a world power seemed to have left its mark on him: the older he became, the more rebellious became his views and his behaviour.

In 1947 he was admitted to the Technical High School in Bamako, in modern Mali. Four years later, he led a revolt against the poor conditions at the school. As a ringleader he was promptly expelled from the school. A few weeks later he would have had his diploma in his hand. Nevertheless, he was drafted into the "Senegal Brigade", the West African unit of the French army. What had begun as a simple demand for simple rights at school became a dramatic turning point in the life of the schoolboy. For the proud young man whose grandfather was an officer in the army of the opposition fighter, Samory Touré, things still got worse. He had to take part in the quelling of the first anti-colonial revolt in the Ivory Coast. He refused the order to shoot and was imprisoned, demoted and dismissed from the army.

Because there was a striking lack of French-speaking soldiers in the colonial forces, he was drafted again and sent to a regiment that was to fight the freedom movement in Indochina. Again he was expected to shoot at people with whom he felt solidarity. Like most of his generation, he was a communist and an enemy of colonial rule. In his revolt he considered deserting but older comrades took him aside and rebuked him, "Young man, use the opportunity to learn the art of warfare. Then you will be able to fight the Whites better." In Saigon (Today Ho-Chi-Minh City) he enlisted for three years. Since he was one of the few "Senegal Brigaders" who could read and write he was transferred to the military broadcaster and an army newspaper. The injustice experienced at close quarters was a burden to him but he realised the way forward. With iron discipline he put aside a large part of his wages because he wanted to acquire his school-leaving diploma by correspondence and study. In 1954 he rejoiced at the end of his military service and over the defeat that the colonial power had suffered in Indochina.

When he started his actual studies in Lyon, he really wanted to study aeronautical and nautical engineering, but there was no scholarship for Africans in these disciplines: anti-colonial demonstrations by African students in France were making waves. In 1956 the colonial power changed its strategy: the colonies had to have a certain amount of autonomy, but under French supervision. The assent of leading politicians to this "colonization lite" fed Kourouma's disillusionment and distrust: "The Africans don't want independence at all!" With a critical eye he followed the developments that at the beginning of the 1960s led to a surge towards independence.

At the end of 1961 and after the conclusion of his studies and a position at a French insurance company, he took a lucrative post with a bank in Ivory Coast. Twelve years after being expelled from school, Ahmadou Kourouma belonged to the elite of the country that at that time had become independent. He did not succumb to the "magic of the unity party" of the Francophile President, Houphouët-Boigny, perhaps only because he did not have the opportunity, as he ironically said in an interview.

On 14th January, 1963 a major police raid shook the country. All functionaries who were not among the President's vassals were arrested, including Kourouma. Unlike his friends, after a short time he was set free. "Because of my French wife they were afraid of a protest from France", he explained. This special treatment however plunged him into a deep crisis: in comparison to his imprisoned friends. He felt himself to have been a beneficiary of the system, even though he was dismissed overnight and given notice to leave his residence. For half a year he tried to find a new job until he realised that there had been instructions from above not to hire him, and that nobody dared defy the instruction. His anger was also directed against the silent West, especially France, who several times had sent paratroops to guide its former colony in the desired direction.

He went into exile. Stemming from his wish to make misuse of power public and to support his imprisoned and tortured friends, he began his first novel, *Les Soleils de l'Indépendances* (*The Suns of Independence*). In Africa, as in France, no publisher was prepared to publish the book; the break with every literary and content convention is very striking. After five years a small press in Montreal indicated an interest. A short time later the well-known French publishers regretted that they had not recognised the significance of the novel, for it marked a decisive turning point in African literature. For the first time, a writer had dealt with post-colonial relations and highlighted the betrayal by the African elite of the vision of a new society that should arise from independence. He expressed the gap between expectation and experience in the young states, "I stupidly thought that with independence thieves would disappear". The novel was not only translated into several languages, about thirty but also, integrated into curricula of schools and universities in Africa and France.

After his return from exile in Algeria, Kourouma wrote a play with the title *Tougnantigui ou le diseur de vérité – The Prophet*. In it he denounced the tyranny and mendacity of the regime. He was unequivocally urged to leave the country, and the prominent author was sent off to an important post in Cameroon. In Cameroon and then Togo, he took up the challenge of administration of an international financial institution. He was aware that people hoped he would fail. In the end he showed his enemies what an independent insurance concern in Africa should look like.

Readers waited twenty-three years for his second novel. In the new work, *Monnè, outrages et défies* (*Monnè, insults and challenges*) he told of a fictional kingdom in the north of the Ivory Coast that was conquered by the French. With biting irony in a sort of Malinke-French, colonialism was bitterly criticised. Kourouma sent a clear signal against Europe's selective perception that all too gladly repressed the horrors of its colonial expansion. He explained the relations between Africa and Europe in his inimitable fashion, "The Europeans are against slavery and we constantly whisper into their ears that they have been the incomparable champions of slavery. They are against colonisation, and we whisper constantly in their ears that they have been abominable colonialists. They are democrats, and we whisper constantly in their ears that in the Cold War they installed and protected bloodthirsty dictators among us. They are against racism, and we whisper constantly in their ears that our brothers who live among them are exposed to demeaning discrimination."

After his second novel that went through several printings, he sharpened his pen against African dictators: *En attendant le vote des bêtes sauvages (Waiting for the Wild Beasts to Vote)*. It is an unsparing critique of the authoritarian presidents that destroy the hopes of African peoples. To expose the perversion of absolute power he chooses the narrative tradition of praise singers, ironically distanced, as practised in the ceremonies of traditional Malinke hunting societies. Just as relentlessly, the author criticises the complicity of European states that laid the groundwork for these regimes during the Cold War.

The older he became, the more radically Kourouma took a position. "It is time for us to wake up", called the pensioner in conversations with African students. His need, in his works, to call those responsible by name, grew even stronger. Correspondingly paranoid, the powerful searched his literary works for similarities to themselves. The first edition of his second novel was pulped and the new edition was delayed for a year by lawsuits against his publisher. In the 2000s he had to leave his homeland again; his public condemnation of the manipulations that led to civil war had brought him the enmity of the government. The bloody division of the Ivory Coast is the theme of his last, unfinished novel *Quand on refuse, on dit non* (When one refuses one says no), that appeared after his sudden death in 2004.

In his literary work, Kourouma put his imprint on the history of modern African literature and inspired many young writers. His influence lies not only in his uncompromising attitude to all oppression, but also in a new utilisation of African cultures and values. His unique style and his subversive wit open one's eyes for an entirely new critical look at social developments in the past and in the future. His trick was understanding through laughter. Ahmadou Kourouma himself liked to laugh at his literary sallies.

Ahmadou Kourouma: *Les soleils des indépendances*, Montreal University Press,1968, *The suns of independence*, transl. Adrian Adams, Holm es & Meier, 1981; *Monnè* Éditions du Seuil 1990;
En attendant le vote des bêtes sauvages, Éditions du Seuil 1998, *Waiting for the Wild Beasts to Vote* transl. Frank Wynne, Heinemann 2003.
Jean-Michel Djian: *Ahmadou Kourouma*, Paris 2010.

WELDEDINGL (Eritrea)

THE MASTER OF THE POETIC ART

BY SOLOMON TSEHAYE

In the year 1803, in the village of Mes'hal, a little boy who would make his mark on the intellectual history of Eritrea like no other was born. His poetry, which has come down to us orally, is witness to his unusual literary gift and impressively demonstrates the strength of words and the role that a thinker can play in society.

Weldedingl was born into an Orthodox Christian family. His unusual name, Son of the Virgin (Mary), reveals the future that his father, Pater Gedul, intended for him: he too should follow in the footsteps of his ancestors and become a priest. However, as he himself told it, the youth had a vision that revealed to him that he should become a poet, a *masségna*. Veldedingl did as he was bid and henceforth saw his destiny in the composition of *massé* and *melqes*, the highest form of poetic art in Tigrinya, the language of Eritrea. *Massé* were performed at weddings and other festivals, *melqes* by contrast, at funerals, but they are not purely praises or laments: both could also include social criticism. What is special about these poems is that they mainly arise extemporaneously, but in any case without models, as was customary in oral cultures.

Already with his first *melqes*, Weldedingl excited considerable attention. At the age of seventeen he came directly from watching over his sheep to the funeral of a rich woman of the aristocracy, whose husband had a lover. To the astonishment of the many funeral guests, the young man declaimed a memorable poem that he called *May I attempt it*:

> *May I attempt to compose a lament,*
> *May I attempt to tell her story,*
> *She was the daughter of a man of rank,*
> *And she slept in a golden bed.*
> *Daughter of a respected woman,*
> *Owner of cattle.*
> *Is it not a pity*
> *That a wealthy woman*
> *Who nourished the poor and the needy*
> *Could not evade death?*
> *I wonder about the other woman:*
> *While people mourn she rejoices*
> *And does not comprehend that sooner or later*
> *She will suffer the same fate.*

This performance at an unusually early age was the explosive prelude to an exceptional career. A few days later, the unmasked lover sent for Weldedingl.

"Did you see me rejoice at the funeral that you could say something so dreadful?" she asked him indignantly.

"No", he answered quietly, "But deep within you, you were glad. That is only human." He explained to her that the words had poured from him, without his having planned it. Enraged at this answer the woman cross-questioned him.

"If that is so, then you can give a poem about that fly there." She had hardly finished the sentence when the young man began:

> *Fly*
> *Aimless wanderer*
> *Formed from milk and moisture*
> *You shame the best cook*
> *By diving into the pot.*
> *Flying to forbidden places*

You see women's intimate places
Shame on you, cunning fly.

The woman was speechless, especially because of the last lines. To make sure that no more unwelcome words came from his lips she quickly gave the boy a tip for his performance and thankfully sent him away.

After his debut at the funeral celebration, which was quite unforgettable, Weldedingl quickly became in demand as a *masségna*. He got as far as *Aite*, a title that in the traditional society of the Tigrinya people was given only to chiefs and important personalities. Soon he was considered a poet with prophetic abilities because he made predictions that turned out to be correct. The story of Bahregas Godefa shows what influence he had.

Bahregas was the son of the priest Kinfu and ruled over the area of Eggba Hames in southern Eritrea. In the 1840s he seized the villages of Ma'ereba, Addi Baekel and others to expand his dominions. Thereupon the chiefs of the villages that were related to the seized places met and discussed what should be done. At the end of the meeting they came to an agreement that Bahregas' invasion must not go unpunished. What the council of elders had concluded was sealed with Weldedingl's *massé* called *Priest Kinfu's Son*:

Priest Kinfu's son did wrong and foolishly,
He set Ma'ereba on fire, we cry,
He set Addi Baekel on fire, we cry.
...
We wager that
For what he has done from arrogance and lust for power
He will pay with twice as much dishonour.
He thinks we here are men in name only.

When Bahregas heard of the decision of the chiefs he was afraid. Quickly he sent presents to the various chiefs in the hope that he could thereby divert the punishment. The chiefs refused to take the gifts. Some of them considered the overture as an attempt at bribery, and saw the danger that such further advances could divide the community. At this assembly, part of the gathering argued for concluding peacefully, since the offender seemed to have calmed down and wanted to unite with them amicably. Another part recalled the content of Weldedingl's *massé* and came to the conclusion that retaliation must certainly succeed, for the poetic prophecy left no doubt about it. All the villages of Akkele and Guzay took part in the retaliation except one, Akhran, whose chief had been bribed by Bahregas. With 'Addi Shiho in shame' the poet recorded this betrayal for future generations.

If it provoked considerable surprise the way Weldedingl had spurred the elders on to a joint struggle, he left the biggest impression in his home village of Mes'hal. After the death of the chief *Aite* Gebreamlak, a feud broke out over the succession between his eldest son Hailu and the latter's brother, Emmetu. The majority of those entitled to a vote were on the side of the younger son. In the strife Weldedingl, in a poem, took up a position in favour of Hailu, which decided the election. In the course of his reign, Hailu became more and more authoritarian, yet the poet kept faith with him. After Hailu's death he created a powerful *melqes* in which he honoured him as protector of his people, without suppressing the fact that Hailu reigned with an iron hand. More interesting for the people was what he prophesied for the potential successor: that Emmetu would reign with intrigues and unfair methods. The consequence of this prophecy was that Emmetu lost the election and was henceforth hostile to Veldedingl. This made no impression on the poet, even when Emmetu became chief, to the contrary.

Sometime later, Weldedingl was called to the neighbouring village of Akhran, where he was to perform a poem at the funeral of the chief, Kentiba Yalew. In his *melqes* he openly unmasked Emmetu. The latter had intended to invade Akhran, but Kentiba discovered it so that the plan could be thwarted, as it was depicted in the poem *Kentiba Yalew*:

Mes'hal Akhran is a flourishing village,
This makes many chiefs envious,
So they want to destroy it, in vain.
They are too weak to accomplish anything.
A mouse is not confident in the neighbourhood of a cat,
A cow is not confident in the cave of a lion.
Even if Yalew is no longer among us,
His son Bairu won't let himself be overthrown.

Before Weldedingl got back home, Emmetu had already heard of what had happened and had him arrested on his return. Out of fear of the

41

reaction of the populace, he was freed again but in punishment, Emmetu had his best cow slaughtered. Thereafter, relations between the two most important dignitaries in Mes'hal were very strained .

At that time the troublesome poet was invited to the funeral of the wife of a well-known blacksmith. Even though the craft of blacksmithing was of great significance for the traditional society, at that time it had become – and had been for some time – regarded as low caste and of little value. As such the nephew of a woman of the nobility, who had died at the same time, produced a *melqes* that from today's viewpoint was defamatory, with the title *Pure Blood*:

> *Go in peace, beloved aunt,*
> *Woman of pure blood and noble descent.*
> *How sad, that you are denied*
> *A more worthy leave-taking*
> *By the burial of a blacksmith.*

When Weldedingl heard of this insult, he replied immediately with the poem *Son of a Fool*, which had lasting consequences:

> *Unlike a human being*
> *You spew out only nonsense.*
> *Have you ever used anything*
> *That was not produced by your hands?*
> *The devil is conquered with the cross,*
> *Just as mischief-makers are put in chains,*
> *The field is worked with ploughshares,*
> *Trees are felled with axes,*
> *One needs a sickle for the harvest,*
> *For clothing you need a needle,*
> *The lawless are overcome with cannons.*
> *Deep in the bush, beyond fields and meadows,*
> *You sit, incompetent son of a fool.*
> *You are not a whit better than an ox.*

This critical poem of Weldedingl's changed the attitude to blacksmithing. Even a hundred and fifty years later his *melqes* is cited in connection with discrimination against social groups and the devaluation of certain professions.

Then Emmetu died. As he had lived in enmity with Weldedingl and had undertaken constant raids against villages in southern Eritrea, everyone waited eagerly for the poet's presentation. What he recited went beyond what was customary in a *melqes*:

> *You will be buried today,*
> *But you have had people beaten and imprisoned*
> *On the advice of ignoramuses and imbeciles.*
> *I know of some good deeds,*
> *But I will not speak of them today,*
> *Not today! Not today!*

For the family of the deceased it was a shock. If the dead were sent off with such scathing words his soul could not possibly find peace. They were all anxious about what had moved the famous poet, what he had postponed with his "not today!" For the mistakes of the deceased, they begged his forgiveness and replaced his slaughtered cow. Finally, they sent invitations throughout the land to a new memorial celebration. At the celebration, Weldedingl performed a new *melqes*, in which he appreciated the Emmetus' merits, but in the last stanza acknowledged:

> *But never will I forgive the one*
> *Who imprisoned me and had my cow slaughtered.*
> *May the funeral guests concur in my call*
> *For his complete obliteration.*

Despite the affront, the funeral was regarded as finished. The poem however became a component of the Eritrean collective consciousness.

With his extraordinary talent and his attitude of mind, Weldedingl made an impact on the thought of an entire people. His struggle against injustice and his critical attitude made him not only a prominent representative of his time, but also a model for other generations and other societies. For this reason, the *Masségna*, who died in 1885 and left nothing in writing, is today among the most quoted poets in Eritrea.

SARRAOUNIA

(Niger)

A QUEEN IN OPPOSITION

BY M. MOUSTAPHA DIALLO

In 1889 in the small town of Lugu in present-day Niger, the young wife of the King of the Azna died in childbirth. All the efforts of old Dawa, who was master of healing like no other in the district, could not prevent it. In the arms of the deceased lay a little girl. The mourners despaired of her chances of survival without her mother's milk, the only nourishment for a baby. Far and wide there was no nursing mother who could serve as a wet nurse, but Dawa set himself against this second challenge of fate. To the general surprise, he decided to personally take over the infant, and not entrust it to the women, as has been the practice since time immemorial. Amazed, but trusting fully in the abilities of his friend, who was distinguished for his prudence and his intelligence, the King agreed to the unusual plan.

In the care of the recluse, little Mangu got through the critical first months. The milk of Dawa's mare proved to be a good substitute, and the old man showed unexpected skill in dealing with the infant. When the first months were past, Dawa asked the king of Azna if he could keep the child and raise it because he sensed something special about the baby. The father agreed and was glad that his daughter would have an exceptional upbringing. The people were curious about how the little one would develop. What kind of girl would she be? Later, how would she fulfil her duties as princess and wife? And would she not be as unapproachable as the old man? Dawa concerned himself only with the question of how, from this little girl, so tried by fate, he could make a strong woman and a worthy guardian of the heritage of the Azna. From tradition he knew of earlier queens who had defied their male rivals, and no one could later say that his ward was not the equal in birth of other rulers.

In November 1884, while little Mangu took her first riding lessons and practised knife throwing, representatives of the European powers, Turkey and the USA met in the State Chancellery in Berlin. From a variety of motives they had accepted the invitation of that great manipulator Bismarck, to discuss the regulation of trade on the Congo and Niger rivers. After tough negotiations, the General Act of the Berlin Conference was passed on 26th February, 1885. This decree concerning foreign states was the basis for the division of Africa into colonies and the starting gun for the so-called "scramble for Africa", euphemistically called the "race for Africa".

While the European powers fought breathlessly over the "delicious African cake", as the particularly ruthless Belgian king Leopold II frankly called it, the ten-year-old Mangu, now firm in the saddle, acquired insights into human interaction, the world of animals and plants and a first introduction to natural medicine. She now knew which plants heal cuts, which help with stomach ache and which against fever; what plants the arrows are prepared with that lame animals in hunting; and in what combinations one can produce deadly poison from the bodily fluids of animals. Her mentor laid great stress on spiritual education, which included the pantheistic world view, generally called traditional religion, of the Azna, as well as matters of political leadership. With seemingly spontaneous questions he explained to his pupil social values, the cohesion of the community, the role of a ruler and much else. Thus, the first time they went hunting and she played with her hat, he asked her, "Why does one wear a cap on one's head?"

"Because it protects you from the sun," the pupil readily answered.

"Then why isn't it made of iron or wood? That would give more protection."

"Then it would press down too hard."

"It is the same with the chief: he must be endurable. Otherwise, sooner or later he will be shaken off," the teacher concluded the first lesson.

At that time he made known to her that very probably she would be the next queen and that therefore she could never bear a child. "You will take your father's place. For that the people need your entire strength. At that time you will not be the mother of one, but of the entire country. Above all then, as spiritual leader you have a great responsibility. It will be up to you whether the centuries old heritage of our forefathers is lost or lives on. Our ancestors will stand by you, if you conduct yourself as all kings before you."

What that meant, she would only discover later. Whether she was sad about it was not passed down. The meaning of renouncing motherhood she presumably was no more able to evaluate than the heavy burden that already lay on her young shoulders. However, she was determined not to disappoint expectations, and proud that she had been selected for such a great task. She had the feeling of becoming a whole size larger within a short time.

Mangu was not yet twenty years old when her qualification as a leader would be decided. On that fateful day the neighbouring Fulbe of Sokoto, who had taken over from the Arabs the idea of religious war, together with Islam, made their first attempt to force the true faith upon the "unbelievers" of Azna and at the same time expand their own dominions. After a fervent morning prayer, in the consciousness of their divine mandate they had made their way to Lugu, to seize the capital of the king of the unbelievers.

Among the Azna, in the gray dawn, the practised eyes of the sentry had discerned unusual activity in the savannah and recognised the danger. Shouting loudly they sounded the alarm on the drums and in a trice the people were violently startled from their slumbers in the cool morning hours. Quickly the old men and the women woke the children and sought shelter in the furthest corners of the fortress, while the men ran to their posts and grabbed their arms at the double. In this tumult it was observed that Mangu also had a weapon and mixed with the archers. In the front line she amazed friend and foe with her resolution and skill. Like the English at the sight of the Maid of Orleans, the Fulbe were alarmed at this unexpected appearance, whose fearlessness seemed to double the spirit of the Azna warriors. And like the English in the defeat at Orleans they recognised in the resolute female warrior a witch incarnate and lost the religious faith with which they had marched so light-footedly into enemy territory. Even more light-footedly, the self-styled holy warriors now made a disorderly retreat, in which they stumbled over each other and accidently left behind several weapons for the enemy.

Thus was born the legend of a sorceress, who turned aside the arrows of the enemy and led those of her own to their goal by spiritual means. For the Azna it was the baptism by fire of a new "Sarroaunia", in the Hausa language, queen, a political and spiritual leader. While the warriors exuberantly celebrated their new comrade in arms and the women put their hands before their mouths in astonishment, Dawa sat unmoving among his comrades and quietly enjoyed how spectacularly his foster daughter had proved herself. His earlier first impression had not changed. At least as proud was her father, who could now contemplate the future in peace. When he died a few years later his daughter was unanimously chosen to succeed him.

As queen, Sarroaunia Mangu astonished all with her thirst for action and her talent for organisation. Besides the obvious strengthening of the city walls and the development of female warriors, she put great store by the education of the youth as traditionally conscious and self-confident Azna. That a new wind was blowing, she also indicated by the choice of her partner, who was a griot, a member of the caste of singers and guardians of history, and therefore of lower rank. Not least, the Azna warriors, who would not stay behind if a woman bravely went ahead of them, were particularly inspired by Sarroaunia's regency.

She was also a challenge to the other side. After the first shock, the Emir of Sokoto thought of revenge, for the "Sublime Leader of the Believers" and descendant of the great Usman dan Fodio could not allow such a defeat to stand. After all, from what one heard, this woman's mode of life was a unique provocation! The sickly Emir prepared a new, vast expedition. His honour, the great name of his dynasty was on the line.

From the west, more precisely from the base camp of the French in Senegal, a much bigger danger threatened. The so-called scramble for Africa was entering its decisive phase: in all parts of the continent people were arming themselves against the increasing demands of the foreigners, by whom they were blinded by deceitful treaties, even though as a rule they received them hospitably. From the great kings in command of as many as forty thousand soldiers to the little people who could only defend themselves against the invasion by emmigrating, a resistance took shape against the colonial expansion, but through

47

their superiority in weapons and forced recruitment of the men in the conquered countries, the Europeans conquered region after region, even though several struggles lasted for more than two decades.

In 1898 after three failed expeditions France sent out troops under the command of the officers Paul Voulet and Julien Chanoine from Dakar towards the east, to snatch Lake Chad from the English and thus unite into one territory their possessions in the west with those in central Africa. This expedition went down in history for its exceptional brutality – villages were burned down, even girls and women were hanged. Voulet and Chanoine proceeded with such ferocity that the French government was led to send out a superior officer to arrest those responsible for the crimes that were disgracing the reputation of France. Out of control, the all-conquering colonial machine roared down on the Azna and their neighbours.

Soon the young queen got the first reports of the bloodthirsty mission. There was no doubt of the military superiority of the intruders from overseas, and they had long since given evidence of their lack of feeling. Anxiously, the queen conferred with her closest confidante, Dawa.

"We are in great danger, father. This time the enemy is overwhelmingly powerful and devilish."

"What does your heart tell you?" the old man asked gently.

"I cannot imagine surrender. I would rather die. But can I demand of the people that they sacrifice themselves? Because these wild beasts have already wiped out larger kingdoms."

"A leader who leads from the front line can expect everything from his followers. But we must ask the oracle. I will go to Boka right away."

At this time a great meeting of representatives of the Hausa states took place in the Gobir region. In view of the disturbing news the dignitaries had met for an urgent strategy summit. In their imposing, gleaming robes the senior chiefs sat together and deliberated over what action they should adopt against the conquering advance of the unbelieving invaders from overseas and their black minions. The tension was clear, because besides the concern over the future, there were rivalries between the advocates of resistance and the supporters of an agreement with the Whites. After the ceremonial greetings the order of the day was put forward, and then Serkin Issan hurried on: "The most recent information in Diundu is shocking! Soon Sarroaunia will be seized. Therefore we should set up an army and fight with it against the accursed invaders..."

"Why should we help this witch?" interrupted the man opposite. "We have the unique opportunity to finally get rid of her, and without loss to ourselves. I would be happy to watch with my own eyes how the Whites break the spine of the proud."

"Do you believe that the Whites will then make an about turn, or have you carefully broken your own spine?" asked his neighbour's opponent. "This woman certainly rejects our religion, but she has never tried to force us to hers. As a neighbour she is far preferable to me than the barbarians, who want to take over our land and are not put off by any cruelty. We should lay aside our communal differences and with our united strengths send the common enemy back to where he came from."

"Your words do you honour, Serkin Ahmadu. But it would be pure suicide to oppose the white devil. Or should we go into exile, like the gallant Ali Buri, who came here from far away Joloff and died? Even the notorious Samory with his great army has recently been captured. Sikasso, the proud fortress, has fallen. We have not nearly so many troops, and the war is not of our making. We should protect our families. As long as one has life one has hope. But for the dead, all is lost."

"That is the wisdom of cowards," grumbled two people further down the row. "Death is a thousand times better than wasting permanently under foreign domination. I have never given in if a woman fought, and I will definitely not bow down before a foreign dog." No common resolution of the various points of view was possible. The overwhelming majority decided for the realistic path, that nothing could be accomplished against superior weaponry. The defeats of great rulers were too discouraging and the massacre in Diundu was too fresh, exerting a paralysing effect. Nevertheless, from individual kingdoms there were three dozen warriors who joined Serkin Issa, and wanted to rush to the help of Sarroaunia.

In Luku, old Boka had consulted the oracle and now entered the queen's apartments. In seclusion, Sarraounia had waited with Dawa for a sign from the gods. No hint was to be drawn from the serious, professionally composed face of the old medium. What he had to report promised nothing good: he could make no sense of the message from the ancestors. Perplexed and deeply upset, he explained that he had used all the possibilities for requesting, always with the same puzzling result. This time the forefathers were no source of hope and encouragement. Anxiously, Dawa stared at the ground and shook his head. "But they have not foretold our defeat!" said the queen defiantly. She got her strength to resist from anger at the bottomless arrogance of the "red ears", as the whites were called, as they got red when they were angry, and from the unshakeable certainty that she could not live in a servile state.

On 27th March, 1899 the murderous column reached the Arewa region. Humbly, Serkin Arewa had sent a reception committee before the city gates to bid the fearsome company welcome and speak mildly to them.

"What do these monkeys want, Makaki?" the commandant, boasted with success and gluttony, and asked his black interpreter.

"Here they greet guests with milk drink and cold water" my commandant," explained Makaki, in his usual submissive manner.

"They want to poison us, these malicious blacks!" Voulet said insultingly and angrily trampled on the calabash, thereby giving the startled bearer a sticky cooling off.

While the shame-faced messenger wondered what to do, the white man gave him a cut with his whip on his smooth-shaven round head. The humiliated man inwardly cursed his ruler and ran to escape another blow, putting a distance between himself and the mounted monster and closely followed by the other members of the welcoming committee, who, like him, wanted to get out of the way of the unpleasant guest. Out of breath they came to the king, bowed hastily and quickly withdrew, struggling to compose themselves. Unusually verbose, the king of Arewa received the white visitor and offered him all imaginable amenities. Pacified by his acceptable reception but full of distrust, Voulet worked himself out of his evil smelling boots and gave his orders. Like the maggots in ham - and he not only had characteristic similarities with the maggot, he wanted to rest here with his hungry gang from the exertions of the previous days and lay in stocks for the next march.

When Sarroaunia heard how hospitably the enemy company had been received in Arewa, she swore never again to set foot in the palace of that worthless traitor. A short while later she had a letter sent to the French commander. In it she informed him she would cover her throne with the hide of a mangy dog if she found it entering her territories. Snorting and spitting like a cross dromedary, Voulet swore to capture the insolent sorceress as soon as possible and humble her to the lowest. However, he took care not to say anything about his plan for when his African soldiers had found out from one among them, that they were headed for the dominions of the sorceress, they became extremely agitated, and it had almost come to a mutiny: they had been promised easy plunder and great lands, so they raged. There had been no mention of a crusade against black magic, and they wanted nothing to do with THE WOMAN. It required strenuous persuasion and threats to quieten the disturbed crowd.

To brighten the subdued mood, Voulet ordered a feast. In the night they were all sleeping off their drink when suddenly they had no air. Sand was flying with full force into the wide-open eyes and mouths of the awakened men. A heavy storm had arisen and raged against tents, stools, cushions and everything that the expedition carried with it. Disoriented, the soldiers ran about and shouted, each in his own language, "Musso!", "Jenne", and "Nkomo" – "the woman!", "the devil!". "the spirit!". Even the ignorant commandant realised that they attributed the unleashed power of nature to Sarroaunia's work, and at last he could fully realise the significance.

After an hour, when the storm had passed, the white commandant discovered the extent of the catastrophe. In the chaos several bearers, women and even soldiers had made off. For the deserters the tumult had come just at the right moment. They had been thinking of flight for some time, and already before the storm, two bearers had used the inattentiveness of the watch at the camp to disappear. They wanted to inform Sarroaunia about the strength of the troops and the time of the attack, and to implore her to fight to the last breath, because death would be better than what otherwise awaited her.

The news of the unexpected spies was especially crushing. The expedition consisted of eight Frenchmen, two hundred and seventy armed soldiers, most of them with fixed bayonets and seven hundred bearers. The worst was the cannons, whose balls demolished every wall. With this, Sarroaunia's defence strategy was futile; she would sit fast in the city walls like a mouse in a hole. Before the next sunset a new plan must be developed, for at dawn, the day after that, the enemy would stand before the city gates. Not only did the cannons present an almost insoluble problem; but the second question was where to send all the inhabitants who could not take part in the battle and where the provisions, with everything else, would be kept.

In the night the queen let the drums be beaten. In the camp of the colonial soldiers their boom startled everyone from his slumber. Voulet uneasily asked what it meant. With a nervous glance the interpreter explained that it must be urgent news that only adepts could interpret. In Tugana, the second city of the Azna kingdom, they knew that all available men had to be in Lugu by daybreak. The three dozen warriors under Serkin Issa's command also knew that they must hurry. While the commander loudly abused "the savages" and from the "damned bush", on the other side sinister music was heard: in Tugana they were acknowledging reception of the midnight news. To Voulet's questioning look, Makaki answered only with a nervous shrug of the shoulders. Sleep was not to be thought of: despite a strengthened watch the conqueror felt himself encircled.

By daybreak the warriors from Tugana had arrived. A short time later the warriors among Serkin Issa's followers came. They had until sundown to solve the logistical problem. Feverishly, the warriors followed the woman's instructions to organise food stores, cooking utensils and animals. Shortly before sunset, when all possible measures had been taken, the inhabitants and their allies assembled in the courtyard and waited for the queen's address. Still today the griots sing of her passionate speech that gave the listeners courage and banished their anxiety before the unequal struggle. Instead of her usual clothing and insignia she appeared in war dress before the crowd: a headband made of lion skin, covered with cowries and sewn-in mirrors gave her face a feminine appearance, and a girdle of gleaming leopard skin over her armless hunter's smock, artfully ornamented with amulets, underlined her readiness for battle, while two armbands of leopard's claws on her upper arms and two broad silver bands on her wrists emitted tremendous energy. Her athletic appearance, which impressed everyone, was completed by skin-tight dark red breeches and light brown boots that emphasised her height of a metre eighty. She gazed at the assembly and spoke in a sonorous, resolute voice.:

"Brothers and sisters of Azna and other peoples of the savannah! We face a great test... Tomorrow will decide whether we continue to live as free people or eke out our existence in slavery... We do not have a big army. But the scorpion is not the biggest animal in the savannah, and yet it is one of the most feared. Like the scorpion we will stick to the dirty foot of the invader until he goes away... If we do not see each other tomorrow at this time, then we will go to meet our forefathers with heads held high, and a deed will be bound to our name that future generations can be proud of. Only one thing is worse than death: a dishonourable life. Tomorrow we shall live free or die in honour."

On 16th April, 1899 the Voulet-Chanoine expedition got under way. At the sight of the listless foot-dragging column, the commandant was overcome with one of his regular attacks of rage. Immediately, he gave the order for a marching song. Sullenly, the mercenaries struck up the supreme song of the Great Nation. In a pronunciation that confirmed that they could make no sense of what they were croaking, they sang of the beauty of France, which they had never visited, and praised themselves for their unwanted membership in the great nation. For Voulet, on the other hand, the monotonous cacophony of the Black singers was the most edifying of music.

A few kilometres before Lugu they saw a dark streak on the horizon. On her black horse Sarraounia was coming towards them with her men. "She is really crazy!" cried the commandant, in a mixture of astonishment and unwilling admiration for such rashness. The mercenaries' breath failed them and they held on desperately to their weapons. The first cannonball made the unequal strength obvious. Just to get within range of the enemy ranks, the Azna warriors and their allies struggled fruitlessly for an hour. Against grape-shot and rifles they were powerless with their few fire-arms. Towards midday they retreated into the woods and attempted to decoy the column in that direction. When the mercenaries stubbornly refused to set foot into the "sacred forest" of the Azna the commandant could not chase Sarraounia's warriors. Finally, to punish the defenceless people, he marched instead into Lugu – and confronted a town empty of people. The inhabitants had fled into the forest before the battle, but left behind gold and silver jewelry in the queen's apartments, as booty for the attacker.

After the onset of darkness the quiet in the French camp was suddenly disturbed. Out of the dark Sarraounia's archers shot arrows into the unsuspecting company. And just as softly as they had emerged they disappeared again into the darkness. Among the mercenaries two who had been hit rolled screaming on the ground. The military doctor arrived quickly but declared helplessly that the arrows were certainly poisoned and he had no access to any antidote. With terrible pain and before the eyes of their horrified comrades both died a short time later. The warriors continued the attacks throughout the night. The still triumphant mercenary troops hid and waited for morning, trembling in fear. Embittered and worried about the support from his demoralised troops, Voulet decided to break camp at dawn. He gave vent to his anger at the accursed sorceress on the buildings. With a balance of four dead, six wounded and seven thousand expended cartridges the expedition left the town.

When they returned the Azna and their allies found everything destroyed. The vandalism however could not cast a cloud over their pride at what they had done. The singers are silent about how many sacrifices they had to mourn. Their spirited effort for freedom inspired the griots to new songs: songs that have been in the collective memory ever since.

Three months later, on 14th July, 1899, the French national day, Commander Klobb caught up with the expedition after a pursuit of more than two thousand kilometres. Without warning Voulet shot at him, and then declared to his uncomprehending subordinates, "I am no longer a Frenchman. I am a black prince. I will establish a new kingdom with you." Two days later he was shot by his own mercenaries. In France the downfall of Voulet was explained as "Sudan-itis", an invented illness that was blamed on the African sun.

Sarraounia could not halt the colonial expansion but her bitter opposition to the overwhelming enemy turned her into a shining figure, whose light has outlasted the dark times of colonial oppression. For this reason a Sarroaunia is still appointed today. Sarraounia embodies not only the many-sided struggle against foreign domination in Africa, but also the confirmation of cultural independence and the equality of man and woman that was firmly anchored in many pre-colonial societies in Africa. Besides the writer Abdoulaye Mamani from Niger and the Mauritanian producer Med Hondo, among others, a school, a club of young writers, a radio presenter and a women's solidarity organisation have raised monuments in her honour.

Bibliography:
Abdoulaye Mamani: *Sarraounia*. Paris 1980;
Med Hondo: *Sarraounia. The battle of the black queen*. (Film). 1986.

MIRIA R. K. MATEMBE   (Uganda)

THE DREAM COME TRUE

BY BANANUKA JOCELYN EKOCHU

The tall, dark energetic figure with round cheeks got down from her bicycle as she drew near the shops. A glance down the street in both directions assured her that nobody was watching her so she pushed her bike swiftly into the bushes and stuck it into a thorny thicket - for which she received a long narrow scratch on her right hand that bled a little. "Oh no!" she cried, "now I will have to lie whenever I give anybody my hand because for certain, they will all ask me how it happened." It could not change anything. She would have to think of a lie because it was clear to her that she would be very sorry if her elderly relatives in the city centre found out that she rode a bicycle. Only recently had she first dared to appear in trousers, and the sensation she had caused by that had not yet been forgotten. She could not afford any further "scandal". "Not yet," she said to herself because she had firmly decided not to be intimidated by anyone and let herself be forced into traditions that still lingered on in a modern world; traditions in which a girl was less valuable than a boy and denied her the right to take part in the stimulating life that the society allowed only to boys.

After she had made certain that her bicycle was well concealed, she went back to the street but had to quickly hide herself behind a tree when she saw a couple of women coming by with baskets of mangoes and roasted corn balanced on their heads. "What will they think if they see me coming out of the bush?" She could easily imagine what stories they would happily spread. What was she doing in the bush, and with whom? That would undoubtedly be the question, and the women would imagine answers that could cause harm. The evil tongues in the village would not be silent for a week, and her mother would punish her for bringing shame to the family.

As soon as she had made sure that the coast was clear, she came cautiously out of her hiding place. She went to the shops and made her purchases. On the way back she pulled her bicycle out of the underbrush and rode back home, in the luxuriant environment of Rutooma village in the Mbarara District of western Uganda. The village was surrounded by banana plantations that promised an abundance of food. Here, Miria Rokuza Koburunga Matembe was born in 1953. She was only "another girl", nothing special. Miria lived in poverty in a family of nine children. For their daily needs the family resorted to agriculture. There was no other source of income.

At the age of six she went to school and proved to be very gifted. As well as a pleasant character she had a natural self-confidence, which led her to ask questions and express her opinion. Miria went through all her exams with brilliance and quite in contrast to many of her fellow pupils, she was not kept back once. She loved school and was always happy to go back again the next day. She was happiest when she brought home a good report. With enthusiasm she read it out to her mother, who praised her for her diligence. That was in fact the only source of joy in her life. As she grew up she realised that other children possessed things that were forbidden to her because of her family's reduced financial circumstances. Her primary school uniform, for example, was the only proper dress that she owned as a child. This dress, she wore all the time, when she went to church or the hospital or anywhere at all outside her village. Shoes in her family were an unimaginable luxury.

Much as Miria's family was poor, there were also some more affluent families in Rutooma village, such that Miria and her brothers and sisters perceived themselves as inferior. She found it painful that she had to go to church in her school uniform while other children appeared in their Sunday best. Most children enjoyed Christmas when they got new clothes and dishes of rice and meat. It upset Miria that there was no chance that she would get a new dress.

As such she found ways to avoid the agony of going to church on Christmas in her school uniform. "I worked in the house until the others left. Then when I went a bit later the church was already full and I found a place behind the door. As soon as the closing hymn was announced I waited until all were devotedly singing and then I slipped out and ran home, before my schoolmates and cousins could find me in my school uniform."

Even though her family was so poor, Miria thanked God for her parents when she recalled how she had been brought up. "My parents had a big share in the firm foundation on which I was able to become what I am today. We children learned to live according to two principles. First, it was never to want something that our parents could not afford. That was not easy because they could not afford much but it helped me not to yearn for the unattainable, to make do with little." Second, Miria and her siblings would never assume a superiority that they had not attained. "My father was of the opinion that there were different levels at which one could realise one's desires. To be able to wear shoes, for example, one must first of all become a teacher or a nurse. Pupils did not wear shoes. You could not count to ten if you could not count to one."

Later Miria's father went to Buganda in central Uganda as a casual labourer. He had to earn additional money because the earnings from the sale of fruit and vegetables were not enough. From time to time he came home and entertained his children with interesting stories, to which they very happily listened.

After he had saved some money her father came back home and built a chop bar in the Bwizibwera Trading Centre that everybody in the village called the Hotel. "He cooked the meals himself and also served them. My mother stayed at home, looked after the land and supplied us with food. Mother also sold a little of what she cooked to earn some money. Thus both my parents together earned the money for school fees and uniforms."

Miria was already aware in childhood of the injustices of society. As a five or six-year-old she recognised that a special status was granted to boys while girls were overlooked and disqualified as "only a girl".

"Though I understood little the ideas that underlay the discrimination, I vehemently rejected them. I had an aunt who was married to a violent man and frequently reported his beatings to us at home. My father, her loving brother, insulted her most of the time that she was with us and insulted her that she was useless, which in his opinion was the cause of her husband's beatings. I felt sorry for her."

However, what shocked Miria most was her aunt's reaction to her brother's insults: "But I am not useless. I brought a bride price to this house and bore my husband sons." In Miria's understanding, the aunt had no sense of her own worth. She valued herself only in reference to the bride price paid for her, for the sons she had brought into the world and in relation to her husband.

When she was older Miria realised that most of the problems that she observed among women were to be traced back to their gender. Her mother was a member of the Mother's Union, an association in the Anglican Church of Uganda for women who had married in the church. When women came to her with their troubles she gave them advice and also prayed with them. Miria began to understand that these women suffered under their husbands and male relatives. She found it absolutely unjust and upsetting and Miria herself was not spared this injustice. When her mother was away she did not go to school but did the house work for which her mother was normally responsible, yet her older brother went to school because he was a boy. He therefore did not have to do any house work as long as a girl or his mother was there. This injustice did not stop here. Because her family did not have enough money, it happened from time to time that Miria and her brother were sent home from school. Miria's parents did everything to ensure that her brother could go back to school within two days.

"I had to stay home until my school money could be paid, which took about two weeks. This made me so angry that at the age of twelve I decided to study diligently and become an advocate for women's rights."

This dream would be almost over before it had properly begun. Miria and her brother Sam were candidates for the primary school leaving exam in the same year, although he was older than her. She passed with shining colours but Sam failed, yet again. While she had already gone to the famous Bweranyangi Girls' Senior Secondary School, Sam had to repeat the last elementary year. When he arrived in the senior school the following year, Miria was already in the second class.

Everything was going well for Miria until one day she saw her mother at the school. Miria was delighted that her mother had come to her school because it was a very rare sign of affection. Her joy did not last long when she discovered the reason for this visit.

"She had by no means come to visit me. It was about something quite different. She had come to take me away from the school and destroy my dream." Not many years later, when Miria told her story, the great sadness she felt at the time was reflected in her eyes. Her mother explained that now that Sam was in secondary school, the family could not afford to pay the school fees for two children. At that time there were no fees for attending a teacher training college and therefore Miria, who was "only a girl", could enrol there and study for free.

Miria could not grasp this audacity. She was frustrated and felt herself betrayed. There she was, a very intelligent girl who dreamed of becoming a lawyer and promoting women's rights, having her own mother wanting to destroy this dream because of her brother, who was not as clever as she was.

"I told my mother bluntly that I would not go to any teacher training college because there, they trained teachers and not lawyers. Miss Hall, the school principal, thought I should listen to my mother but I wanted to know nothing about it. It was clear to me that I could hardly change anything for I did not have money of my own for school fees."

Miria had a fit of rage, which however did not impress her mother. A few minutes later, among all her tears and anger, a thought came to her. She had heard others talk of stipends. If her parents were not in a position to pay her school fees she could get a stipend. She asked her mother, "Where does one get a stipend?"

"I think, from the District Education Office in Mbarara," her mother replied.

"Then let's go there and apply," Miria said.

Her mother was uncertain whether this was such a good idea because she did not speak English. How would she talk to the school authorities? Miria told her not to worry about it.

"Just go there with me, and let me do the talking." Today she rates her mother highly for agreeing to do it. The school principal permitted her to try.

Two hours later she sat on a bench in front of the District Education Office, only a few minutes before the beginning of the mid-day break. Neither of them knew how the procedure went and so they watched while one visitor after the other entered the office and left again. Once, the door stood open and when Miria glanced into the room she saw that the last visitor was about to leave. He was standing, and the Education Officer had also got up from his place. She realised that he was now going on his lunch break.

"I jumped up and wanted to go straight into the office when the Education Officer came out. He saw us and asked my mother, "What do you want?" She could not understand him so I answered, "Sir, I want money for school fees.""

When Miria saw the confusion on his face she began a swift but effective explanation of what a distinguished pupil she was at the Bweranyangi School. Her parents were demanding of her that she change to the teacher training college so that her brother could go to secondary school. She sniffed and wept as she explained that she wanted to be a lawyer and protect the rights of women, for which teacher training could not prepare her. Would he please give her a stipend so that she could continue going to her school?

A week later Miria received a stipend and continued her schooling. She got exceptional grades and went on to Namasagali College, where she achieved the higher school certificate. It was then much easier for her because anyone who had the higher school certificate would be supported financially by the state. There was no more unpleasantnesses about school fees!

During her time at Namasagali College, Miria developed the desire to become a member of parliament. She was so fascinated by the history of the British parliament that she would gladly have become a member of the lower house. A friend of her father's was a lawyer and Uganda's first Minister of Justice after independence. She admired him and dreamed of one day working as a lawyer in his ministry. This dream was not realised because he was persecuted under the dictator Idi Amin and had to flee into exile.

During the long vacation after receiving the higher school certificate, Miria found a place as a teacher at the Rwantsinga Primary School, which was about ten kilometres away from her home. Her life was taking a promising turn. Finally, she could afford to buy something nice for herself, at least, so she thought. Then her father began to collect her pay.

"At the end of each month he appeared at the school on his bicycle, brought me *matooke*, a dish made of green cooked bananas and a pot of about a litre of milk and explained to me bluntly that he had come for my wages - for my entire wages! He calmly informed me that I did not need the money as he had brought me food."

He was not interested in the fact that by evening the milk would no longer be usable and the food would not last longer than a week. He wanted her money, all of it. With it he would pay the school fees for her brothers and sisters. When she wanted to discuss it with him rationally he objected that she needed part of her money herself, and promised her he would sell his bulls and buy her the things she needed from the money.

In my young and trusting mind the question why he didn't just sell the bulls to pay my siblings' school fees didn't arise.

When the final marks were published, Miria again had the highest, and it was time to register at the respected Makerere University. The time had finally come to make her dream a reality; time to begin studying law, to become a lawyer and to protect the rights of women. That was exactly the moment when her father asked for her money. Then he had to sell the bulls and pay Miria back her money. She only had a couple of payments left.

"What do you need the money for?" asked her father.

"I have to buy myself something to wear."

"You have something to wear."

"I need new shoes."

"Yours are still perfectly good."

"I need a wristwatch."

"What!?" thundered her father. One might have thought she had done God knows what. "A watch? Have you forgotten that you should never raise yourself above your own level? Who are you that you have to have a watch?"

Miria had had enough. There had to be a distinction between the respect that one owed one's father and the acceptance of a despotism that disregarded the entire needs of the other. When she received her final wages she managed to keep them away from him. Fortunately, there was still enough time before the beginning of the semester and she bought a few things that she needed. Unfortunately, the money was not enough for a watch.

Soon Fortune smiled upon her again. A couple of days later in a shop Miria met her uncle, who was there in the company of a friend. She excitedly told him that she had been admitted to Makerere University.

Coincidentally, her uncle's friend had a son who likewise was about to begin studying there. "I bought a watch as a present for my son," he said to Miria's uncle. "I'll buy your niece a watch too." His words were music in Miria's ears. She thus acquired her very first watch.

After successfully taking so many hurdles, Miria thought the worst was over but then, the struggle began in earnest. Her father absolutely insisted that girls should not study law.

I ought to have become a nurse or a teacher, he insisted. This time I asserted myself against him and said I must study law but he didn't want to know about it. I listened to him for a while as he proclaimed that no man would marry a lawyer otherwise such a woman would not be controlled. He added that the university had already laid down what course I would follow. I told him that if he wanted me to be admitted to different courses then he would have to go there himself and request it from the administration. Of course it was clear to me that he would not go to the university, and indeed he didn't. I eventually soon began my law studies in the ivory tower.

The university was a new world that brought with it enormous freedom. Students went out together so openly that Miria, who was very shy, wondered what her mother would think if she knew what kind of life the beginning academics led.

"I was always afraid of the other sex ever since my time in Bweranyangi. The road to Bweranyangi led through a swamp. When my mother accompanied me on the first day of school, she stopped there, indicated the swamp and said, "If you ever become pregnant, just don't come home again. Simply throw yourself into the swamp here." It was easy for her to give me this warning, yet she had never explained to me how one got pregnant."

Since then Miria could not get the swamp out of her head. Every time a man approached her she thought of it. Her mother had instilled so much fear in her that she kept away from men, almost entirely.

"Fortunately, nowadays parents don't try to achieve a desired behaviour in their children by frightening them. They either give them advice or unfortunately not even that. That is why so many young people go astray. They are influenced by peer pressure, television and the internet. If I detest the terror with which I was disciplined, I am also against an upbringing without any guidance."

Miria's relationship with her parents was marked by fear. She was as afraid of her mother as of her father. She never discussed with them things that affected the family or herself. Words were uttered only if the parents ordered something or censured the children. By her teachers on the other hand, she felt herself respected, loved and protected and she could always ask them when she needed help. "That is why I was always dilligent and learned with such great success."

Miria also distinguished herself in sports, especially in athletics and netball. She took part in tournaments as a representative of her school or her region. She shone as a speaker and a talented actress. Later, as an adult, she wrote a play that was performed at the national theatre by the celebrated music, dance and theatre group "Ndere Troupe". She dedicated the piece to her teachers who believed in her and were there for her.

At that time Miria lived her religious faith as a born-again Christian. Among them, dancing counted as a sin, which was nevertheless a great sorrow to Miria. When she came to the university she made the decision to dance as much as possible.

"Every Friday, when we came back from the gathering of our Christian congregation, there was a disco in our hall of residence. I couldn't pass up the opportunity! I even asked one of my friends to take my Bible up to the room while I went dancing. At first, nobody seemed to have anything against it, but after a time my friends could not hide their disapproval. They told me that I wanted to serve two masters and I must eventually decide on one of them."

Miria felt injured. She loved dancing and would be cheating herself if she gave it up. She also did not consider it a sin, so long as she did not go dancing in night clubs. What could be wrong with dancing in a student's residence? She thought about it. She eventually decided in favour of dancing and against born-again Christianity.

"Unfortunately, I liked dancing. When I stayed with my Aunt Olive during the vacations after the college closed, a young man invited me to go dancing with him but at the same time asked me to ask for permission from my aunt. She said no. I could not believe it. No, after I had done the right thing and asked for permission? "Would your mother permit you to go out dancing with a man?" Of course I had never asked my mother whether I could go dancing but I had assumed that since Aunt Olive was so modern and lived in the city, she would be understanding. Her prohibition came as a complete surprise to me and annoyed me especially because that very evening, she herself went dancing with her husband."

Her aunt could have proposed that they all go out together. She could have seen to it that Miria did behave properly. On the other hand, Miria had her college certificate in her pocket and considered herself grown up. She was no longer a child like back in the days when she sneaked out of the house with her brother Sammy to dance at the Rutooma Primary School.

"We regretted this adventure the very next day when our eldest brother gave us a sound thrashing. After that we left dancing for a while but in the period between college and university nobody could get between me and the dance floor."

Then Miria went out with young men but she made a quick exit if anybody wanted to get intimate. One evening, in her second year at university, she met her future husband at a *kasiki*, the dance for a bachelor's farewell party.

"At first what I liked about Nicky was that he was such a fantastic dancer. I had no idea that he liked me for the same reason. He introduced himself to me and we danced a couple of times. When I realised how close he wanted to dance I told him that I had no interest in sex. 'Me neither,' he answered. Wow! Finally, here was somebody who wasn't planning to use my passion for dancing to get me into his bed as quickly as possible. He only wanted to go out with me and showed it through his behaviour. I trusted him and didn't drop him, like others earlier. I was moved when at our first rendezvous he took off his nice watch, gave it to me and in exchange took my tiny Oris watch that my uncle's friend had bought me. It was a lovely gesture, and I have lovingly kept the watch.

If I was at home during the vacation, practically all conversations with my father turned on instructions about which men I could not marry. All our conversations revolved around this theme. Out of a clear sky he could say, 'You are to marry when you have finished your education.' The next day he called me, 'Don't marry anybody from the north,' he then said, without any connection to anything, and when I asked him why, he replied that we did not understand their language and therefore could not talk to them. After a while he called me back again. Apparently, it had occurred to him in the meantime that I would not marry anybody from the north (including men from the east). Now he proceeded to discuss a marriage with another ethnic group."

"Koburunga, don't ever marry a Muganda." I was puzzled. Would he allow me to marry at all? I had to find out what the problem was.

"Why, father? What do you have against the Baganda?" I asked him.

"They are proud, they steal and they call us Bunyoro." In my opinion he was unjust, surely in every group there would be proud people, criminals as well as good, honourable people. I tried to talk to him rationally: "But they aren't all like that! There are also good people among the Baganda." He did not want to know about it. He firmly insisted that all Baganda were alike and his daughter should not marry any of them. I did not understand what he was thinking about. So I kept quiet but it was not long until he called me again: "Koburunga my daughter, don't ever think of marrying a Munyoro." It had become a kind of game. I asked him why he did not like the Bunyoro.

"They are greedy," he replied.

"How can you say something like that?" I was beside myself. "You don't even know any."

"I have visited my son and seen how greedy his roommates were. You can't marry any of them." Short and sweet, I realised that my father was a person I could by no means argue with, and I asked myself whether he wanted me to marry at all. His outbursts began to amuse me.

"There is absolutely no question of marrying a Mukiga," he announced one day.

"Why, father?"

"They are such gluttons."

I couldn't restrain myself from saying that among us I had seen men fall upon their food like hungry lions.

One would have thought that there was something wrong with every ethnic group, except naturally for the Banyankore. When I informed him of my intention to marry Nicky, a Munyankore, he still would not immediately say yes. That was during my second year at the university. "You can finally marry when you have finished your studies," he fumed but I retorted that we had already made up our minds.

"Why are you so anxious to get married?" he asked. "This man will treat you badly. You must not marry him," he argued. I answered that there could be no objection to this marriage; then he changed his tactics. "You cannot marry him. He comes from Igara county. You cannot marry a Munyigara because they eat sheep. Look for a husband from Kashaari."

When his arguments had run out, Miria's father called the elders of the family together. He complained to them that his daughter did not respect the paternal wishes but Miria had had enough annoyance in her life, now she was fed up. Despite the dictatorial propensities of her sophistical father she would not give up the man she loved.

"Since my father could not give the elders any overwhelming reason why he should deny my dearest wish, they approved my choice and told him that he should let me marry the man of my choice. After a lot of threats and insults, my father finally gave in and agreed to my marriage with Nicky but he stated an unreasonably high bride price. That didn't intimidate us. We married at the beginning of my third year at Makerere University. When I ended my studies we already had our first child. If I look back on my life I see that it was constantly marked by opposition. In my youth I had already learned to stand up for my rights."

Miria was now wife, mother and lawyer with a diploma from Makerere University. She therefore expected that she would be given the respect owed to her as a responsible member of the society. Far from it! Her mother thought quite differently about it.

"At my graduation party, she angrily left the room because I had dared to drink a glass of beer in the presence of my father! My husband Nicky had himself offered the beer. Later I found my mother in the kitchen where she gave me a severe dressing down for my "unbecoming" conduct."

Nicky proved himself a real dream husband. He didn't seem to be a typical representative of the male species. Miria was treated as an equal, and by a man, her husband.

"I thank God that he blessed me with a husband for whom the equality of the sexes and the emancipation of women are not empty words. The greatest gifts that Nicky has given me in the course of the years are support, free space and encouragement. He gave me the kind of independence that very few African men grant to their wives. He valued my strengths and tolerated my weaknesses, by which he strengthened me for the struggle for the rights of women. He has stood by me through thick and thin."

Miria's original desire to devote herself to women's matters was still in her mind. She had been able to marry a man who valued her and had great respect for her, yet she was conscious that in this respect, she was an exception. Millions of women were oppressed and could not raise their voices. For these women she must struggle. She began her political career in the 1980s as the one responsible for mass mobilisation and education in the opposition party of Museveni, later President. In 1989 she became a member of parliament and for seventeen years she was active as a member of the Ugandan parliament as well as two years in the Pan African Parliament of the African Union. Numberless women hailed her on the political platform as one of those who would make a stir and take the risk so that their voices could be heard. However, many believed that her goal was to get rid of the institution of marriage. This faulty impression was not spread only by men. Her proposal to castrate men who raped their wives or defiled young girls created a huge sensation. Because of the rise in sexual violence, her viewpoint today meets with general understanding. Many are of the opinion that her proposal should have become law.

Over the long period of her parliamentary work, she worked for the passage of numerous laws for the equality of women. For example, the genital mutilation of women, trade in human beings and domestic violence were made punishable, and an organisation for granting credit to women was founded. Equally uncompromising, Miria put through a law against the abuse of children. In Africa, it is unusual that fathers are responsible for their children outside marriage. She struggled to make their support a duty, unfortunately so far without success. She considered her most important achievement to be that she had made women visible and audible. For that, she received the Women Heroines Award in New York in 1998, as one of the "hundred heroines of the world".

Miria belonged to the commission that in 1994/95 worked out the draft for the new constitution of Uganda. It is thanks to her that equal rights for women were written into the constitution. In 1997 Miria did her Master's in Law and Development Policy at the University of Warwick (England). In 1998 she was Minister for Ethics and Integrity in the government of Uganda. That ministry, personally founded by her, is responsible for the struggle against corruption. She was concerned that new members of the government should have to make public their sources of income. As far as the struggle against corruption was concerned, she had to bow to the recognition that in African countries, the political will for it is lacking. She was Minister until in 2003 when Museveni had her dismissed.

"I worked so well that I pushed myself out of the government. For when our President wanted to change the constitution to get rid of the time limits on the presidency, I told him that that was a corrupt act. I told him that to manipulate the constitution to his personal advantage was the highest form of corruption and as the minister responsible for the struggle against corruption I would not support him. Two weeks later he formed the new cabinet, and I was out."

After that she worked for Non-Governmental Organisations. Miria Rokuza Koburunga Matembe co-founded Action for Development, one of the leading interest associations for women in Uganda. She played a central role in the founding of regional women's organisations, including Women Law and Development in Africa and FEMINET (African Women's Network). A short time later she co-founded the Centre for Women in Governance, which set itself as a goal to further the education of women who wanted to be politically active throughout Africa and Asia.

In the year 2007 she received the honorary doctorate from the Law Faculty of the University of Victoria, Canada. At international conferences and organisations she lectured world-wide about the situation of the African woman and about Africa's major evil, corruption. She is the author of the books *Gender, Politics and Constitution Making in Uganda* (2002) and *Women in the Eyes of God: Reclaiming a Lost Identity* (2009).

Miria had four sons, two daughters-in-law that she did not call "daughters-in-law" but "daughters-in-love", two nieces and a nephew.

When she thought back on the path of the life she had followed for so many years, she was thankful.

"I have in the course of the years made so many good decisions but the best was to devote myself to women's affairs. I have realised that the joy of serving others, enriching humanity and the meaning of my life lies in stirring up the lives of other people.... I would like to say to the young people, it is a good thing if you have a dream early in life, a vision that determines your life and your fate. Live your life according to your plan and not in obedience to exigency. A dream helps you to organise your life. In this world impressed by materialism and the greed for power and riches, I may say that life does not expand with success and possessions but in the knowledge of who one is in God, and that one makes one's God-given capabilities fruitful for one's own life according to His wish."

The name Miria Matembe has become a synonym for self-determination and equal rights for women.

SAMUEL MAHARERO and HENDRIK WITBOOI (Namibia)

THE WHITES HAVE VIOLATED THEIR PEACE WITH US

BY AZZO

In 1882 an eighty-four-year old citizen of Bremen put out commercial feelers towards the south-west African region that today is called Namibia. His name was Adolf Lüderitz. After his apprentice years in Mexico and a frustrated project in Nigeria, he wanted to realise his dream in this colonial territory. He would fail again, but his name will forever be bound up with the history of this country and German colonial history.

Like the wholesale merchant Lüderitz, thousands of Germans dreamed of Africa; from the starving subjects to the megalomaniac Kaiser Wilhelm II. For the poor, Africa promised a new life in human dignity; for the privileged classes, it meant riches and above all, the exotic. The fascination with the spices, fruits and other foreign products was so great that in 1898 the Purchasing Cooperative of Retailers of Colonial Goods (*Einkaufsgenossenschaft der Kolonialwarenhändler* – EdK – called *Edeka* since 1911) was founded. The political leadership developed a plan to divert the mass immigration to the USA, towards an African New Germany, to where they also intended to deport representatives of the workers' movement. For the sovereign of the empire it was about

Germany's "place in the sun", about her role as a world power that was to secure survival in a world determined by the law of the stronger: "Anyone who doesn't join in with the colonial powers is ruined" was the watchword of the hour.

The driving and ambitious merchant from Bremen set a breath-taking pace: after one year he had taken possession of an area that was bigger than the entire German realm – 580,000 square kilometres. That he proceeded by cunning and tricks, goes without saying. Soon he acquired the nickname Lying Fritz (*Lügenfritz*). His most famous method was the so-called "mile fraud": in drawing up the title deed he let his partner believe that the unit of measurement was the English mile that he was familiar with – 1.6 kilometres – only to then insist on the longer German mile, 7.4 kilometres. By such subterfuges he quickly became a central figure in the German colonial adventure; for up to now it was no more than an adventure, as the German state kept its distance from it all. "As long as I am the Chancellor, we won't pursue any colonial policy," Bismarck had declared.

While the Germans indulged in their colonial fantasy, the advance guard was already at work. Deeply convinced of their duty, the volunteers of the Rhenish Missionary Society (*Rheinischen Mission*) instructed the natives in the Christian religion. Among their pupils was the son of a chief, one of the leaders of the Herero, who was distinguished by an especially lively mind: Samuel Maherero (1854-1923). Because of his promising abilities, the young Samuel was selected for the intellectual track and belonged to the first to be taken into the newly founded "Assistants' Institute". Some years before, and two hundred kilometres farther south, another chief's son, Hendrik Witbooi (actually, Nanseb Gabemab, 1835-1905) of the Nama people, had distinguished himself. As well as several languages, he mastered Christian theology so well that he later astonished his teachers. When in 1884 he decided to move north with a large group and open up a new area, he resisted the opposition of his father and the missionaries, who feared a confrontation with the resident Herero. Against these objections Hendrik put forward a striking argument: the Holy Ghost had appeared to him and had given him the task. Hendrik's "sacred duty" brought these two leaders together for the first time: the Herero made it unmistakably clear to him that he had lost nothing in their country. They would encounter each other again, for Hendrik would not give up so fast....

From Lüderitz Bay the merchant worked tirelessly at permanent annexation of territory in a hurry lest the German government send soldiers as colonial troops. However, Bismarck stuck by his rejection of colonial engagement: "I won't let one penny go to colonial ventures". This changed abruptly when it became known that the English planned an occupation of the region. On 7th August, 1884 Lüderitz's anticipations were even exceeded: the German flag was raised over an area that was bigger than his own possessions. Now Germany was a colonial power, and typically, he was persuaded that one's own colonialism is better than that of the competition. A year later the initiator had to sell his possessions and leave the colonial enterprise, yet with the town of Luderitz he left behind the most durable trace of German exercise of power in Africa.

The first years passed largely without noteworthy events as everywhere in Africa the people were not troubled by the presence of the pale strangers with unusual clothes and peculiar customs. So long as they did not interfere with the daily life of the locals, one could live with them. Only a few groups like the Bondelswart-Nama stubbornly refused to put up with the sight of the German troops and kept them in suspense with constant attacks. Meanwhile, in 1894 Hendrik Witbooi was forced by the Germans into a peace treaty that he would condemn ten years later. From the Herero too there was no danger. Since the other Herero leaders questioned the legitimacy of his rule, Samuel Maharero had signed a protection treaty, not realising that the "protection" referred only to external enemies who threatened the interests of the Germans. Major Leutwein, later the governor, in this way followed the principle of "divide and rule", in that he played Maharero and his competitors for power against each other in order to establish German rule with the least possible expense and turn the country into a settlement colony.

For Maharero, the protection treaty seemed all the more necessary because shortly before, Hendrik Witbooi had renewed his attempt to realise his "sacred duty". Just how well the governor played his game of deception may be seen in Maharero's son Friedrich's legendary visit to Germany, including an audience with the Kaiser. Within the framework of a folklore display, a popular "exhibition" of people from the colonies in zoos at the end of the 19th century, the twenty-two year old Herero prince came to Germany in 1896. To the great disappointment of the eager public, he did not appear half-naked or in a grass skirt but in a suit. However, this ultimately did no damage to the fascination with the exotic: long after his return he received love letters with presents and at his departure young women stood at the railway station with their suitcases hoping to be taken along. Such scenes were also common at non-royal folklore displays...

In the German empire the colonial project took its course until 1897. After an outbreak of rinderpest that carried off eighty per cent of the Herero herds, the social order wavered. This catastrophe was followed by a malaria epidemic, a plague of locusts and a period of drought. Now they had to hire themselves out to settlers, who, thanks to more effective vaccination programmes, had lost fewer cattle and risen to be employers. Intoxicated with their new power, the small minority of around three thousand settlers profited by the situation and by means of usurious credit – interest rates of up to 500 per cent – acquired even more cattle and land. In the end they possessed more than three-fifths of the land area. To massive expropriation was added the fencing off of broad areas, which brought even more distress to the Herero with their herds. With their new power, the arrogance of the foreigners also increased. Their previous efforts at peaceful co-existence yielded to ever more aggressive autocracy.

In a letter to the missionary society, a missionary named Eigner wrote: "The average German treats a native like a being more or less on the same level as the baboon (their favourite name for natives). This attitude too often results in harshness, deception, injustice and assault, frequently homicide." For killing a native the decreed punishment was imprisonment of between three months and three years; in the reverse case the punishment was death. Eventually, the Herero became conscious of discrimination. In 1901 Maharero sent a complaint to the governor. When this petition changed nothing, and in 1902 the railway was built through their country against the wishes of the Herero, he called all the leaders to a mobilisation.

On 11th January he sent a letter to his former Nama opponent Witbooi: "I inform you, that the whites have broken their peace with me. And for our part we shall do what we can in our weakness... If you have got arms, help me and give me two English and two German guns, for I have no guns." Despite the obvious military implication, he was resolved to act against the deprivation of rights in his own land. Shortly thereafter, he sent Witbooi a second letter, which expressed not only his determination but also the growing consciousness of a mutual challenge:

"Let us rather die together and not die through abuse, imprisonment or various other means. Let all the princes down there know so that they rise up and act." Witbooi found himself divided. On the one hand he felt himself in solidarity with Maharero especially because he somehow rejected the German protectorate: "That one is the master who stands above, and he who stands below him is the subordinate". On the other hand, ten years earlier Witbooi had had to sign a treaty that bound him to military service. In this dilemma he decided in favour of his word as he had given it with the treaty.

On 12th January, 1904, while the German troops fought the rebellious Bondelswart four hundred kilometres away, the insurrection began. In the first days a hundred and twenty-three settlers fell victim to the long-standing, bottled up anger of the Herero and the Bondelswart-Nama. While the rebels left the peasants, the English as well as the German women and children, undisturbed, the colonial power talked about bloodthirstiness and race war, to conceal the actual reason. In Germany this news unleashed an angry call for retaliation.

Instructive for opinion in the empire was the correspondence with Governor Leutwein. Unlike the propagandists of race war, he had asked Samuel Maharero for the basis of the attacks. In his answer, the chief named the injustice and above all, "the violation of our women by the whites. Many men have been shot dead like dogs when they refused to hand over their wives and daughters and threatened to defend them by force of arms". What distinguished Leutwein from the broad range of his countrymen blinded by race was his logical way of thinking. Against the colonial caricature of the African as a savage, for example, he commented on his correspondence with Witbooi and Maharero as follows: "In these letters our 'savages' do not lack logical thought as they also show a feeling for right and wrong". On the basis of his insight into the causes of the rebellion, Leutwein pragmatically initiated negotiations. He was criticised as too soft, and dismissed.

Now the hour struck for the swashbuckling Lieutenant-General von Trotha, the "butcher's boy", as the SPD chairman, August Bebel, called him. His participation in the brutal suppression of the Boxer Rebellion in China, as well as the Hehe Rebellion in East Africa justified the name. With racist fervour he swore to eliminate "the rebellious tribes in rivers of blood". With imposing extra strength from Germany that inflated the colonial troops by almost fifteen thousand men, thirty cannons as well as twelve machine guns and a light signal station that made communication between the troops possible, von Trotha considered himself well armed against the rudimentary weapons of the Herero. Soon the old soldier, accustomed to success, realised that he had underestimated his opponent. After painful defeats through the guerrilla tactics of the rebels, who made use of their knowledge of the country, on 2nd October 1904 he gave his infamous command for genocide: "The Herero people must leave the country... Within the German borders any Herero, with or without a weapon, with or without livestock, will be shot. I admit no more women and children, drive them back to their people or let them be shot." What he referred to by "admit" was the first German concentration camp, in which the prisoners were abandoned to starvation, 7,683 out of 17,000.

What this document demonstrates, apart from the barbaric conduct of its author, is the creation of the legend of the so-called decisive battle at Hamakari – Waterberg – two months earlier. Contrary to widespread representation, the battle of 12th August, 1904 was a military disaster for the German superior power. Aided by the light signals, the German troops had succeeded in forcing sixty thousand Herero, including women, children and old people, to this hill. With no way out, instead of capitulating, the women stood behind the men and encouraged them with praise songs. To free themselves from the trap the rebels released their cows and used the same banners as the Germans, to cause confusion. While they understood the commands of their opponents and reacted appropriately, they made themselves understood among each other in their own language. It took the German officers a long time before they realized that the opposition sniping was deliberately aimed at them, and tore off their badges of rank, which however did not help as soon as they had to give a command. Despite the hopeless inferiority in the ranks of the Herero and their allies, only a thousand people were killed. They suffered their greatest loss after the battle, when they were chased for two weeks through the desert and systematically driven away from the few watering places. At the end of the rebellion, eighty per cent of the Herero had perished, even among the Bergdamara, who were not involved, a third lost their lives. Von Trotha practised cruelty to such an extent that several Nama deserted the German ranks.

When they informed Witbooi of the German terror, he renounced the peace treaty and went into the resistance. Soon after that von Trotha was dismissed by the German regime because of his brutality. With fewer than two thousand fighters the seventy-year-old Witbooi obstructed a heavily armed, fifteen thousand strong army for a whole year and extracted from the new commander, von Deimling, the following praise: "Witbooi has operated as though he had gone through the school for General Staff." Unlike Samuel Maharero, who could flee after the legendary battle at Hamakari to exile in Botswana – then Bechuanaland – where he died in 1923, Hendrik Witbooi fell on 29th October, 1905. For two years individual groups continued the struggle for independence, among them the brilliant leader, Jacob Morenga, the central figure in Uwe Timm's impressive novel. As the son of a Nama man and a Herero woman, he brought into being that common resistance that Witbooi and Maharero had not achieved. Thus he laid the foundation for the national liberation movement that in 1990 led to the independence of Namibia.

What was started at the beginning of the 20th century in German South West Africa, the whole world understood thirty years later. The ideology of contempt for humanity that National Socialism spewed forth showed itself first in all its aspects in the first German African colony. That is true not only for the designation of Africans as "vermin", that was later transferred to the Jews, but also for the racial fury that raged in the first German genocide and the first German concentration camp. In this camp, a certain Eugen Fischer carried out barbaric experiments on the prisoners that later inspired his pupil Josef Mengele: Fischer was also one of the authors of the standard racist work "Foundation of the study of human heredity and race hygiene" (*Grundriß der menschlichen Erblichkeitslehre und Rassenhygiene*). Just as noteworthy are the suppression of the colonial past and the decades-long refusal in Germany to ask for pardon. While the federal government rejected any "formulation relating to compensation" with reference to a new state, in 1990 it felt obliged to send a high ranking delegation in support of the property rights of Namibians of German origin, that go back to the massive expropriations after the rebellion.

In Namibia, the rebellion of 1904 to 1907 is etched into the collective consciousness, as the origin of a new consciousness that brought forth a national identity and made possible resistance to German colonialism as well as the apartheid regime. As such, Samuel Maharero and Hendrik Witbooi remain the most important figures of Namibian history. In the tragedy of their aborted alliance lies a warning for the whole continent that is contained in Witbooi's letter to the perpetrator of the massacre of Hornkranz, Lieutenant von Francois: "By colour and way of life, we Africans belong together, and this Africa, in its entirety, is the land of red leaders. That we possess different kingdoms and countries can mean only an incidental sharing out of Africa."

Bibliography:

Larissa Förster (editor) *Namibia-Deutschland, Eine geteilte Geschichte.* (Namibia-Germany, a shared history.) Wolfratshausen 2004.

Toubab Pippa (editor), *Von der Bosheit im Herzen der Menschen: Hendrik Witbooi und die schwarz-weiße Geschichte Namibias* (From the evil in the hearts of men: Hendrik Witbooi and the black-white history of Namibia.) Lörbach 2004.

Jürgen Zimmerer & Joachim Keller (editors) *Völkermord in Deutsch-Südwestafrika. Der Kolonialkrieg und seine Folgen.* (Genocide in German South West Africa. The colonial war and its aftermath.) Berlin 2004.

SULTAN IBRAHIM NJOYA   (Cameroon)

THE METAPHYSICS OF THE ARTS

BY PATRICE NGANANG

Very few Africans were intellectually as active and brilliant as Sultan Ibrahim Njoya of Bamum, Cameroon – a fact which, remarkably, has long gone unnoticed in research into the history of ideas on the African continent. This paradox is explained on the one hand by the original inclination of the Sultan's thought, and on the other by the orientation of African philosophy, literature and politics towards independence. But first of all, who exactly is Sultan Ibrahim Njoya? Certainly, Njoya (ca. 1860-1933) was the Sultan of Bamum, the most famous descendant of the dynasty of Nchare Yen, who, according to the chronicle *Histoire et coutumes des Bamum* (History and Customs of the Bamum, 1921), the written version of which he directed, had founded the Kingdom of Bamum. From the viewpoint of the history of ideas, he is above all an inventor and a renewer: the inventor of a script, of which he developed eight versions in the course of the years; and of a language with a reduced range named Shümom that he used especially in the palace, but also in writing books and in his correspondence. He is the inventor of a corn mill, a printing machine, that, according to a report cited in *L'Ecriture des Bamum* (The Writing of the Bamum) he destroyed. But he is also the

77

builder of a palace that brings together various stylistic tendencies and is still today very impressive. Further, he initiated the mapping of his kingdom and many other things, including a basic renovation of the laws of Bamum.

Most important and instructive of Njoya's intellectual production is undoubtedly the invention of a script. His fascination with the written sign, and with calligraphy, was probably the result of an encounter with the Arabic script that must have occurred when he allied himself with the Islamic Fulbe living in the north of Bamum, thus deciding in his favour the murderous struggle over the royal succession that had resulted from his enthronement; for he had come to power at an age when he could not yet exert it. Njoya himself tells in *Histoire et coutumes des Bamum* that he had the idea of the script and its form – the signs – thanks to a dream. From its very conception Njoya's script is inconceivable without the figurative art that in itself is a revelation. The gradual development from pictograms to ideograms indicates that the script was based on a well thought-out plan. At the same time, it was an artistic language whose model, the rebus, as Alfred Schmitt described it in *Die Bamum-Schrift* (The Bamum Script), made possible an infinite number of combinations.

The basis of Njoya's script is that it is developed from drawing, and so a broad system of graphic art, that in the course of its progressive formalisation drew on calligraphy, sculpture, as well as architecture and cartography, surveying, in short, all branches of art that Njoya fostered and supported in his kingdom. Such a comprehensive formal system can only arise within a politics that induces the practical experience of happiness, as Njoya understood it. Happiness in its basic sense consisted for him physical pleasure. It is therefore hardly surprising that one of his most innovative books turns out to be an erotikon, the *Lerewa Nuu Nguet*, written from the male point of view to be sure, and from the perspective of the Bamum noble class that has physical enjoyment as its fundamental theme. The various texts that were produced in the Sultan's scriptorium (secretariat) by scribes cannot be understood without reference to these central writings of the Sultan. One of such scribes, (incidentally, also called Ibrahim Njoya or Johannes Njoya, is one of the pioneers of African comics). Over and above their meaning as literary works, these books represent a rich creation which generated artistic and political activity unique in Africa, in the world of the Bamum, who up to today glorifies artists.

Ibrahim Njoya (the Sultan) thus through two fundamental texts, but above all, through his writing system, founded a metaphysics of art. This metaphysics is the basis on which his building activity as well as his political activity is to be understood. His intellectual stature, even though it is often wrongly reported, as well as his fame as creator of a script, contrasts with the fact that today only a handful of people can read it. Njoya's achievements remain insignificant in the history of African ideas because these, in the wake of colonisation, are based on two concepts that had no particular meaning for the Sultan: first on "races" and their cultural differences, to which the Négritude movement bears witness, and secondly, on the "nation" witnessed by nationalism with its recognised and applauded outcomes to which African independence belongs. Njoya's metaphysic of the arts has no place in a history of ideas that on the one hand sanctions Senghor, Césaire and current movements like the African Renaissance and, on the other hand, celebrates Franz Fanon and Amílcar Cabral. Because the starting point of Njoya's metaphysics was original and unique, the African exegetes have condemned it to obscurity. The manuscripts written in his alphabet have been given up to destruction while African literature disdains his writings.

Consequently, Njoya's concept has been politically side-lined by the history of Africa as determined by nationalism. Just as his palace is a hybrid building, combining architectural forms of the Bamileke, the Bamum and also the Germans because it was erected at the boundary between three colonial epochs (the German, the English and the French), on the political level, the Sultan also tried to maintain his rule in the altercation with the colonial powers, who gradually conquered his kingdom. Banned from his kingdom in 1931, he died two years later in exile, yet in the recorded history of Cameroon, he is only occasionally favourably noticed. Either the Sultan is reproached for his scepticism concerning the emerging Cameroonian nation, or it can only, with difficulty, be forgotten that he, rather than participating in the development of a coalition of anti-German national forces, gave preference to his German friends and so delivered up the flower of the Cameroonian intelligentsia, Samba Martin Paul, Ngosso Din and Douala Manga Bell to the gallows. That in the history of Cameroon Njoya is pronounced guilty of collaboration is a dark stain from which, despite his originality, he cannot be cleansed. Nonetheless, his works bear witness to the determination of an African to mould history, for which he used the means at his disposal, and this, in the shrewdest manner during one of the most turbulent epochs Africa has ever known. His works also put before our eyes a concept of Africa that takes art so seriously that an entire structure of thought is built upon it – a metaphysics.

Bibliography:
Alfred Schmitt, *Die Bamum-Schrift* (Bamum Writing), Wiesbaden, 1963.
Patrice Nganang, *Der Schatten des Sultans* (The Shadow of the Sultan), Wuppertal, 2011.

WANGARI MAATHAI (Kenya)
TO RENEW OUR EARTH

BY VIRGINIA PHIRI

On 1st April 1940, in the little village of Ihithe in the foothills south of Mount Kenya, a girl who would write history was born. In the luxuriant landscape of this fruitful area, with its pure air and clean water courses, the little Wangari and her two older brothers grew up well looked after. From her mother, with whom as an only daughter she had a close relationship and whom she helped in the fields and in the house, she learned to treasure nature as the source of life. Apart from her mother, her aunts and the women of the village were her role models.

When she was sent to school in 1948 she already had the traditional education behind her. Among an overwhelming majority of boys, who were given preferential treatment, she quickly learned to assert herself. With highest marks at the age of twelve she moved to the boarding school of the Catholic Mission of Mathari and accepted the Catholic faith. In this school she spent the 1950s far away from the turbulence of those times, when the Mau Mau war against the British colonial regime was going on in Kenya. In 1956 she attended the nearest mission school, the Loreto Limuru High School, where African girls from all over Kenya came together. She firmly intended to study at Makerere University in Uganda, but it turned out otherwise.

In view of the approaching independence of Kenya and the lack of local expertise, the Joseph P. Kennedy Foundation created a scholarship programme for outstanding Kenyan students that would enable them to train for professions that had previously not been practised by Kenyans. In 1960 Wangari was offered such a scholarship. At the age of twenty she ventured out into the wide world, which at that time, was an unusual step for a woman. In the USA she was admitted to the Catholic St. Scholastica College in Atchinson, Kansas where the nuns are more liberal than in Kenya. Curious and adventurous, the young woman from the Kenyan provinces tried many things. She went dancing with enthusiasm, wore fashionable clothes and even straightened her crinkly hair. After her Bachelor's degree in 1964 she applied to the University of Pittsburgh for a Master's programme in Biology. In these years she came into contact with environmental themes for the first time. When a group of environmental protectionists opposed air pollution she joined them. The success of the environmental activists left a lasting impression on her. After her Master's programme in Biological Science in 1965 she received an offer from the University College in the capital Nairobi to work there. Thirsty for action, she returned to her home country, oblivious of the problems that awaited her.

In the faculty she was informed that the promised position had been given to somebody else. She had underestimated the reservations against women in the world dominated by men, and the extent of thinking in ethnic categories. For months this highly qualified young woman found no position. Significantly, her first placement was offered to her not by a Kenyan but by the German guest professor, Reinhold Hofmann. When he went back to Germany he suggested to her that she conduct the research necessary for her doctorate at his home university, Giessen. She did research there and for two years in Munich after which she went back to Kenya in 1969.

In the same year she married her long-standing friend Mwangi Mathai, which proved to be a fateful decision. In 1971, in the same year that she had her second child, Wangari made history: she was the first woman in east and central Africa to earn the title of Doctor. Despite the double burden, she made a career by becoming Dean in 1974 and three years later, as Professor, she had a foothold in the male dominated academic elite.

Wangari supported her husband in the parliamentary elections of 1974. As the husband of a highly visible academic, he felt under pressure to appear in a comparable position. Through her involvement in numerous organisations, from the National Council of Women through environmental organizations to the Red Cross, she had a major part in her husband's electoral success. Soon however, she realised that her husband did not keep his election promises. He did not care at all that the jobs that he had boldly announced in his campaign had not been created. Now her own reputation was at stake because she had canvassed for him in his electoral campaign. With her own capital she founded the company Environcare Ltd that established jobs through a programme for planting indigenous trees. Thus began the first indigenous tree nursery. However, after a short time the money ran out. Environcare had to apply for bankruptcy but the convinced advocate for the environment did not lose hope.

The United Nations Environment Program (UNEP) was aware of her work and invited her to the first summit meeting of the Human Settlements Program in June 1976. From the stimulation she received from this conference she was newly motivated and proposed a new project to the Council of Women. On 5th June, 1976 she made a breakthrough: on this International Environment Day, Wangari Maathai initiated the campaign "Save the Land Harambee" (Let us pull a rope together). That was the birth of the Green Belt Movement. Encouraged by the success of this undertaking she took the next step: throughout Kenya the women were called upon to plant indigenous saplings in their surroundings. For every sapling that took root they got 0.40 US dollars. Thus the Green Belt Movement also contributed to the improvement of the financial situation of women, who as a rule are financially dependent on their husbands, and strengthened the self-confidence of the participants.

In the midst of success, Wangari experienced the greatest disappointment. Her husband left her, and not only that, he also disgraced her. In suing for divorce he accused her of cruelty and adultery and even made her responsible for his high blood pressure. Despite the preposterous accusations, he won the divorce. Once again it was proved that it is impossible for women to get justice in a patriarchal society. Moreover, as a politician, he had influence on the justice system. In her indignation over the judgement Wangari said in an interview that the judge was either incompetent or corrupt. When she refused to retract her comment she was accused of contempt for the law and sentenced to six months imprisonment. After three days confinement, her lawyer succeeded in having her freed. Now her husband demanded that she give up the name Mathai. Just as stubborn as she was resourceful, she parried this attack by adding an "a" and proposed the name "Maathai". Thus Wangari would go her own way.

The high costs of the divorce process put her in financial difficulties. As a single mother with three children, for whom her husband paid no support, she had to look for a more lucrative place than a university professorship and moved to the UN Economic Commission for Africa, with headquarters in Zambia. The job involved travel throughout the continent. On the basis of this professional burden she made the decision to leave her children with their father. When her financial situation was normal again she took the children back and returned to the university.

In 1979 Wangari was a candidate for the presidency of the National Council of Women but she lost the election because of her ethnic background. Besides, as a representative of educated women independent of men, who involved herself uncompromisingly with justice for those of her sex, she was distrusted by the state. In 1980, when she again stood for election as president, she only won the office against the voices of the organisation *Maendelo Ya Wanawake* (Progress for Women). That government-aligned organisation, which saw in Wangari a political opponent with the wrong ethnic affiliation, now received state funding rather than that of the Council of Women. In consequence, Wangari concentrated harder on environmental projects for which there was funding.

This experience with politics strengthened her fighting spirit and in 1982 she competed in a by-election for a parliamentary seat. Her candidature was rejected with the shabby excuse that she had not been registered as a voter in the previous election. She went to court against it and won but it was too late to hand in the application documents. At the same time she had had to give notice to the university in order to be able to apply for the parliamentary election and in the meantime her place was filled. Fortunately, a short time later a Norwegian forestry commission requested partnership with the Green Belt Movement and appointed her as co-ordinator. Women frequently came to the office from rural areas and complained that there was no firewood to cook the meals. For Wangari, it became even more important to offer checks on the destruction of the environment through the cultivation of trees. It was therefore a stroke of luck that the Green Belt Movement received financial support to the amount of 122,700 US dollars from the UN endowment fund for the Decade of Women, which was for that time, a very large sum. Within a few years, the small project of the Council of Women became a country-wide movement that mobilised thousands of women to plant millions of saplings.

When the Third World Conference of Women was held in Nairobi in 1985, the Green Belt Movement was one of the highlights of the programme, even though it was pushed to the side-lines by the state organisations. Wangari Maathai was in demand as a speaker who knew how to persuade the participants of the success of her women's and environmental activities. After this conference the Council of Women received further financial support for the Green Belt Movement, which spread to other African countries until finally a Pan-African Green Belt Network was formed. People came to Kenya from many countries to educate themselves in the problems of environmental protection.

In view of the growing popularity of this engaged scientist, the government called upon the Council of Women to limit its work to projects purely for women and to discontinue the environmental programmes, which also addressed questions of human rights and democracy. Thereupon Wangari withdrew from the Council of Women and devoted herself all the more to political work within the Green Belt Movement.

In 1989 it came to open confrontation with the government when Wangari learned of plans to build a sixty-storey building complex in the middle of Uhuru Park. The skyscraper would comprise the central party headquarters of the Unity Party KANU, offices, a shopping and recreation centre as well as parking places for 2,000 cars. The central forum would be crowned with the statue of President Arap Moi. In the name of the Green Belt Movement and on several occasions, she sent protest letters to national officials, international organisations and the press. "Certainly the English and the Americans would never accept a skyscraper in the middle of Hyde Park or in Central Park, then why would the inhabitants of Nairobi accept it?" she argued. The reactions were violent. In parliament, angry delegates debated for forty-five minutes over her action and hurled volumes of abuse on her. That a divorced woman publicly criticised the government was the height of provocation. Nevertheless, more inhabitants of Nairobi joined the opposition. Wangari's complaint was rejected by the Supreme Court. On 15th November,1989 the first sod was cut. At the independence celebrations in Uhuru Park on 12th December, the President, who had already assured the opponents of the building that they had "insects in their heads", personally attacked Wangari. He said of her that if she were a true woman in the African tradition, she would respect men and keep her mouth shut. Shortly thereafter rooms were denied to the Green Belt Movement. This was followed by raids on her private house, from where she directed the movement. The New York Times, the Los Angeles Times and the Independent reported in full, and international environmental protection organisations became aware that for the first time, African environmental activists were demanding to be heard. In January 1990 the builders withdrew from the project. For Wangari Maathai, that was a great victory that made her internationally famous.

In 1991 the opposition politician Oginga Odinga founded the Forum for the Restoration of Democracy, which Wangari joined. It advocated the restoration of the multi-party system and general elections. What followed was dramatic. Many signatories to the declaration found their names on a death list! Many went underground, Wangari Maathai and others turned to the press. After the press conference she barricaded herself in her house. Three days later the police succeeded in forcing their way in and arrested her. Together with her co-combatants she was accused of disseminating malicious rumours, incitement to revolt and treason. The international community mobilised itself on their behalf. In the face of sharp criticism from eight American senators including Al Gore and Edward M. Kennedy, the government gave way. After one and a half days in prison, all were freed under caution. In November the charges were dropped. From this it was clear that public demand for free elections in Kenya was legal and no longer punishable.

After this, Wangari was asked by the mothers of political prisoners who had been punished for exactly this demand, to join them in pressurising the government, and so achieving the release of their sons. She presented the Attorney General with an ultimatum and the mothers met in a corner of Uhuru Park that they called Freedom Corner in a three-day hunger strike. This spectacular action attracted unusual attention and created a broad wave of solidarity. On the fourth day the police stormed Freedom Corner and advanced against Wangari and the mothers with teargas and batons. They employed the strongest means the African tradition prescribes for such cases: "On the contrary some of them did something very brave. They undressed and showed the police their breasts... in their anger and their desperation they made the police to understand: "in showing you my nakedness I curse you as I would curse my son, because you mistreat me so badly."

As the Freedom Corner was barricaded, the women got a space in the neighbouring cathedral, the seat of the Anglican archbishop, where they continued their action. The mothers relieved each other in the hunger strike: if one became too weak the other went hungry. The hunger strike, in which Wangari took part whenever she could, lasted for a year, before finally the imprisoned sons were released.

In 1998 Wangari Maathai learned from her information network that the Karura Forest before the gates of the capital was to be parcelled out: the Unity Party KANU had conveyed plots of land to political minions and luxury residences and office buildings would be built there. Wangari started a campaign for the preservation of the Karura Forest, which for Nairobi, with a population of millions, had an important ecological function. The beginning was a letter to the Attorney General with the demand that the building work be stopped immediately. This was then followed by tree planting at the places that had already been cleared. The International media and organisations, especially the UN Environment Office in Nairobi, were informed and the struggle over the Karura Forest was supported around the world. On 8th January, 1999, by way of demonstration, a tree was to be planted at the entrance to the forest. The activists from the Green Belt Movement were met by six members of parliament, journalists, international observers and representatives of human rights organisations. Unknown men attacked them brutally. Wangari, four members of parliament, a journalist and two German observers were injured. The police did nothing.

What the police did not know was that the event was filmed, the report was broadcast on television. A storm of anger broke out, even the UN Secretary General expressed clear criticism. In Nairobi the students organised a solidarity demonstration. When they were attacked by the police they fled to the UNEP compound. Even there the police struck. There were street battles and the university was closed. On 16th August, 1999 the President finally prohibited the sale of public land. Even so, the clearing of the Karura Forest and in other places continued until the regime change of 2002. As candidate of the opposition parties united in the Rainbow Coalition, Wangari won a seat in parliament and the new President Kibaki named her Deputy Minister for the Environment.

For her non-violent struggle for the protection of the environment and human rights, Wangari Maathai received the Nobel Peace Prize in October 2004. For the first time, what was held to be impossible became possible: an African woman received the most famous prize in the world. All Kenya and the rest of the world celebrated. In her acceptance address she said: "My inspiration comes from my childhood experiences and observations of nature in rural Kenya. These were influenced and nurtured through the education that I was privileged to enjoy in Kenya, the United States and Germany. As I grew up I saw how the woods were deforested and replaced by commercial plantations that destroyed the local biodiversity and the ability of the woods to store up water."

The Nobel Prize gave her new incentive. In 2010 together with the University of Nairobi she founded the Wangari Maathai Institute for Peace and Environment Studies that has made the networking of academic research with traditional knowledge its duty. On 25th September 2011 Wangari Maathai died. President Kibaki ordered national mourning for the 29th and 30th of September. The woman, who for decades was harassed and abused by the state, received a state funeral. She had arranged to be cremated – in a coffin of water hyacinth, papyrus and bamboo, not wood. In 2012 fourteen of the supranational organisations united in the Collaborative Partnership on Forests established the Wangari Maathai Award for sustainability, endowed with 20,000 US dollars.

Wangari Maathai concluded her autobiography with words that are her testament: "We find ourselves in good company, thanks to many others throughout the world who keep the Blue Planet in their hearts. We have no other home. Any of us who have seen the damage to the environment and the suffering cannot allow themselves to remain inactive... We owe it to today's and the coming generations of all living beings to rise up and change!"

Bibliography:

Wangari Maathai, *Unbowed, a Memoir.* Knopf, 2006.

Afrika, mein Leben. Erinnerungen einer Unbeugsamen (Africa, my Life. Memories of a Stubborn One.) Cologne, 2008.

Die Wunden der Schöpfung heilen. Wie wir zu uns selbst finden, wenn wir unsere Erde erneuern (To Heal the Wounds of Creation. How we discover ourselves, when we renew our earth.) Freiburg, 2012.

Taking Root: The Vision of Wangari Maathai. Film by Lisa Merton and Alan Dater, 2008.

MARGARET OGOLA   (Kenya)

WITH STETHOSCOPE AND PEN

BY MIKE KURIA

Margaret Ogola, a well-known personality in Kenya as much as the Nobel Peace Prize winner Wangari Maathai, is impressive for her lifetime of work in two entirely different areas. Stethoscope and pen were her tools. As a doctor, she advocated for AIDS patients, for health care and for the interests of women and families. As an author, her stories concentrated on the history and the current situation of women in Kenya. For her novels she was distinguished by the Jomo Kenyatta Prize for Literature and the Commonwealth Writers' Prize. For her humanitarian activity she received the Schweizer Familias Award. When she died of breast cancer at the age of fifty-three on 22nd September, 2011, only a few days before Wangari Maathai, President Kibaki rightly honoured both women as great Kenyans.

Margaret was born on 2nd June, 1958 in Asembo, a village on the banks of Lake Victoria. She was her parents' fifth child. After attending the Thompson's Falls High School in Nyahururu, where she graduated as the best of that year, and the Alliance Girls High School, she studied medicine at the University of Nairobi and did specialisations in surgery and paediatrics. In 1990 she concluded her education with a Master's degree. Margaret got married, had five children and adopted two children, AIDS orphans from her extended family.

Throughout her life Margaret Ogola was interested, above all, in the weak and the disadvantaged. She sympathised with them and her entire professional career was devoted to the improvement of their condition, whether as a paediatrician in Nairobi, or as a leading consultant in many Non-Governmental Organisations and in committees of the Catholic Church of Kenya, where she had a voice in the formulation of health and family policies. From 1994 she was Medical Director of the Cottolengo Hospice in Nairobi for children with AIDS. From 1994 until 2002 she worked for the Kenyan Conference of Catholic Bishops, initially as Director of the Family Advice Board and then as Executive Secretary for Health and Family Life. In the last years of her life she fought for care of AIDS patients. Among other things, she worked for the Hope for African Children Initiative, which was interested in AIDS orphans in several African countries and she built up the SOS Clinic for the care of AIDS patients in Nairobi. At international conferences, for example at the UN World Conference of Women in Peking, she acted as spokeswoman for the women of Kenya and strongly advocated for all women at all societal levels in their struggle against poverty in relation to equal access to education and work and to family planning programmes that respect the value of African women and their children.

Based on her Catholic convictions she was a feminist activist for human rights and a pioneer fighter for access to health care for all people. Margaret Ogola made a meaningful contribution and would surely have left deeper traces in Africa if a longer life had been granted to her.

Margaret Ogola wrote four novels. *The River and the Source*, her first novel, which won the Jomo Kenyatta Literature Prize for 1995 and the Commonwealth Writers' Prize for the best first novel in Africa. The book has also been on the school syllabus in Kenya. Her second novel, *I Swear by Apollo*, was published in 2002. Her third one, *Place of Destiny* (2005) received the Jomo Kenyatta Literature Prize in 2007 and her fourth, *Mandate of the People*, was published posthumously in 2012. Together with her husband she wrote the non-fiction book *Educating in Love*, and with Margaret Roche she wrote a biography of Cardinal Maurice Otunga with the title, *Cardinal Otunga, a Gift of Grace*.

The River and the Source embodies Margaret Ogola's belief in what, in her speech to the World Conference of Women in Peking, she called the "unconquerable spirit of African women". Her world view arises from a knowledge that has its origin in the cultures of Africa. She makes Africa the centre from which the world is to be viewed. *The River and the Source* illustrates her social concern for women, embedded in the African and Catholic conception of the holiness of marriage, motherhood and family. When I interviewed Margaret Ogola she explained to me that motherhood bestows power, that she would not acquiesce in the disturbance of the institution of the family and that fathers should be the leaders of their families. "If I put myself forward anywhere, I cause an average-size scandal when I say that before everything else, I am married, have four children, and my children inspire me to wake up every day and to do what has to be done. My approach to this theme is very African. I believe this is the most important thing in my life. No matter how many degrees I have; no matter however successful I am in my literary activity, if I fail as a mother and my children grow up without the inner balance that only their mother can give them, then I have failed shamefully, and nothing can redress it. I don't find that I have been in any way at a disadvantage because of my children. On the contrary, they have given me the incentive to push much further than if I were alone or only together with my husband. When I read that motherhood is a hindrance and women must be freed from motherhood so that they can prove themselves against men in the world of work, then I am a little sad."

Margaret Ogola insisted that Africa's people must find their own solutions suited to their specific problems, for example, to such sensitive questions as the lack of gender justice, the spread of AIDS, birth control, poverty and cultural traditions. In *The River and the Source* Margaret Ogola demonstrated and celebrated the fact that the struggle for gender justice and the emergence of strong, revolutionary women in Africa is not a colonial or a post-colonial legacy. The novel describes the road to gender freedom as a river whose source is traditional Africa and which flows from the past into the future.

At the beginning of the twentieth century Akoko, the main protagonist, gets married to Chief Owuor Kembo, with whom she has two sons and a daughter. The chief is an unusual man, for in spite of his mother's insistent pressure, he refuses to marry more women and beget more children. Akoko's first son Obura is killed in Tanganyika in 1918. When his father too suddenly dies, the second son Owang Sino takes over the office, but soon chokes on a fish bone. Owang Sino's son, called Owuor after his grandfather, is a small child at the time of his father's death. The *chik*, tradition, does not allow a child to become a chief, and so the position passes over to his uncle, in this case, Otieno Kembo.

According to tradition, Otieno Kembo should only remain chief until the young Owuor has grown up but Otieno Kembo does not give up power and appropriates the family property, including Akoko's own possessions. Akoko knows that "as a woman, widow and mother without a son, with a small baby as her only direct male relative, she is at a very serious disadvantage." However, she will not give in and decides to proceed against the chief and calls upon the *sirikal*, the colonial administration. She makes the trip to Kisumu, which was then the seat of the colonial administration. For Akoko and her descendants, this trip marks the beginning of the struggle for greater gender justice and for a more human society. Akoko thus becomes the source of the spirit of opposition, for the river that Margaret Ogola has flowing from generation to generation until in the year 1992, it meets Wandia, a Kikuyu woman who has married into this Luo society. Akoko is the source of the great river that "begins its journey as a small stream, at first without apparently meandering from its course, occasionally disappearing underground, and yet is always there, forever moving to the sea."

The female main characters are subversive and conformist at the same time. The greatness of the author lies in how she creates figures of women who have doubts about the long-standing patriarchal values and the injustice towards women that they involve, without distancing themselves from their society or permanently shaking the stability of the society. These revolutionary women are not driven by cynicism about African traditions or by a condescending superiority complex. Opposition to the injustices to which women are exposed begins with Akoko's going to Kisumu. The white male colonial officials, with support from local male personnel, side with Akoko and allow her brother-in-law to be enthroned and another appointed as chief until Akoko's grandson is old enough for the office. The first person to follow the path into a new world opened by Akoko is Akoko's daughter Nyabera. After her husband's death she is disinherited by his family, is unfortunate in a new marriage, and has suffered several miscarriages until she leaves the village and goes to a Catholic mission centre where she accepts the new religion. Thanks to the mission school her daughter Awiti is able to become one of the first women teachers in Luo country. Among the Luo she thus becomes an "object of curiosity" since "a woman who did other work than cultivating the fields and raising children was previously an unknown phenomenon." She marries Mark Antony Oloo Sigu and has seven children with him. The process of change initiated by Akoko reaches a peak when the degree of medical doctor is bestowed on Awiti's daughter-in-law Wandia, the first woman to earn this title in Kenya.

Despite the individual successes of the protagonists, critical voices could reproach the author because she does not fundamentally interrogate and analyse the ideology and the social structures that undermine women's struggles for liberation. More interestingly – and not surprisingly – the women are supported by the men who mean most to them, namely their husbands. Margaret Ogola also thought that women's struggle against sexism should begin at home and for that to be successful there, resistance cannot be based in the simple opposition of men against women. Women must win the support of the important men in their lives and if they have this support, and are not hindered by artificial, social and patriarchal barriers, they will be successful. In other words, African women need neither excuses nor favours; they need free access to all possibilities.

This is not to say that Margaret Ogola considered the patriarchy necessary in all its forms and features. On the contrary, the novel *The River and the Source* mentions the negative elements of patriarchal practices and expectations and argues that this baggage should be discarded, for example in the betrothal ceremony. Tradition ordains that the bride has to present herself as "the image of bashful modesty," gazing down at the ground, hands folded in front of her mouth." Akoko however proceeds self-confidently, with a firm step and head raised high, hands by the side of her body, and looks at her fiancé as if to appraise and challenge him. It is an aspect of Margaret Ogola's African way of approaching gender injustice that she does not present a chief who compels his wife to adjust in the name of the patriarchy; far more is implied in the fact that Akoko's strong character so impresses the chief that he is interested only in her. In that it is his mother who wants to persuade the chief to marry another wife, the author shows the patriarchy in Africa as a system supported by both sexes.

Margaret Ogola showed that the woman in the traditional Luo society is, above all, reduced to her reproductive function. This attitude is propagated and supported by men and also by women, as in the example of Chief Owuor Kembo's mother's demand that he should marry another woman because Akoko does not get pregnant as often as expected. If in such a society it is nevertheless possible that strong and resistant women can go their own way, then the author has social change triumphing over the limitations that tradition imposes on people. Awiti rises up against the traditional restrictions, not thanks to the mission school or the help of a western missionary and philanthropist, black or white, but because she was brought up by a strong, imaginative Luo woman.

Margaret Ogola is consequently neither against change, nor does she maintain that in Africa one may not intervene for more justice and social progress. She represents much more the view that African women are very well placed to recognise injustice as such, and that in the effort to improve their situation they can seek out and request assistance wherever it may be. Margaret Ogola opposed not only the temptation to construct an Afrocentric feminism as the antithesis of Eurocentric feminism, she also anticipated the reproach that she imitated western societies with her argument for strong, free women.

She took time to explain the numerous African customs that she depicted, rather than simply condemning them. So for example, she showed that there is a logical and intelligent explanation for what in feminist discourse is pejoratively described as wife inheritance. With reference to this practice, known among the Luo as *tero*, Margaret Ogola showed that a man who inherits a widow in this way had no claim to the woman; it was rather his duty to beget children to preserve the name of the dead and prevent his widow from attaching herself to a strange man, which was considered shameful in the society. In an interview she told me, "In my view, this practice is often wrongly assessed because the historical background is left out of account. If one takes the inheritance of widows out of its historical context, then one misleads people.... I don't say that we must hold on to our culture at all cost, for things change, but one should not see it as something that happened by being imposed by somebody. On the contrary, it happened for the protection of women and children."

Her second novel *I Swear by Apollo* – the title refers to the Hippocratic oath – tells the story of two orphans, Alicia and Johnny. They have lost their mother Becky through AIDS, after their Canadian father had deserted them. Their uncle and especially their aunt Wandia, the doctor from *The River and the Source*, bring them up. Johnny becomes a Flying Doctor and Alicia a distinguished music teacher. Margaret Ogola makes it clear that the traditional African structures, in which relatives look after each other can be useful resources in the struggle against AIDS. When I interviewed her she said, "I think that on this young continent of Africa, with the problems we have, our family sense is our greatest strength. With its help we can, I hope, overcome the AIDS epidemic and the problems arising from it. But I am sad when I see that the family cohesion is more and more undermined."

Nonetheless, Margaret Ogola also wanted to send a signal of political hope. When *I Swear by Apollo* was published in 2001, she ventured to believe that in Africa a woman could become a President and that was before the election of the two, and so far, the only women Presidents on the continent, Ellen Johnson Sirleaf, elected President of Liberia in 2006, and Joyce Banda, who came to power in Malawi in 2012, after the death of the previous President Bingu wa Mutharika. The scene of the action is an African country ruled by a "stern and fearless" female President. Her main concern is the struggle against "institutionalised corruption."

Her novel *Place of Destiny* is concerned with another much feared cause of death in Africa, cancer. As with AIDS, many people in Africa with this diagnosis often avoid talking about their illness. Only in recent times, since the two former Ministers of Health, Beth Mugo and Anyang Nyongo, made public their breast cancer and prostate cancer respectively, is cancer no longer a taboo subject in Kenya. Margaret Ogola's *Place of Destiny* is about Amor, a successful businesswoman, who discovers from her doctor that she suffers from advanced liver cancer and has only four to six months to live. She is happily married to Mwaghera Mrema, a historian, and has four children. The diagnosis of cancer forces her to confront death and dying. In her culture it is a taboo, for the tradition predicts that an evil that one intentionally thinks about, talks or even writes about, certainly will come to pass and cause grief to the person concerned.

Margaret Ogola's book encourages people suffering from cancer to talk about their illness and to spend time thinking about their approaching death. Amor spends time organising her business affairs, talking to her children, encouraging her husband to remarry after her death, and urging their son to take over the business. As she accepts her fate and often talks about it, the family can prepare themselves for the sad event.

The book has autobiographical features, for when Margaret Ogola was working on it she herself already had breast cancer. Shortly before her death she was able to finish yet another novel. In *Mandate of the People*, which was published posthumously, she described an election campaign. Adam, an entrepreneur from the city, competes in a rural electoral district, the home area of his mother. In a political environment in which ethnic origin is the decisive factor, together with the youth of the district, he proposes a development plan. What is new is that their successful application of ideas depends on professional qualification instead of on ethnic heritage. Despite the hostility of political opponents the candidate wins the election. Margaret Ogola thus expressed her hope that tribalism, that hinders lasting development, can be overcome.

This message was very important to her. In all her earlier novels she had already taken up the idea of a society without tribalism and ethnic prejudice. Always there are female protagonists who break through ethnic barriers as they marry men from other ethnic origins, adopt children from other families or consciously detach themselves from tribal traditions. Margaret Ogola wished that Africa might recognise that narrow-minded ethnocentrism has no future, and that the citizens of the continent require a world-scale society and this all the more, because in Kenya after the elections of 2007/2008, more than a thousand persons lost their lives in a senseless brutal conflict between ethnic groups. Ogola attempted to give Africa hope, well before Obama made the slogan "*Yes we can*" popular.

Bibliography
Margaret Ogola, *The River and the Source*, Nairobi, 1995;
"   *I Swear by Apollo*, Nairobi, 2002;
"   *Place of Destiny*, Nairobi, 2005;
"   *Mandate of the People*, Nairobi, 2012.

ALICK NKHATA (Zambia)

A LIFE BEFORE ITS TIME

BY ELLEN BANDA-AAKU

In the heart of Lusaka, the capital of Zambia, a busy street leads past the Zambia National Broadcasting Corporation. The street is named after Alick Nkhata, the broadcasting pioneer and ground-breaking Zambian musician who, in the course of his life, was also a teacher, farmer and war veteran. Instead of a hat on his head, he always had his guitar and a radio close by; for underpinning all his activities and effort, was the love of music and broadcasting.

Those who knew Nkhata describe him as a sociable, sympathetic, generous and intelligent person with an infectious laugh. He laid the foundations for broadcasting and radio in Zambia and tried to preserve the traditional music for later generations. He was also inventive; as a musical pioneer in the 1940s and 1950s, he adapted the traditional indigenous music to the modern, by using western instruments such as the acoustic guitar. Nkhata's eldest son David said of his father, "He lived before his time".

Alick Nkhata was born on the 2nd of February, 1932 in Kasama, in the middle of Bemba land in the northern part of Northern Rhodesia, today's Zambia. He was the youngest of four children of Beatrice and Aaron Kapandula Nkhata. Nkhata Senior was one of the many Tonga migrants from Nyasaland, today Malawi, who had moved there at the beginning of the 20ᵗʰ century in search of work.

When Alick Nkhata grew older he went to school in Kasama. At the outbreak of the Second World War he joined the East African Forces and arrived in Burma as a copy typist and entertainer. At the end of 1945 he was discharged with a diploma that classified him as of exemplary behaviour, conscientious and reliable. There are very few records of what happened to the soldiers in the Northern Rhodesia regiment of the King's African Rifles, and apparently Nkhata did not talk to his family about his war experiences. Only occasionally, if knowledge of first aid was needed, did he go back to what he knew from his time in the military. Besides his army uniform, he brought home from the war the Order of the Star of Africa as well as a tattoo on his upper arm that he claimed, was dedicated to his parents.

After the war he did teacher training in Kasama at the Lubwa Mission School, the first teacher training institution for Africans in Northern Rhodesia. At that time the colonial administration encouraged educated black Africans to become teachers. Nkhata studied together with Kenneth Kaunda and Simon Mwanda Kapwepwe, later President and Vice-President of Zambia respectively.

In 1946 Nkhata married Christine Kapoya Kapotwe. They had eight children. Even though he had such a large family, the gates of his house stood open wide, and his home was always full of people. In the 1950s Nkhata lived like all Africans in Northern Rhodesia, in a special quarter designated for blacks. In order to earn something there he kept a small shop where he sold goods for everyday needs. There, without thinking about it, he took goods from the shelf and shared them with friends and relatives. His generous heart also governed his love for music; often Nkhata took young musicians under his wings and promoted them.

Already, as he was growing up, Nkhata was devoted to music and playing the guitar. After the war he worked together with the well-known British ethno-musicologist Hugh Tracey, who was credited with the discovery of the *kalimba*, a thumb piano, which he associated with the traditional musical instrument from southern Africa, the *mbira*. To record African music, Tracey and Nkhata travelled throughout south and central Africa, in a Bedford van outfitted with recording equipment. After Tracey had left Northern Rhodesia Nkhata continued alone. He used some of the material collected in his own compositions.

In 1948 he went to South Africa on a veteran's award to study music. He recorded a series of duets with the guitarist Shadrick Soko and founded the Alick Nkhata Quartet. The other members of the band were James Shitumba, James Lenga Lenga and Titus Mukupo, who replaced Black Kapotwe (Nkhata's brother-in-law). Out of the Alick Nkhata Quartet came the Broadway Quintet, in which younger musicians like Sumangaliso Tutani, Jonas Marumahoko and Timothy Sikova from Zimbabwe took the places of the older band members. Later the Zimbabwean guitarist Zacks Gwaze, former member of the Golden Cool Crooners from Southern Rhodesia, joined the Quintet. Gwaze, who today lives in Botswana, is a famous jazz guitarist and played with such well-known musicians as Hugh Masekela.

Jazz, jive, sinjonjo, calypso and traditional African sounds inspired Nkhata's music. He sang and composed many pieces himself. He made other songs, which originally would have been played with traditional instruments, into dance music by introducing acoustic guitars. Because he produced the music of different parts of the country in new form, pieces that were originally regionally limited became universally known.

Nkhata sang his songs in various languages, among others Bemba, Chewa, Lunda, Nsenga, Tonga, Nyanja and English, or he combined several languages. For example he sang *Shalapo*, a love song, in Bemba and English. This kind of combining local African languages with western languages is a very popular trend among musicians. Franco, the great musician from the Congo, mixed Lingala with French in his music. Young musicians in Africa today, such as P Square from Nigeria and Exile from Zambia, similarly combine African and western languages in their music. Through songs that dealt with social themes in different musical styles, and fascinated listeners because they were about their everyday experience, Nkhata sensitised people about social problems. In the song, *Imbote* he warned, in an amusing way, of the dangers of illegally brewed alcoholic drinks that could dry up the human gut. *Abanakashi aba mu njanji* makes satirical fun of women who blindly exchange their traditional customs for European values and fashions.

Nkhata also wrote political songs. When independence for Northern Rhodesia was drawing near he founded the UNIP Band, an electioneering group that propagandised through their songs for the United National Independence Party (UNIP) – the party that eventually won the election. The UNIP Band consisted of members of his Quartet and other musicians recruited by Nkhata. During this time he also ran the Northern Rhodesian broadcasting stations, which were based in Tanzania and broadcast directly to Zambia in support of the struggle for independence. In addition, on account of his easy-going personality, Nkhata was often invited to mediate between the political parties contesting the election.

After independence Nkhata composed songs in support of the government and its policies. To celebrate the independence of Northern Rhodesia and the birth of the new Zambia, the Anglo American Corporation of Central Africa financed a film with the title *Zambia '64*, about the newly independent country, and Nkhata wrote the music for the film. In the 1960s he received the commission to write a song that would encourage the population to contribute to the building of the country's first university. Gifts in the most varying forms, from cash to *kitenge* (printed coloured cloths) to live cattle, streamed into the fund from all parts of the country. Once again, Nkhata's music had done its work.

Characteristic of Nkhata, his wit and his talent for composing the suitable song for every occasion, is a radio broadcast recorded in 1953 in his two-room house in the African quarter of Chilenge in Lusaka. In the broadcast he informed "London" that he was giving a party in honour of Queen Elizabeth's accession to the throne. "We celebrate here in respect, and I wish that she could celebrate with us. The house is small, it has two rooms, one of many hundred houses in this overcrowded quarter. The room is small, we haven't much space here to move around in. It is lit by paraffin lamps, food and drink are on the table; European and African. Some drink European drinks, others our traditional African beer. We are of various origins, and we celebrate by singing. Now comes a song that I have written for this occasion. I was inspired for it by a traditional African piece." Then he let loose with a Bemba song celebrating the crowning of Queen Elizabeth the Second.

In 1950 when Nkhata travelled back to South Africa he had begun to work at CABS (Central African Broadcasting Services), the broadcasting station set up by the colonial administration for Nyasaland and Northern Rhodesia, which also employed Africans. CABS had grown out of a station in Lusaka that broadcast news during the Second World War and transmitted information to families and friends about their relatives. At that time also, the mass production of "saucepan radios" began, radio receivers running on batteries for the African market. In those years more and more Africans moved to the cities for better prospects for work and education and they bought themselves radio sets. Nkhata was already a well-known musician and as a radio announcer, he reached an even larger public with his broadcasts and his music.

In 1957, with Cyril Sapseid, a white veteran of radio and a musician, Nkhata founded the Lusaka Radio Band, members of which he recruited from the police and the army. Nkhata sang and played the guitar and Sapseid played the piano. The Lusaka Radio Band made music for broadcasting organisations.

With the development of the Federation of Rhodesia and Nyasaland, in 1959 CABS became the FBC (Federation Broadcasting Corporation), whereby European broadcasting was based in Southern Rhodesia and African broadcasting in Northern Rhodesia. Nkhata was sent to the Southern Rhodesian station in Salisbury.

At a time when many African countries were struggling for their independence, the Federation was pushing in the opposite direction to the population, and the colonial government used the radio to spread its propaganda. This put the African radio presenters in a bad light for the African listener, who identified them with the content of the broadcast, accused them of being on the side of the colonial masters, and thus viewed them with mistrust. Nonetheless, the colonial masters too did not value them highly, for their roles were limited to translation and announcing and they received a much smaller salary than their European colleagues. All the same, the African radio presenters, with education at their disposal and at home in the popular culture, were extremely significant as the central connecting link between the African audience and the colonial broadcasting organisation.

In the 1950s, Nkhata was presented in a BBC television documentary. In 1953 he was sent to London for further training at the BBC and in 1957 a photo of him appeared in a local newspaper in which he was pointing on a map to Los Angeles, where he was to go on scholarship for a year of further studies. It was decidedly unusual for an African to be sent abroad and so Nkhata was in the headlines.

The pressure on African broadcasting employees not to work for the colonial power continually grew and Nkhata left the FBC in 1962. With the musicians whom he had engaged in Southern Rhodesia he went back to Northern Rhodesia and supported the campaign of the UNIP led by Kenneth Kaunda. Even before Northern Rhodesia achieved independence Nkhata, together with five other African radio presenters, got a position with the American foreign broadcaster, Voice of America and he moved with his family to the United States. He was one of the first presenters of the Voice of America programme, African Panorama. In 1964, when the UNIP won the election and the first African government of the independent state of Zambia had been formed, Nkhata was named as the first black Director of the Zambian Broadcasting Services, ZBS.

On his return to the Zambian Broadcasting Services, as the national radio broadcaster was now called, it was still important to Nkhata to promote local music and culture. The radio was as before, a central medium for spreading music for the masses. Nkhata used his musicians from the Broadway Quintet together with some from the UNIP Band and founded the post-colonial Lusaka Radio Band, which played music with a national character for the radio. The Lusaka Radio Band changed their name to Big Gold Six when they were sponsored by a tobacco company that produced a brand of cigarette called Big Gold Six.

With all his passion for radio, Nkhata tried to make the Broadcasting Services into a first class broadcaster. He pushed for the building of new purpose-built structures for the accommodation of the radio and television services. After independence there were only a few employees at ZBS with formal qualifications. While he himself had none, but rather a wide-ranging experience in broadcasting work, he was convinced that experienced, motivated technicians, whether with or without professional certificates, deserved appreciation, especially since the broadcaster depended on them. Nkhata insisted that such personnel be retained and paid appropriately. The criteria for employment that had been established from a western point of view, in his opinion, were not always useful. As a broadcasting man who believed that radio should inform and support the listener, and as someone who wanted to further expand the ZBS audience, he took the view that an African broadcaster must know the local and cultural context of its listeners, if it wanted to arouse the interest of the listeners and communicate with them. Nkhata had been in broadcasting long enough to know the requirements of the African public. That perhaps was why he believed that the future belonged to commercial radio, in contrast to radio financed by taxes. In Zambia, more people would listen to the radio if they did not have to pay taxes for it, he thought.

Because the promotion of local music was close to his heart, he laid out a plan according to which the state radio should play ninety per cent indigenous music and only ten per cent foreign music. With the establishment of private radio broadcasters this rule went largely ignored; but Zambian music is so popular that it nevertheless takes up an important share of broadcasting time.

In 1972 Nkhata was named the head of the Culture Department, where he likewise was engaged in the promotion of Zambian culture. Two years later he left this position and became a farmer. He was disappointed that the Culture Department was made into a division of government and that the government, instead of following his recommendations for an independent broadcaster, placed the ZBS under the Ministry of Information.

Even after his withdrawal, Nkhata remained true to his love of music and of broadcasting. Besides his occupation as farmer he was also active as a free-lance worker in radio. Private organisations like, Colgate-Palmolive Zambia Limited, engaged him for broadcasts sponsored by them. In the late 1970s he worked with the first members of the Alick Nkhata Quartet, including James Shitumba and Black Kapotwe, and gave his music a new lease on life. Aside from being song writer, band leader and music producer, Nkhata was also still active in the promotion of local music. He was planning the establishment of a recording studio in which Zambian artists could record their music when his life came to an abrupt end.

Alick Nkhata lost his life on 19th October, 1978 in a tragic manner when he fell in a raid by Southern Rhodesian forces on a ZAPU (Zimbabwe African People's Union) refugee camp, which was close to his farm in Mkushi in the Central Province of Zambia. It is an irony of history that a man who had been sent to the other side of the globe in the war was killed close to his home as a civilian. At his funeral, the Gold Six Band played in farewell, one of his most famous pieces, *Ifilamba*, Tears.

Through radio and music Nkhata contributed much to Northern Rhodesia and the then young nation, Zambia. He helped to transform the radio from purely a channel for information into a medium of support, social involvement and promotion of culture. On the radio he brought the local music home to the people. An important number of traditional Zambian music pieces and musical instruments were saved from oblivion by his efforts. To the extent that he put traditional songs, legends and proverbs into a modern idiom, he enriched Zambian culture and made it possible for the Zambian people to have a comprehensive knowledge of their own music. His greatest legacy perhaps lies in his passion for music making and the messages that he has sent us in his compositions. His music of social criticism is still relevant after fifty years, and the influence of his songs on Zambian music and the Zambian musicians is still traceable today. In the year 2011, at a memorial service for the deceased Mwanda Wa Bayake, a well-known guitarist from the Congo, who by chance also worked in broadcasting, a young guitarist played Alick Nkhata's *Uluse Lwalile Nkwale* – in memory of the great guitarist of the 1950s in East and Central Africa.

Almost four decades after the death of the great musician and broadcaster, Nkhata's most important legacy is his music, which is still played throughout the world. He is remembered for his songs, but also by a busy tarred road that leads past the buildings of the state broadcasting system. Alick Nkhata never saw the complex of buildings of the Zambia National Broadcasting Company with his own eyes, but they were his vision, for which he advocated and had the foresight, fifteen years before they became a reality.

Bibliography:

Alick Nkhata, Coronation Night in an African Homestead, CABS Radio Broadcast, 1953. South African Music Archive Project. http://www.disa.ukzn.ac.za/samap/content/coronation-night-african-homestead-southern-african.
Electric Jive, *Zambia* '64. http://electricjive.blogspot.co.uk/2012/09/zambia-64-soundtrack.html

ANGELINE S. KAMBA (Zimbabwe)

SOURCE OF INSPIRATION

BY CHIRIKURE CHIRIKURE

Since time immemorial, in African societies, as also in other societies, the greatness of a person is measured in particular ways. It is a matter of intellectual abilities, of the capacity to develop ideas and apply them, and how the thinking affects the family, the community and the environment. With the onset of colonialism the abilities of an individual in Africa were measured by new criteria. Success in official school education became the fundamental yardstick but the greatest challenge was to find a balance between traditional and modern ways to make a contribution to society. For the first generation of Africans who passed through the official programme of western school education, this challenge was much greater than it was for later cohorts.

For women this challenge was even more difficult to overcome because, regarded by society as mothers and carers, in a modern world they were nevertheless encouraged to go to school. The balance between the expectations of society and their own plans and goals was for women an enormous challenge. Zimbabwe was no exception. One young Zimbabwean woman succeeded in bridging the gap and becoming one of the first to achieve outstanding success in school. With a professional career that was unusual for her time, she received honour and recognition beyond the borders of Zimbabwe, on both intellectual and social levels.

For many she proved to be a true source of inspiration. This woman is Angeline Saziso Kamba.

Angeline was born on 15th October 1935 in the Methodist Thekwane Mission (in what was then Southern Rhodesia), where both of her parents were teachers. For primary school she went to various establishments in Plumtree, first to the Dombodema Mission, where her father was the Principal, then to the Empadeni Mission. For secondary school education she went to St. Mary's Girls Institution in Lesotho (at that time Basutoland). In 1954 there were only four girls in her class. A Southern Rhodesia scholarship enabled her next to register for a bachelor's degree at Pius XII College in Roma (today the National University of Lesotho), where at that time one could earn a degree from the University of South Africa. In 1957 she completed her bachelor's degree and thus was only the second African girl in Southern Rhodesia, today's Zimbabwe, with a college degree. She returned home and registered in 1958 for the first year of teacher training at the University College of Rhodesia and Nyasaland, today the University of Zimbabwe, where she was one of only two African women in the entire college.

On 27th August, 1960, she married Walter Joseph Kamba, at that point in time a lawyer, who would later carve out an academic career and eventually, shortly after the independence of the country, become Vice Chancellor of the University of Zimbabwe, a position that he held for ten years. She had three sons, Denis Thabo, who died early, Mark Adrian Chawapiwa, who lives in Glasgow, and Julian Tendayi, who lives in New York with his family.

At the time of her marriage and while her children were growing up, Angeline Kamba worked as a library assistant, first at the US Information Agency in Salisbury, then at the University of Rhodesia and Nyasaland. At this time she took a year off to do a Master's course in library science at Columbia University, New York, which she completed in 1966.

From 1967 until 1980 she lived abroad with her family, in exile. These were years when she aspired to broaden her horizon, and at the same time, years of political unrest at home. During this time she had positions as librarian in various institutions in Great Britain, including the Institute for Advanced Legal Studies and in the library of the University of London. She spent the longest time at the University of Dundee in Scotland, where she and her family lived for eleven and a half years. She herself described this time as "a period of tremendous growth, from both the intellectual and the professional point of view".

During their exile Angeline and her husband made an important contribution to Zimbabwe's struggle for independence. However, the greatest opportunity to employ her acute understanding as well as her international experience was offered after the attainment of independence. She returned home with her family and in February 1981 was made Director of the National Archives of Zimbabwe. This was a historic moment because she was the first Black, and at the same time, the first woman to head this institution. Under her leadership the national archive shed its earlier colonialist and elitist character and was transformed into a true national-historical establishment. She was the guiding force in the reactivation of the programme for World Heritage and Tradition. Under her direction, the archive, which in the years before independence had become completely isolated, was again received into the bosom of the international community, above all, into the International Archive Council, where she played a leading role. Angeline was even elected its vice-president.

During her time in office the National Archive was host to important international conferences, and mounted public exhibitions that contributed immensely to the development of national identity after independence. However, in November 1990, after contributing so significantly, Angeline left the institution.

During the years 1993-1995, at the invitation of the Director General of UNESCO, she accepted an important international assignment as a member of the World Commission on Culture and Development. The members of the Commission were chosen according to their personal abilities and represented different nationalities and disciplines. Under the chairmanship of the then Secretary General of the UN, Perez de Cuellar, the Commission was to explore the relationships between culture and development and draw up guidelines for UN and UNESCO activities. The published report, *Our Creative Diversity*, was presented in November 1995 and kindled debates on this theme of culture that continued into the present. Angeline was involved in the debate and gave lectures in various national and international fora and also appeared in discussions on television. She also collaborated on the production of an hour-long film to publicise the Commission's procedures and the report itself.

Angeline always participated in projects on the theme of cultural diversity, for which she herself says, she has a great passion. This passion of hers was further stimulated by her activity as member, then chair, of the International Rice Research Institute that comprises all the rice cultivating countries of Asia. She said that this work that she carried out from 1998 to 2003, "made possible a clearer view of cultural diversity".

In the meantime, in November 1990 Angeline was appointed to be part of the Public Service Commission (PSC) Board of Zimbabwe, where she was active until her retirement in November 1998. The PSC is a constitutional committee, whose members are nominated by the President of the Republic of Zimbabwe and is responsible for personnel management in the public service.

One of Angeline Kamba's later callings was from 2003 the directorship of the Harare International Festival of the Arts (HIFA), a festival that takes place annually, established as a foundation in the year 1999. The HIFA is one of the few success stories that have survived the time of Zimbabwe's economic and political disturbances, and is in fact the best organised festival in Africa, south of the Sahara. It takes place yearly for a period of six days and offers a variety of presentations and performances in the areas of music, dance, theatre, literature and art. The participating artists come from Zimbabwe, from throughout Africa and the rest of the world. The festival grows bigger from year to year. In the year 2012 more than 1,500 artists appeared from thirty countries. During the six days that the festival lasted, a total of more than sixty thousand entry tickets were sold.

The devotion, the enthusiasm and the management of Angeline Kamba and her team brought about this success. This is all the more significant as in most years the festival took place in a difficult environment, for Zimbabwe went through social and political chaos as never before. Politics was polarised to a high degree, and art was under severe scrutiny from the state. The economy was so destroyed that unemployment was over ninety per cent and the majority of the population did not even have the basic necessities of life. Despite all these challenges the festival held its ground as one of the few remaining windows into the country.

Angeline Kamba left the HIFA board in 2011. Since then she has been anything but idle. For example, she worked in local committees and non-governmental organisations and sat on the councils of the Midlands State University in Gweru and the Catholic University of Zimbabwe. Her international activities included participation in the presentation of the Caine Prize for African Writing, in the Observatory of Cultural Policies in Africa with headquarters in Maputo (Mozambique), and in the non-governmental organisation, Non-Violent Action and Strategies for Social Change.

During all these years Angeline Kamba wrote and published numerous articles in newspapers and books. She gave talks at seminars and conferences. Her writings give a valuable insight into her vision and opinions. The Shona people of Zimbabwe have a proverb that goes, *Chitende chinorema ndechine mhodzi*. This can be approximately translated as "the bottle gourd that is heavy carries seeds." This means that the true qualities of individuals often reside in their personalities. One recognises a sincere person by his inner worth and his personal effort. For that, respect is due to him or her.

Angeline Kamba is an African personality whose achievements raise her above many others. Already as a young woman she crossed over barriers and made a name for herself as an excellent student, who attained outstanding academic qualifications. She was the second Zimbabwean woman ever to receive a college diploma, and all that, against the reigning cultural and social prejudices.

She married and brought up children, but never allowed domesticity to overwhelm her. In her academic achievements she added further distinctions. In the course of the years she moved from one influential post to the next and left impressive traces each time. In most of the jobs that she held in her mature years she was confronted with political and social hurdles that required much tact. With her unique courage and determination she indicated her wish to speak on numerous platforms of the world and knew how to avoid ever being pushed aside. Through these personal accomplishments, her ability and her preparedness to share her knowledge, she became a true source of inspiration for many people in her country and throughout the world. She is in fact a heavy gourd, whose seed will bear fruit for the good health of Africa's future.

It is only right and proper that on 24th November 2010 the Faculty of Arts of the Midlands State University conferred on her an honorary doctorate in archaeology, heritage and museum science.

Bibliography

UNESCO (publisher): *Our Creative Diversity*. Report of the World Commission on Culture and Development, Bonn: German UNESCO Commission, 1997. unesco.org/culture/en 1995.

MARIAMA BÂ (Senegal)

A PRAGMATIC LITERARY PIONEER

BY VÉRONIQUE TADJO

When Mariama Bâ's first novel appeared in 1979 the critics were unanimous: *So Long a Letter* is a major work of African literature. The original style and the social range of the themes handled make the work a classic of world literature. After the novel was recognised at the Frankfurt Book Fair with the Noma Award for Publishing in Africa, which was being awarded for the first time, translations into several languages followed. Today it has reached millions of readers. With *So Long a Letter* Mariama Bâ made a crucial contribution to the development of women's consciousness in Africa. Her novel is a landmark for the appearance of French speaking African women on the literary scene. In a period when literature was dominated by men, Mariama Bâ pushed open the door for a generation of women writers, who came onto the scene in the 1980s and changed the literary landscape of Africa. Mariama Bâ's greatest service consists in the fact that she began to speak for women who for centuries, in the traditional as well as in the post-colonial society, had remained dumb. To correctly understand the impact of her work it is useful to have a look at her biography.

Mariama Bâ was born in 1929 in Dakar, Senegal. Her mother died when she was a small child. This blow of fate the little girl perceived as a great injustice. She grew up with her grandparents in a strongly Islamic, very conservative and privileged milieu. A stately building, standing on the family land served as a mosque. Her father belonged to the small educated elite, and was a minister in the autonomous government that worked for the country's independence towards the end of the 1950s.

Against the wishes of her grandparents, Mariama Bâ attended the girls' school in Rufisque, a suburb of Dakar. She distinguished herself not only by her good performance in school but by her rebellious behaviour. She resisted the traditional structures and especially the alienation that was the goal of the curriculum in the colonial schools. In one of her first youthful writings she announced, "My brain is bleached, but my head remains black. And in my civilized veins my undeniable blood pounds like an untameable horse".

In 1947 she finished her training as an elementary school teacher and taught for twelve years, before she changed to school administration for health reasons. After her ninth child she divorced her husband and wrote her first novel. On 17th August 1981, three months before the appearance of her second novel, entitled *Scarlet Song*, she succumbed to cancer.

With her novel *So Long a Letter* Mariama Bâ chose an unusual form that alternates between autobiography, diary and novel. The book, the story of Ramatoulaye, a fifty-year-old Senegalese woman, who, after the death of her husband, Modou Fall, writes a letter to her friend Aissatou, who has emigrated to the USA. In the seclusion of the mourning period, in which the widow cannot leave the house for forty days, Ramatoulaye meditates and reviews the course of her life. She tells her friend about her problems when after twenty-five years, Modou married a second wife, Bintou, who was the age of their daughter, and plunged Ramatoulaye into emotional and financial distress because he abandoned her and their twelve children.

As in Ahmadou Kourouma's novel *The Suns of Independence* (*Les Soleils de l'Indépandences*), that appeared ten years earlier, *So Long a Letter* bore the impress of the disillusioned literature of its time. The novel denounced the African elites who had declared the foundation of a new society after their return from abroad, a society freed from the colonial yoke and from backward customs. Yet in this society not only did deep inequalities remain, and a narrow-minded political view was retained, the majority of women remained excluded from divorce proceedings and from public life. In addition, polygamy remained just as widespread as the caste system and all possible injustices.

What Mariama Bâ's book strikingly expresses is, Senegalese women, that is, African women in general, are certainly mothers, sisters and wives, but they will never be treated as equal members of society. They feel themselves betrayed by their former comrades in arms, who, settled in the comfort of the privileged, had entangled themselves in numerous contradictions and abandoned the hopes of earlier years.

The struggle of African women for full equal rights is presented here from the woman's point of view, as a concrete example of a mother with her children. Here is where Mariama Bâ's skill is revealed: what previously counted as a social side-show takes centre stage; the world of women and the domestic reality that were pushed to one side becomes a major political problem. The aim is a fundamental change, for it concerns the structure of the family and the most unyielding forces of the society.

In calling polygamy into question, Mariama Bâ criticised not only Senegalese society but all African societies in which women do not have the same opportunities as men to realise themselves and to contribute to the development of the continent. She shows the negative influence of tradition on society through the example of the story of the friend, Aissatou, to whom the letter is directed. Aissatou comes from a family of goldsmiths and her husband, Mawdo, is from the Fulbe people. This difference eventually leads to divorce because tradition forbids marriage ties between the *Géer* – nobles, warriors or farmer – and the Ñeeño – to whom the lower castes, goldsmiths, bards and leatherworkers, belong. Many Ñeeño also oppose such marriages. Because of the consciousness of origins, as pronounced as it ever was, and strong family ties, in Senegal, this strict separation has until today not been entirely overcome.

For Mariama Bâ it was not a matter of attacking tradition in general, but of the harmony between tradition and modernity, a theme that is still current today: "Rootedness and openness. Rootedness in the value of our own tradition, in what is good and beautiful in our cultures; and openness to other cultures, to universal culture." She pointed an especially critical finger at the short-comings of the so-called "modern society". For example, she rejected materialistic thought because from several points of view it resulted in deterioration of values. In her view, the adoption of the western lifestyle often leads to a society that promotes immoderate consumption and sets material acquisition above the goal of social equality. The family, the foundation of social order, is particularly affected by this: "But if the families crumble, then the children, who are the germ cells and the future of the country, will not enjoy a good upbringing. These children will not become well educated, knowledgeable people, who can guide the destiny of the country."

Mariama Bâ was equally critical of the conduct of women.

Bibliography:

Mariama Bâ; *Ein so langer Brief.* Frankfurt /Main 1996.

Der schalachrote Gesang. Frankfurt /M 1995.

Alioune Touré; *Succès littéraire de Mariama Bâ pour son livre; "Une si longue lettre"* Interview. In: *Amina,*Nov. 1979.

SOPHIA KAWAWA (Tanzania)

A LIFE FOR TANZANIA'S WOMEN

BY HELEN KIJO-BISIMBA

One afternoon in 1968 there was a public meeting near our elementary school. From childish curiosity we ran to the place, which was already crowded with people. Among all the men sitting at the table we noticed a young woman. This was unusual because women were rarely in jobs, and even more rarely, involved in political functions. Particularly astonishing was the fact that she held a baby in her arms! We heard a few old men say, "Why doesn't the woman stay home and look after her children? This is no place for women with babies." Others found it very courageous of the woman, whom one of the men introduced as Sophia Kawawa. She was one of the leading representatives of the Tanzanian women's union, *Umoja wa Wanawake Tanzania*.

"She has travelled all the way from Dar es Salaam to us in Usangi," declared the man at the microphone. That caused great amazement, but we also were aware of whispers of appreciation. This was mainly because of the effort of undertaking a trip of over six hundred kilometres, at least seven hours by car, that is, if it was not raining. So everyone waited expectantly for what this unusual woman would say to us. Her words made an abiding impression, especially on us young girls. Even the old men, who would have preferred to send her back home, paid her due respect and had a high opinion of her fluency and determination. "But that is a pugnacious young woman! And she isn't wrong about many things," I heard them say. "Where does she come from? Certainly from a powerful family," surmised others.

Sophia Kawawa grew up as the youngest child in a perfectly normal family. She was born in 1936, in the Rusuma region in the south west of today's Tanzania, at that time Tanganyika. Her parents were farmers and grew cashew nuts, beans, maize and vegetables. As a child, her father had fled with his mother to Tanganyika from the war in Malawi. Her mother brought ten children into the world, of whom only four survived, so that Sophia was confronted early with human suffering and developed a special sensitiveness for the difficult situation of women. It was thanks to her brother, a teacher, that she belonged to the few girls of her generation who were sent to school. When her father died her sister paid the school fees so that she did not have to stop school. After completing secondary school she met her future husband, and married in 1951. She lived in Dar es Salaam and became a housewife, for at that time careers for women were not available and they were controlled by their husbands. Sophia became a volunteer assistant at the Red Cross and worked together with other young women in a centre for people with leprosy. At this time she joined the Tanganyika African National Union (TANU), the Julius K. Nyerere party that was founded in 1953 and fought for independence from British rule. Her early activity in this party formed her political consciousness in quite distinctive ways, for during the early years the female party members played a special role.

As women were not employed and therefore did not have to fear sanctions, they formed the majority of the party. Men were of course enthusiastic listeners to Nyerere's speeches but they did not join the party because of fear for their jobs. They however sent their wives, who became members. If the men joined the party they were careful not to let that information be known at home. One of the women, Bibi Titi Mohamed, reported that she represented three hundred and fifty men. A further explanation for the high number of female party members is the sympathy they felt for TANU's radical claim for independence. As a result of their dominant numbers the women developed a strong self-confidence, and were able to make their influence felt later when the men acquired more posts.

After joining the party Sophia Kawawa took a leading part in the Tanzanian Women's Union, UWT, which was a wing of TANU. She quickly realized how few educated women were represented in the party and the union. Resolutely she recruited as many educated women and female academics as possible to join TANU and the UWT – among them, for example Lucy Lameck, one of the first women ministers in Tanzania. At the same time she encouraged young women to learn to read and write. First as district chair and later as national chair, she built contacts with European partners and used them for the further development of Tanzanian women. In this way she hoped to bring about changes in all areas of society that would in the long run improve the situation of women.

In her efforts for women Sophia Kawawa demonstrated great ingenuity. As the mother of eight children she knew from her own experience how difficult it was to combine job and children, and how limited the sphere of activity of mothers could be. She therefore introduced the idea that women should take their babies with them to the meetings and be allowed suitable breaks; she also arranged for baby sitters, paid for by the UWT. A big step in the direction of equal rights was her initiative in persuading lawyers of both sexes to advise women without means in legal matters and represent them in court. Previously, the court costs had hindered women who came from disadvantaged levels of society or were financially dependent on their men from obtaining justice. Sophia Kawawa belonged to the initiators of the "Centre for Legal Aid for Women", one of the first achievements in the struggle for women's rights in Tanzania. This was bound up with a developing public consciousness of the legal disadvantages of women.

In 1988 Sophia Kawawa opened a second front in the war against discrimination against Tanzanian women: the Islamic style of administration of justice, as it had been practised on Zanzibar for example, in the Kadi courts, for centuries. She promoted the abolition of polygamy and law of succession that disadvantaged women in that it granted them a significantly smaller portion of the inheritance. There was boundless indignation throughout the country. "Who does this woman think she is, to presume to correct the Koran!?" raged the Islamic scholars, who forbade the meddling of women in religious matters.

In 1990 she sprinkled salt in the wounds when she related polygamy to the spread of AIDS. She remained unimpressed by the disproportionately powerful wave of indignation. At the end of the 1990s, after a tough struggle, she succeeded in having the family law changed so that an unmarried woman who had been at least two years in an extra-marital relationship with a married man, and her children, had a right to support. In this way a check was put on the practice whereby men could evade their responsibilities in respect of a lover and her children. A further victory of the women's union under the leadership of Sophia Kawawa was the change of the labour law, removing discrimination against unmarried women, in that antenatal care was no longer limited to married women.

Sophia Kawawa's effort for the interests of women went so far that she initiated the alteration of a law that was based on the principle of equality. In 1974 the Tanzanian government decided that females as well as males after their school leaving certificate should spend a year of national service in the army and in social institutions and work for two years before they could begin university studies. As president of the women's union she objected that this decision seriously endangered the future chances for girls. A lapse of three years, she argued, would have the result that many girls would not study after their school certificate because during this time they would marry and have children. She recognised the danger from her own experience: despite their good marks they went to school only until they were reasonably mature and had their first child at seventeen. In fact, in 1977/78 the three-year duty was changed so that girls could go to university immediately after the national service. This was barely noticeable, but nevertheless, an important contribution to the advancement of women.

Sophia Kawawa's thinking and activity were determined by the desire to overcome the domination of men. Her daughter Khadija quoted her, "Education and job are your husbands!" She produced this sentence for us in 1972 when she was invited as guest of honour to our graduation ceremony at the Weruweru Gymnasium (High School). She thus made sure than not only both her sons, but also her six daughters completed an academic education and she was proud that all of them had made professional careers. The emancipation of the woman should however not be achieved at the cost of her roles as wife and mother. "She was always there for us, always loving, comforted us, and we confided in her as a friend," reported her daughter and added, "She also taught us our roles as wife and mother."

With this understanding Sophia Kawawa took up the struggle for the rights of women without ideological noise, long before the slogan "women's rights are human rights" was pronounced on the international stage,and long before the UN Convention on the Elimination of all Forms of Discrimination against Women of 1979. Remarkably – or therefore? – hardly any notice was taken of her. She is hardly mentioned in the relevant literature; in a Google search her name shows up in only a few, early and inconsequential articles. Even the posthumous renaming of Lindi Street in Dar es Salaam as Sophia Kawawa Street had almost no effect, as the new name was hardly used. When she died on 11th February 1994, at the age of fifty-eight, she had been recognised only once, for her contribution to the unification of Tanganyika and Zanzibar in the Republic of Tanzania. Only in 2011 was she honoured for her service in the struggle for independence and in 2012 for the founding of the women's union.

Tanzanian women of today have Sophia Kawawa's engagement to thank for a whole series of improvements. At a time when legal decisions discriminated against women and lack of education jeopardized their presence in public life she made herself the mouthpiece of women. By her struggle she demonstrated that changes are possible, if people stand up for them.

Bibliography:
Susan Geiger, *TANU Women. Gender and Culture in the Making of Tanzanian Nationalism, 1955-1965.* Portsmouth, N.H. 1997;
Nakaziel Tenga and Chris Maina Peter,The right to organise as mother of all rights: the experience of women in Tanzania. In: *Journal of Modern African Studies* 34 (1996) pp. 143-162.

DJÉRASSEM LE BÉMADJIEL (Chad)

THE DREAM OF WATER

BY OUAGA-BALLÉ DANAÏ

The Great Hall of the Ministry for New Technologies in N'Djamena is absolutely full. Numerous government and foreign representatives, men, women and children have come to see the winner of the Great Prize for Innovation. The excitement is palpable, and glances betray curiosity: "Who will get the prize?" The great room hums like a beehive. Among the laughter, loud voices and music from the loudspeakers the festive atmosphere can be read in the faces and the excitement! Success and failure are two sides of the same coin.

The moderator announced the government Minister. Two hours of waiting, two hours of suspense, two hours of patience, the usual thing. Now the ceremony can begin. The monotonous voices of officials that issue from the speakers' rostrum send me into a state of paralysis. In the whole room people are suffering from the oppressive April humidity; at the end of the long series of speeches deep sighs of relief are to be heard. "A speech is like the beauty of a woman," my father used to say, "...it causes injury to anyone who can't appreciate it". The moderator began with the runners-up. Every name is followed by a storm of applause -- then comes the fearful moment. An uneasy silence reigns when the name of the prize winner drops. This time the applause lasts an eternity, eyes seek out the lucky winner, in vain. Only when strong arms raise me high do I understand what has happened: my mother's prayers have been heard. She had said that for her it would be the greatest thing ever if I came home with the prize with the neighbours looking on in amazement – apart from my birth, of course.

The speaker described the "method for control of flow and generation of electrical current" that I had developed, "an autonomous method", for him a "revolution in the water economy". From now on one could pump between forty and a hundred cubic metres of water from a well without needing a source of energy. All one had to do was turn the tap. After he had made a speech in praise of me, decorated with superlatives, I had to receive the prize from the hands of the Minister. Eyes fixed on my red shoes, I walked past the glamorous hostesses drawn up in a line. I was so excited that I was quite blind to their beauty. Every step towards the rostrum brought me closer to my dream. When I held the prize in my hand I was so overcome that I could only utter barely audible thanks to my parents. The one thing that I was conscious of at this moment was a fat tear that bounced off my shoe and soaked into the ground.

The tear opened the gate to the past. In my dreams the earth is a monster. She nourishes people, but often denies them her gifts. This image is imprinted on my memories of my homeland, a country of hopelessness in spite of immeasurable riches. With the blessing of the gods, my homeland receives the tears of heaven twice a year. Beaten by the dry wind under a leaden sky, its broken crusts yearn in vain for the healing rain. Men, women and animals traverse great distances to silence their hunger and thirst. I remember the rare frenzy that gripped the village when heaven opened its sluice-gates. The people ran hither and thither to collect the precious moisture, while the marabouts in their white robes strutted through the lanes to make it clear that it was their prayers that had achieved this wonder.

They say, "He who possesses water rules the world." In my homeland they told a story of two brothers about this. The story always began, once there was a pair of twins. Their father bequeathed them so much land that one could not see the end of it, and a watering place that served them all. Both families lived together in harmony, until the day when the younger disregarded the blood ties and fenced in his land. No one can know what burns in the heart of a man, say the elders; and the hardest of hearing is he who will not listen. To reach the watering place, the family of the elder brother had to cross over his land. Unimpressed by the suffering of the people on the "other side", the younger brother insisted on a toll for crossing. Boundaries destroy relationships and divide people. Deeply offended, at first the others submitted, then they secretly opened a way through the fence. "It is our land and our life! In no way will we pay when we use what we have inherited from our mutual ancestors!" they fumed. Now their opponents put up impregnable fences. The "other side" stormed with anger. Finally, a bitter fight broke out between the two communities. Each side exceeded the other in stratagems to get control over access to the water. The earth was so sodden with blood that the blue water of the oasis turned yellow. Only the silence of force was to be heard. After any brief victory, the evening's laughter was followed by the morning's tears. The stronger the discord grew, the drier the area became. Exhausted from so many years of fraternal war, the elder twin went southward with his family in search of a new homeland but some of his sons did not follow the patriarch. Today they still plunder the land of their forebears and reclaim their inheritance.

Water is at the centre of my life and determines the rhythm of each day. My very first steps in the world were directed by the need for water. Very early in the morning, around four o'clock, my mother tied me on her back; we had a twenty kilometre long march ahead of us. Energetically, she set out on the stony path to the single oasis. The farther we came, the farther away the oasis of peace seemed to be. My mother sang. Her voice fought against the obstacles. Early in the morning we reached the oasis, proud that we were among the first. The water running over the stones and twittering of the birds relaxed our weary limbs. The inviting greenery allowed us, for the blink of an eye, to forget our fatigue. At the spring, life flourished. Everyone exchanged news, however unimportant, including my mother. The whole time she shifted impatiently from one foot to the other. Then finally she was in line. The long wait in the queue was followed by the laborious drawing of the container. My mother groaned under the burden of its weight, while as in a ballet her slim hands pulled constantly on the rope and wrested a small amount from within the spring. The glass-clear bubbles of water glittered like gold nuggets in the light of the first rays of the sun. At the end the thief of the blue gold had filled the life-dispensing leather bottle, which she carried home on her head, while I was rocked by the regular rhythm of her steps and the cheerful sound of her voice. The bottle was in a wretched condition. Water ran out, mixed with my mother's sweat and flowed over my face. It had a salty after-taste and helped me bear the scorching sun.

I never saw my mother tired, at least, I never heard her complain, even when we had to leave our village because my father was transferred to the capital. In the city my mother did not have to walk so far to fetch water; now it was one kilometre away. When I accompanied her for the first time, I was ten, and I saw how happy she was. Ever since that day I wondered why we had no running water; why my mother had to toil so much; why many people had to suffer so long from scarcity of water, while many parts of the city were well provided for.

They say dreams are children's lighthouse. They illuminate their daily life with the strength of their imagination of the future. In my fantasy I saw my mother simply turn on a water tap. I saw peasants who conveniently watered their fields and cattle herders who watered their animals without trouble. I carried this dream with me as a pregnant woman carries her unborn child. From High School to Engineering School it grew and gradually took a clearer form. After finishing my studies I spun further at the fabric of my dream. This morning's teardrop is the redemption of sleepless nights, self-denial and frustrations. The complaints of my wife Rokia and the scorn of the neighbours still resound in my ears. Now, the prize proclaims a new era!

Two months later, my father came home with the post, a letter from Geneva. With shaking hands I opened the envelope and hardly believed my eyes: "Dear Mr. Djérassem Le Bémadjiel, we are pleased to inform you that our Council of Experts has agreed to your request for participation. It is an honour for us to welcome you to the 39th International Exhibition of Inventions in Geneva in April 2012..." I fell on my parents' necks. Then I ran to my room to bring the good news to Rokia. The whole house was in uproar. Soon the neighbours came and asked the reason for all the jubilation. Throughout the entire afternoon Rokia and I scoured the letter with our eyes, as if we could have overlooked something. That night was the shortest of our lives, for we made plans and painted ourselves a glittering life prospect. Geneva became the city of our dreams!

The next day my father went out with me to the nearby corridors of administration. Next we went to the Ministry for New Technologies. The secretary looked us over from head to foot, as if two strange beings had wandered into her office.

"What do you want, sirs? This is not a pigeon loft."

"It is about my son..." stammered my father.

"Why, what about your son?"

"Ah..."

"You had better settle your family problems at home."

"No. He has won the competition for inventors."

"And so?"

The young woman's arrogance made my father lose his self-control. She was not even as old as his daughter, his second child.

"What do you mean "and so"? Isn't this the Ministry for New Technologies?" he shouted.

"If you want to see the Minister ... his meeting calendar is quite full. I will find out what can be done."

Very slowly she rose from her chair and went into a nearby room, apparently the Minister's anteroom. With a startled expression she came back out. "Sorry. The honourable Minister can receive you in one month at the earliest."

"Only in a month!" I cried. "The fair is in three weeks!"

"Then go to the office manager." Without waiting for our answer she turned and went back to her desk. The interview was over.

In the office manager's anteroom they told us that he was out of the building. We waited until the office closed, in vain. For a week we showed up at the Ministry every day and got the same answer from the secretary every time. The discouraging wait could not move my father, his stubbornness is contagious. In the second week a friend advised him to take care of the passport right away, so as not to waste valuable time. Our experiences at the passport office were shocking! The same arrogance and the same disdain. Without airline ticket and reservation, no passport! Then how can I get a visa?

From day to day my hope for the visit to the Geneva Fair dwindled. Bad news descended on me like locusts on a flourishing field. My whole family suffered under my anger with the authorities. My mother could not eat, my father did not sleep. Rokia was deeply disappointed. The trip to Geneva was turning into a nightmare.

"Only four more days," sighed Rokia.

"Don't be sad. There will be other opportunities," I consoled her resignedly, but she just stared gloomily in front of her.

"Ladies and gentlemen, in a few moments we arrive in Geneva."

The friendly voice of the stewardess roused me from my half-consciousness. While the plane prepared to land, I let the events of the past three days pass in review before me.

I was sitting on a bench in the inner court of our house and brooding over the frustrating experiences with the authorities, when suddenly my friend Carlos appeared. For him to visit at such an early hour was unusual. "How far have you got with your papers?" he asked. "I'm making a documentary film about you that will be broadcast today on the evening news. My chief agrees. What do you say to that?"

He signalled to his people and gave instructions for the filming and interviews with the family and the neighbours. One hour later everything was ready, and we made an appointment for 17:30 o'clock. I was flattered by Carlos' idea, but I was sceptical. Who would be interested in my history with the authorities? What difference would it make if it was reported that I could not travel to Geneva? My fears were confirmed. The film came at the end of the news broadcast, the whole thing lasted for barely one minute, my conversation with Carlos took exactly half a minute.

When I was about to go the announcer asked me to wait. Live on camera he explained that the government had just informed an important personality that the administration would support young people and my odyssey would have a happy ending in the coming hours and, and, and... My feeling as I left the broadcaster was sublime.

The next day I was overwhelmed by the events. An official car with a friendly chauffeur, a diplomatic passport within an hour, a flight ticket with urgent reservation, a breathless rush to take leave of friends and relatives, the elegant VIP lounge in the airport, the press, at twenty hours the flight to Paris and then on to Geneva.

"Welcome to the 39th International Exhibition of Inventions. We expected you two days ago. You have won the prize of the Ministry for Industry and Innovation of Nizny-Novgorod and the RegionMetTrans GmbH for innovative technology. We missed you yesterday at the prize giving. But we hope that you will enjoy your stay and can interact with your colleagues."

The voice of the Fair official sounded as though from another world. I felt offended by the stupid smirk of the Secretary of State for New Technologies who had accompanied me to Geneva. Behind the window panes a light rain drew a veil over the city, and on the opposite side of the bay the lights dancing on the water seemed like a promise. "If only this water could purify the hearts of men!" I thought.

YOUSSOUF OURO GUÉZÉRÉ TCHATCHÉDRÉ   (Togo)

FOR OUR CHILDREN

BY SAMI TCHAK

It is not always easy to present to outsiders portraits of heroes who are rooted in the collective consciousness of the people and whose everlasting light is connected in large part, to a tragedy. Often such heroes are carried off by death in the middle of their struggle or at the very height of the dreams and expectations that inspired them, which strengthens the messianic power of their words, even if these are far beyond the powers of imagination by which the nations and their leaders are guided. Che Guevara, Patrice Lumumba and Thomas Sankara are prominent examples of such sanctified heroes, whose struggle cannot fail to move anyone who takes an interest in them. Who could say that they would not have shown the other face of a political leader if they had been in power longer? --- that face of the dictator, who is so persuaded of his ideas that he carries them through at the cost of the individual's rights to freedom and human life --- Robert Mugabe in Zimbabwe and Sékou Touré in Guinea are shining examples. They would have been glorious figures if, after the independence of Zimbabwe and Sékou

125

Touré's majestic "No" to de Gaulle, they had been murdered. Yes, it is often death that makes people into heroes because they can no longer turn into the opposite of what they have been admired for. On the other hand, there is also the example of a hero who has remained true to his vision to the end of his life: Nelson Mandela. A great man, who has not exhausted himself in the exercise of power; who retained so to speak, his wonderful humanity through twenty-seven years of imprisonment and probably from this experience was able to acquire the understanding for an exemplary life.

However, among us, lost in ordinary every-day life, there are also people who, away from the media uproar and in complete anonymity, deserve to be recognised as heroes, not because they were unusual, but because they grasped that as ordinary men or women, they could do something that directly or indirectly would benefit others who were even less privileged than themselves. It is not necessarily a matter of self-sacrifice. They were not concerned to carry the cross for the damned. No, they are people who, without renouncing comforts, refused to sink themselves in the egoism of professional, social, and economic success. They used their relatively privileged positions to raise up others. Their achievement is to be measured less by quantity than by the exemplary character of their activities, by their determination despite all hindrances. One could call them every-day heroes and humanity is more indebted to these heroes than to the international stars. Humanity lives because of the every-day heroes who exist in every society and whom one will never see with a decoration on their chest or around their neck. It is not unimportant to show what they are like. That is what I want to do in the following portrait.

Youssouf Ouro Guézéré Tchatchédré was born on 13th June, 1965 in a very small village called Kamonda in central Togo. I know the village very well because I had also entered the world there five years earlier. Youssouf is among the people I have watched grow up and who regarded me as an older brother and adviser. I took notice of him very early because from the beginning he gave evidence of being a gifted youth, whom his teacher displayed as a model pupil. Later, when I became a teacher myself --I taught philosophy to the pre-baccalaureate class – he came to my notice again, although I had not lost sight of him and we always remained in contact, often seeing each other in our village. He had remained the same: diligent, reliable, intelligent.

Nevertheless, in view of the dim prospects on the job market in Togo I worried about him. I was afraid that even with a good university degree he would share the fate of young people in Africa who are sacrificed on the altar of so-called economic sense in order to fulfil the injunctions of the International Monetary Fund and the World Bank.

Having begun school in 1972, Youssouf completed his certificate in 1986, while I was leaving Togo for France. He studied Geography and Sociology at the university in Lomé, the capital of Togo. After a Master's in Geography and a licentiate (first state examination) in Sociology he went back to his home village in 1991 to look after his sick father. The fatherhad three wives and many children, but Youssouf was the only one with an academic education, and so the main support of the whole family. He was conscious of this responsibility very early.

At this time Togo was convulsed by an economic and political crisis. The wretched transition to democracy, which happened only on paper, had led to bloody disturbances and a general strike that lasted for a year. So Youssouf remained in his village and devoted himself to farming, as he had done in his school days. He made ends meet through agriculture and rearing poultry but he was always determined to apply his academic skills to concrete projects, to utilise his knowledge of geography and sociology, to get beyond the situation of simple subsistence and do something that would also benefit the village community.

With a friend who had studied management he therefore founded the Office for Organisation and Business Management, to help the illiterate to make their livelihoods more secure and develop savings. They did not let themselves be diverted from their undertaking by lack of support and solvent customers. The experiences during these difficult years would prove useful. Soon the children's aid organisation *Plan Togo* took notice of him. He worked in this organisation on a limited contract as adviser and trainer. With the death of his father his family responsibility increased. After four years he rose to co-ordinator for the whole district. In the year 2002 he received the distinction of "Best Collaborator" of *Plan Togo* with a prize of two hundred thousand CFA francs (three hundred euros). With further support he enjoyed travels abroad, which took him to five West African and three West European countries.

The village boy had made it. Now he was one of the privileged, about whom before this he had only heard. He was no longer affected by the economic ups and downs of Togo because he had the status of international leaders, who are paid from other sources. Yet in his privileged situation he did not forget what he had always dreamed of, finding ways and means to make himself useful to society. In 2005 he made a private trip to London to persuade a big recycling firm to be partner in a project called "Empty Ink Cartridges". Since no large organisation was behind it the project did not come off. During this trip he made contacts with the organisations *London Play* and *Right to Play* and on his return found the aid agency *Africa Play*, that wanted to strengthen the rights of children to play and free time so that they can develop into socially responsible personalities. In 2012 he gave a lecture on "Play and free time in developing countries, the example of Togo" at the 17th meeting of the International Union for the Promotion of Play in Hong Kong. On the occasion of this meeting he succeeded in getting support to the amount of six thousand euros. This money made it possible not only to provide play equipment but also to finance the training of school mistresses at home and excursions in which a hundred and fifty children took part.

A highlight of this project is *Kédiya*, a "program to promote reading and knowledge against poverty." Kédiya is the name of a special tree with many aerial roots that can reach an advanced age and serves as palaver tree in the villages of the region. With this programme Youssouf came closer to his dream of standing against the dictatorship of material need and saw his reward in the smile of a disadvantaged child who did not dare to cherish a dream.

Despite the difficulties in a country like Togo he succeeded in realising several projects devoted to the improvement of the situation of children. To the most important belonged not only the building of septic tanks and bridges in small villages, but also sponsorship of western organisations that made it possible for children to attend school. In addition to this, there was the struggle against migration into the towns resulting in forced prostitution, as well as the financing of clinics that offered the villagers an education and jobs.

In a country that belongs to the poorest in the world, such an effort is essential. In little Togo, he belongs to those people who understand that real success resides in making a future possible for others, and thus in working for a better future for the society. With each project Youssouf Ouro Guézéré Tchatchédré fulfills his dream and shows that one can help others to their dreams.

PATRICK AWUAH

(Ghana)

IN DEFENSE OF A NEW ETHICS

BY MAMLE KABU

At an open air seminar held within the grounds of the new campus of Ashesi University on the hills of Berekusu, a guest professor from the University of Ghana was speaking. The participants in the seminar listened intently, and then one raised a hand and asked a question. The professor gave him an answer but the questioner was not completely satisfied and he expressed his own views, perhaps a little more bluntly than the renowned professor was used to. After all, we were at Ashesi, Ghana's private university that is proud of its freedom of thought. Be that as it may, the elderly professor considered it his right to put the young man in his place. This was still Ghana! How shocked he must have been when another listener raised his hand and angrily interjected, "Excuse me sir, but that is our President."

To take Patrick Awuah for a student on his own campus is a mistake that anyone could all too easily make. The reason for this is not only his youthful air and appearance, but also that he waives displaying any of the usual external signs of his leading position. In spite of it, he puts himself on the same level as others and leads by good example. Anyone who is surprised that he is the President of the best known private university in Ghana will certainly be astonished at the great responsibility he has taken upon himself, namely the firm conviction that his generation has a responsibility in respect of Africa and future generations and must set the direction for the economic development of the continent.

Patrick Awuah gave up a lucrative job as programme manager at Microsoft in the United States, came back to his homeland and founded a university, not just any university. His university has the goal of nurturing a new generation of leadership that will further Ghana's development. He was influenced in this by the example of Asiatic countries, which changed from developing countries to industrialised states within a generation.

Patrick Awuah was born in Takoradi in the Western Region of Ghana and lived in Ghana until he was twenty. His father was an engineer and he too studied mechanical engineering. Originally Patrick wanted to be a pilot or an astronaut but pilots cannot wear spectacles and astronauts must, or so it seemed to him, be American or Russian. Thus it came about that he worked for Microsoft for eight years. During this time his son was born, which led him to think about what meaning Africa would have for his children and his children's children. If he should go back home with his family, in what kind of Africa would they have a future? He therefore decided that he would live in his homeland.

Originally his idea was to produce software in Ghana, by means of his own competence in software and with additional investors, which could also be exported. However, he soon realised that he had to start lower down, at the base, indeed with education. The education system should promote more skill and talent, such as would build leaders who could put Ghana and Africa on course for development. He decided to play his part in the building of such an education system. He also had in mind the problems so noticeable in infrastructure, health, education and other areas. Why was there so often no electricity? Why weren't the media doing their job? Why was there so much that didn't work? Why was so much invested in the training of doctors in Ghana, but so little in paying them adequately after their studies so that they went abroad? Who was responsible, and who made such decisions?

The answers all led to the governing elite. "Every time I arrived at the same answer," he said. "It all turns on the governing elite; on the people who bear the responsibility. If you want to be thorough you must ask further, why the governing elite behaves in this way. Why are so many of them corrupt? Why are they so concerned with their own advancement and why do they care so little for the society? My answer is, it lies in the education system."

Patrick Awuah saw here three basic problems. First, the educational institutions in Ghana instilled knowledge more through stubborn rote learning than through analytic investigation. Secondly, the spectrum of subjects was too limited. The students studied only a single subject, while in foreign universities an abundance of subject areas was taught. Patrick Awuah himself studied, besides mechanical engineering, art history, political economy and literature at Swarthmore College in the United States. As to why this variety is important, he gave the following example. "If you are managing a hospital, knowledge of business management is useful. You are then in a position to set up a cost-benefit analysis that tells you how much you spend in a year for doctors' wages and how much you spend on cleaning the building. In our country there are hospitals that spend so little on cleaning that the lack of hygiene negates the doctor's work and demoralises the doctors and nursing staff. If only a small increase were invested in hygiene we would achieve much better success in healing. That is a simple example of how important it is that doctors, who at some time or other run our hospitals, learn about something more than just human biology."

The third problem for him is that educational establishments in Ghana are purely academic: "Universities have abandoned the idea that they should teach ethics or build character. Their ethical principle is, don't get caught. To be sure, there are cultural institutions: family, education systems and religion. I use the term "culture" with necessary caution because institutional and also national cultures intersect and correlate with each other. The named institutions must take this task seriously and concern themselves with the question of what kind of society we want and how we can educate the people who can make this kind of society a reality. As a pedagogue I must take both to heart, intellect and personality.

Ashesi was thus created on the pattern of universities like Swarthmore College, devoted to the concept of General Studies, which attributes great significance to ethics and personal development. Training includes civic participation and sensitisation to problems of the environment. Many such colleges possess a code of honour. The basic principle is that one does not cheat, which means that examinations can just as well be written at home. The principle is that if the students have internalised the idea that they themselves are the ones who most profit by it, and their social environment shares this attitude.

Patrick Awuah is convinced that in the long run the linking of science and ethics has a direct influence on leadership and government. It disturbs him that this approach is not recognised by Ghanaian universities. "Of course, ethics is not established through simple rote learning of course content, and for that very reason, moral questions like plagiarism or sexual harassment are not adequately dealt with. The consequences of such a narrow education are revealed in the style of leadership of the "products of education", and so the vicious circle continues. Only five per cent of the population of this country goes to a secondary school. Eventually they hold important offices and many then make highly immoral decisions. It is simply a scandal that the elite behaves in this way. I want to change this, to act as a catalyst. Ashesi will prove that Ghana's universities can train more competent and more ethical leaders. I hope that other universities will follow our example".

In one audacious step, Ashesi introduced a code of honour for examinations. There is no supervision by the faculty. Instead, the students themselves oversee each other. At the end of the examination everyone signs a declaration that he or she has neither cheated nor observed cheating by others. Cases of irregular behaviour are investigated by the faculty and the deans and judged by a committee of students, professors and representatives of the administration.

From time to time, graduates of the university are invited to colloquia about ethics in professional life. Referring to real life examples, they discuss how one practises one's profession, maintains integrity and still achieves one's goals.

In addition to its honour code, Ashesi's liberal arts (and sciences) approach is also catching on. Under this system, students apply to the university, not to a department. . At the beginning of their studies they are obliged to engage with a broad spectrum of themes. During the first year they all follow the same course of study. This includes a seminar on leadership, writing skills and analytical thinking, sociological and political theory, economics, mathematics, finance and programming. Then, elective subjects are offered and the students decide on one of these as their major. The involvement with a variety of subject areas qualifies them for a broad range of professional careers, for they can apply their knowledge anywhere. "The job market reacts very positively", says

Patrick Awuah. "Whoever employs Ashesi graduates employs people who can deal with complexity. Enterprises that engage our graduates confirm that indeed they find solutions to difficult and complex problems and develop innovative approaches".

In my interview I asked him how he deals with the fact that most of his students are coming from a rote-learning background. "Shock therapy," is his answer. During the orientation week the students must design something independently. "From the first week, we make it clear to them that this place is different. Here we engage your mind and encourage you to engage the minds of others to come up with solutions to problems".

This "shock therapy" is also offered to school pupils. During one summer vacation sixty pupils from secondary schools throughout the whole country came to Ashesi for a week. In teams of four they worked out the construction and basic programming of robots using custom-made Lego kits. Ashesi students stood by as tutors. Each team built a robot and used it to accomplish simple tasks. "The pupils' self-confidence grew enormously during this one week. There was no single correct solution, but rather, a series of correct solutions. Each robot behaved a little differently from the others. It was good that the pupils could have this experience. Imagine being challenged this way for four years! That is our approach."

To the question about how his innovations at Ashesi could evolve into a lasting effect at the national level, he named as an example, a relatively new, very successful system called Mobile Money, whereby money can be transferred by mobile telephone. Ashesi students were involved in its development and since then, they have been working on comparable technological innovations. A social impetus of this kind should happen more often as more students register at Ashesi. Currently, there are six hundred, and it is planned to raise the number of students to two thousand, which means five hundred graduates per year. Most of them are goal oriented. Patrick Awuah believes that they will make a great difference to Ghana.

There are two possibilities for expansion. "Other universities can adopt our model, or further educational institutions can be established on our model. In addition, many people in the world go through on-line education and we will examine how we could employ it effectively".

Another question of concern to Patrick Awuah is that of purpose. "Why have I decided to move things forward in Africa? Probably it has to do with my studies at Swarthmore." The Mobile Money project mentioned above presents a further example of how an ethics-inclusive, liberal arts education promotes integrated thinking, an indispensable prerequisite for good governance. One of the participating Ashesi students was stimulated to consider what use the sixty per cent of the Ghanaian population that have no bank account could make of it. "Such questions result from encouraging our students to understand themselves as part of a greater whole. In our leadership seminars we discuss what makes a great leader. What rules and laws should there be in an ideal organisation? How must the economy be structured so that everyone is treated fairly? If we do not lead people to pose such questions in the course of their education, why should they pose them when they are in leadership positions?"

Concerning challenges and disappointments, there are always a few students at Ashesi who will not accept the ethical concept and eventually leave the university. Patrick Awuah acquired considerable support from various donors, but some have meanwhile stopped their donations because they want to see faster results. He would like more support for his long-term approach.

The experience with the robotics seminar led to the consideration of how the lower educational levels could be integrated on a long term basis. "There we are still at the beginning. We need contacts in the upper levels of administration who will give us access to the schools. For a single individual like me it is very difficult to manage that. I sometimes wish I could advise policymakers more. People listen to me here and there, but I feel they could listen more. And also I don't have much time to do it. That is another big challenge, the enormous pressure on my time".

One wishes that a man like Patrick Awuah had more than just one lifetime for his work. The unusual energy with which he pursues his goals suggests that something more than just his studies at Swarthmore have made him into the man he is.

He ransacks his memory. "I experienced something when I was a child, at the beginning of the 1980s when chaos ruled in Ghana. Every day I went to vacation classes. It was a long way. At five in the morning I got up. After six, on foot and by bicycle-taxi I finally got to school. On the way I always had to cross the Kwame Nkrumah Circle, where a seriously disabled person was sitting. In front of him stood a metal box for alms. I regularly gave him money, and one day, shortly before Christmas I

actually spoke to him. I put my coins in his box and said *Afenhyia pa!*
"Merry Christmas!" In tears he wished me a very merry Christmas. Then
I realised that his greatest wish was to be recognised as a human being,
and to be valued as somebody with whom one could speak. I had thought
that I had it hard, but this experience set me straight. Perhaps that was
it. People who are privileged should be thankful for it and not act as
though poor people are less human, and as though it were enough to
merely give them alms."

Patrick Awuah is always self-assured and governed by cool logic, but
there is also something else – passion. Emotion, as when he recollected
his memory from thirty years ago. "People must maintain their dignity,"
he said softly. "That is more important than everything else".

JOHN BALOYI (South Africa)

AGAINST THE POWER OF THE ART TRADE

BY VONANI BILA

In Limpopo Province in the far north west of South Africa, in the tiny village of Mashamba, you will find the art gallery of the sculptor John Baloyi. For many people of the surrounding region John Baloyi was a role model, somebody who grew up in difficult circumstances like themselves but realised his dream to live as an artist and bring art to the world of the under-privileged in rural districts far from the big cities. In his view, art was more than just an object of speculation for a clever art dealer. "Art and culture should not be a matter for the rich," he said emphatically. "They are the bearers of our historical consciousness, our identity". Coming from his mouth, such pronouncements had special weight because of his career.

Born in 1964, John Baloyi had to leave school at fifteen and earn money as a mine worker in Johannesburg. Under the brutal apartheid regime he shared this situation with innumerable youths who had the "wrong" skin colour. By the age of nine he had to help his father make mats, baskets, stools, walking sticks and coffins. Like so many youths without prospects, Baloyi later sold *dagga*, marijuana, to make ends meet. In the difficult 1980s, when the monster of apartheid was struggling against social change, he met Jackson Hlungwani, a sculptor and founder of an independent church. Thanks to this encounter, Baloyi freed himself from the clutches of *dagga* and began to get involved with sculpture, which had had a special fascination for him since childhood.

In discovering his spirituality, he developed a consciousness that changed his understanding of art. The young man from a simple background no more saw works of art as just any objects that one can sell to Whites, but as components of a culture , as an expression of a way of life, of a living community in defiance of great oppression. Art occupied an ever greater place in the bleak life of the man with the infectious laugh. Against all reason he dreamed of a gallery of his own. He told nobody about this dream. Who in this world at the farthest margin of society would take him seriously? Here it was a matter of bare survival.

In 1990 his dream took on more definite contours, for the freeing of Nelson Mandela seemed to announce a new era. Now everything would get better. Now John Baloyi made the decision to start a gallery in his own house. As to the question of how he would do it, he said with a sly smile, but decisively, "Like the ants, in small steps and without thinking about time." Imperturbable, he set aside a small part of his modest income whenever the needs of the family allowed it. He could have earned more money if he had carried out all the orders for his sculptures. For that he would have needed much more wood. Against all economic reason however, he refused to cut down trees. "I don't destroy trees, but bring dead wood to life. Art that is produced on the back of nature is accursed work," he explained calmly. His artistic production was not aimed at the maximum possible market; he worked on several pieces for ten months without knowing whether he would find a buyer for them. Thus he originated monumental sculptures three metres high and two metres wide, such as Godzilla Enraged and House of Spiritual Exile.

Of particular importance for Baloyi is the social function of art. This is why he carves living creatures like kangaroos, dolphins and camels, that children in the surrounding villages never see. He also brings them in contact with world history, with artistic representations of historical personalities like Napoleon and Caesar. Together with his mentor, Hlungwani and other artists, he began a campaign to develop a new consciousness of the value of art. In view of the stream of tourists that flows into the neighbouring national park, the art activists sent out a clear message, "It is wrong to view the animals in Skurza (Kruger

National Park) without bothering to glance at the art of the area." Soon their studios became a tourist attraction in Limpopo.

Despite the increasing public interest, the building of the gallery made slow progress. To drive his project along, friends helped him to apply for state support. The application was denied. For the government that invested millions in prestige buildings, the idea of a gallery in the countryside excited as much notice as the sneeze of a louse. Baloyi did not let himself be discouraged by this indifference.

In 2015 John Baloyi sent out invitations to the opening of his gallery, the first in the area of the small towns Elim, Mbhokota and Mashamba. After ten years of hard work he had reached his goal. The guests discovered an unconventional building that in itself constituted a work of art. Through a maze of small spaces one passed along artistically painted walls that introduced a modern form of mural painting. Round windows from car tyres and coloured steps completed the impression that one was entering another world, the world of art. You would never imagine that the floor had been made of clay and cow dung. In the spaces stood works that stimulated the visitor to intense reflection: a drum with legs and tail, figures with titles like Vanquished Soldier, Saluting Spirit, Heavy Load and many more. The whole building radiated a passion for art and a message that the spectator could not ignore. One respected this small man all the more because this day visibly compensated for years of toil and self-denial. To crown it all, the writer Albie Sachs facilitated the purchase of the wood sculpture Godzilla Enraged, which ever since keeps watch over the Constitutional Court building in Braamfontein, Johannesburg. At Wits University, there is another work, Guardian Angel, with which Baloyi recognised the commitment of the scientist Peter Hunter to students from deprived backgrounds. Other works are to be found in Germany, Holland, Belgium, Botswana, Japan, Australia, Korea, Italy and England.

With his gallery Baloyi put a completely unnoticed region on the cultural map of South Africa, for now this no-man's-land was a destination for art lovers and tourists. But this was just a first step; just as he exhibited works of colleagues and initiated co-operation with the artists in the region, he also saw the gallery as a beginning of deliverance from the power of unscrupulous art dealers, who buy art works at derisory prices and sell them to rich customers. For this reason he not only offered the artists a home where they could break through dependence on this art market, he set about modernising this home; he bought a generator that facilitated the work of his colleagues and himself and planned a bore hole for water, because up to today the inhabitants of Mashamba share the water of the Ritavi river with the animals. He could not realise this intention. In May 2006 Baloyi died in a traffic accident, aged just forty-two.

John Baloyi dreamed of a time in which the life of a black middle class would offer better conditions for artistic activity. If his dream has not come nearer – for still today the income of a white South African is on average six times higher than that of a black, at least the artist made an important gesture against the power structure. The gap left by his death is shown by the dramatic deterioration of his gallery, whose roof has partially collapsed. In Mashamba he is missed not only as a sociable man who was always fun to have around, but also as an energetic visionary. The South African art scene lost an exemplary figure, one who on his own pushed against the neglect of rural artists and of the greater part of the population.

JIMMY B (Sierra Leone)

MUSIC FOR PEACE

BY BRIAN JAMES

From the roof of his beach house he gazed at the water. He leaned back in his chair, contemplated the sun, which was going down over the restless sea, and surrendered to a serene calm. Below on the street, cars went to and fro. If anybody were to stop and cast an eye at the solitary figure they would immediately recognise him, even with the baseball cap pulled far down over his face. Whoever saw him would slowly realise that a flesh and blood celebrity was there before him, would stare at him furtively or openly whisper his name "Jimmy B" or "Godfather". Some might speak to him and thank him for his services to local music. Others might tell him how much they liked his last film. Still others might perhaps talk about the guerrilla warfare between two of the biggest hip-hop stars of the country, the frequently violent conflicts between their respective fandoms and would want to know what he was doing about it. After all, James Bangura is the "Godfather". If anyone can be expected to have the situation in hand, he is the one.

But the cars go by too fast for anyone to recognise him, and he prefers it like that. He has retreated here to find peace.

Down below on the beach a boy of perhaps eleven years old offers to carry the bags of a white woman in a light summer dress. He gazes at the boy's face. His roguish smile and precocious behaviour are strangely familiar. The longer he looks, the more the boy's features are transformed into his own. Instead of the woman he sees another woman, a white tourist, and the passing vehicles are not Toyota 4Runners but older, slower VW beetles and Rovers. The boy he is looking at is a younger James, thin and quite small for his age. He is not wearing shoes. Yet he can persuade the tourist that he is exactly the right man for this task. The bags are heavy but he covers this up with cheerful grins. Hopefully it will get him a couple of pennies; he hasn't eaten for a long time.

His home is the steps at the front entrance to a shop that is closed at night. Since the death of his father he gets by on his own. In the pitiless streets of Freetown it is an everyday matter that an orphan perishes, is overcome with misery, that his soul is shattered and turns a small boy into an embittered, apathetic man who wants to take revenge on the whole world. Somehow the child James survived.

The image of the past grows hazy. The shop, the steps and the dark streets fade away. A room forces its way into his memory - in Los Angeles, 1988. The baseball cap pulled down over his face, James drums his fingers on the sides of his plastic chair. The feeling that something is about to happen makes him uneasy but he makes no comment. All the young men in the room feel as he does. Some he recognises, others have just arrived, but the same hope can be read on all faces and the same fear of rejection. In many respects Los Angeles is just as hard and unyielding as the streets of Freetown. To get a foothold in the film industry is as difficult as everybody says it is, only more so.

The door opens. James can hardly hide how nervous he is when a large, gangling man in a jeans jacket comes in. He is one of the casting agents of the Cemex Agency. Extras are wanted for a film whose production costs are in the millions. The title of the film is *Coming to America*. With players like the elegant young comedian Eddie Murphy, Arsenio Hall and other top-class talents, its success seems guaranteed. Like all the young men in the room James hopes for a chance to work on it – and earn a couple of dollars. He figures the chances are good. The story of the film began in Africa and unlike the others, he in fact comes from this continent, as his strong accent bears witness. The man in the jeans jacket selects a couple of boys, including James. That is still no guarantee but it is possible that he will actually be seen in the film.

A couple of days later he was about to get himself a sandwich at the set canteen when John Landis walked by, the man who led the production of Michael Jackson's music video "Thriller" and was now the producer of this film. James had never been so close to John Landis and he made up his mind to speak to him. Of course he knew that a mere extra should not speak to the producer. Of course he knew that such an enormity could cost him the job but he wanted to seize the opportunity, just like the barefoot little boy on the beach, and he had no intention of letting it go to waste.

"Mr. John Landis," he called out. The much taller John Landis stood still and looked down at him.

"Mr. John Landis, my name is Jimmy Bangura. I come from Sierra Leone in West Africa. I would like a role in your film, a role in which I am seen, no matter how small it is. I want my friends at home to see, then I can be proud."

Landis looked at him in amusement. It definitely was not every day that a young, over-excited African with a strong accent asked to play a part in his film.

"What was your name again?" he asked.

"Jimmy Bangura, sir."

"We'll see," he replied, and went on.

Just as expected, the world premiere of *Coming to America* was a smash hit. Only a few noticed a palace guard in a khaki uniform who opened the door for the prince acted by Eddie Murphy and closed it behind him. James is in the picture for exactly three seconds but he had to smile when he sat in the cinema and saw himself on the screen. He was aware that it was just the beginning of much bigger things.

Since the beginning of the 1990s, war had prevailed in Sierra Leone. The rebels, who accused the regime of greed and corruption, struggled, so they said, so that Sierra Leoneans could have better lives, yet in the capital Freetown more and more horrors were heard of from the war areas.

In this atmosphere of political unrest and uncertainty James returned home. He was no more the same James who had left Sierra Leone many years before. In the meantime he had been named Jimmy B. A sparkling ear stud glittered in his right ear and the baseball cap so typical of him was pulled down over his face. He had become a star. As he alighted from the plane he declared that in the more than twenty years "Mama Salone", as Sierra Leone was called by its inhabitants, had not changed nearly as much as he himself had. The airport was in just as desolate a condition, the airport employees in their shabby uniforms dawdled around and beggars crowded around the arrival gate with outstretched hands. The feeling that he had achieved something yielded to sadness.

In the years before that, Jimmy had made a career in the music industry. He discovered his musical talent and produced records for established musicians in the United States. Subsequently, he began a career of his own as a solo rapper. With his combination of fast hip-hop rhythms and African percussion he delighted a large community of fans. Soon he became Jimmy B the Superstar, and received international awards but with all his fame he never forgot his roots, and returning home always remained his goal.

In a country like Sierra Leone, in popular opinion everything that originates from the place is of inferior quality, and this attitude also holds for music. Next to war news reports, Whitney Houston, Tupac Shakur, Michael Bolton and other American artistes ruled the air waves. They were heard at parties. Their music resounded in the night clubs. When "Jika Jika" by Jimmy B, a local rapper, was issued there, reactions were muted. Yet Jimmy had not just come back to thrill people with his music, he brought mixers, loudspeakers, microphones and a complete state of the art recording set-up, all bought by himself. He had assigned himself the task of fundamentally changing the music scene.

A huge jet black vehicle with four-wheel drive and tinted windows rolls into Williams Street. Like in other districts of Freetown the houses are squalid and the streets littered with potholes. A naked child looks on unconcerned when the car stops in front of an unremarkable two storey building. Jimmy climbs out and contemplates the house. He pays attention to neither the dirty windows nor the cracked walls. What he sees is the building that will house Paradise Studios; his idea, his spiritual "child".

After he had renovated the building and set up the recording studio, Jimmy went talent hunting. He is optimistic; he knows that he only has to look: the talents are there, buried under the dirt of poverty, non-existent opportunities and contempt. With a lot of effort Jimmy surveyed a host of hopeful people and selected fifty women and men. They came from schools, slums, clubs and universities and had just one thing in common: their youth and their rudimentary skills in music making. The Paradise

Family originated from them. Not all of them had what it takes to be a Superstar, but a few would soon be very well known in Sierra Leone and outside the country. In the months that followed Jimmy put all his equipment at their disposal, worked with them personally and trained them.

The Paradise Family quickly developed into a serious competitor for supremacy on the air waves. Hip-hop music with a pinch of local rhythms and rap in local jargon was something new and instantly became popular. The names Daddy Saj, K-man, Vida and Cool Don Kay became trademarks of Sierra Leonean music in the country and beyond its borders.

A dilapidated mini-bus or *poda poda* that served for public transport rattled along the Congo Cross highway. The young man on the back seat paid little attention to the sound of a Celine Dion classic that rang out from the vehicle's surprisingly powerful loudspeakers. The *poda poda* stopped in front of a group of girls in school uniforms. They climbed in laughing, and the minibus travelled on. One of the girls asked *Driver," you nor geh none Salone music?"* The young man listened. Surely this very age group is fixated on western romantic love songs; that is why at this time of day, right after the schools closed, the driver had played Celine Dion. The driver thought about it for only a moment, took the cassette out of the player and put in another one. In the car the lively rhythms of a rapper by name Daddy Saj were to be heard. His voice was not as trained as Celine Dion's, and he did not attempt complicated vibratos, but the girl liked his impressively performed song, which he ended with a greeting to the Godfather Jimmy B and the rest of the Paradise Family. The young man who observed the change in the local music scene with such amazement could not know it, but one day he would meet the "Godfather".

Ever more local artistes confidently took the microphone as the enthusiasm for "Salone music" took hold. The musical revolution happened practically over night, while the people were depressed by thoughts of another revolution, the civil war. The rebel army known as the RUF (Revolutionary United Front) no longer carried on a war just against the government forces but also against the men, women and children for whom they claimed to be fighting. News of unimaginably brutal violence committed by both the warring sides against the civilian population reached the most distant corners of the world.

Jimmy Bangura, dressed in an elegant navy blue suit, was taken to the offices of the President of the Republic of Sierra Leone, Alhaji Ahmad Tejan Kabbah. Like so many other Sierra Leoneans he knew of Jimmy's popularity and the impact of his music. He gave him an audience because Jimmy had submitted a proposal on how he could support the on-going peace process. Jimmy's idea involved something deemed impossible. Whether it would succeed was uncertain, but in any case it was worth a try.

Weeks later a United Nations helicopter clattered through the air. Accompanied by UN soldiers, Jimmy was flying to Makeni. Makeni, which is in the northern part of the country, was a rebel stronghold at the time. The rebels were informed who was coming. But Jimmy was not at all sure what awaited him.

The helicopter landed in the night. Jimmy climbed out and looked around. There was no electricity, the place was lit by flickering oil lamps and campfires. The two rebel soldiers who had been detailed for his reception greeted him rhapsodically. It was the first time that a prominent personality had appeared before them, and for a moment they seemed to forget that it was their custom to commit violence against every Sierra Leonean who didn't fight on their side. The two of them chatted casually, but Jimmy knew of the rebels' brutality and had seen the scale of their destructive rage. He forced himself to suppress the sick feeling in his stomach.

The rebel soldiers escorted Jimmy into the sparsely lit township and talked to him about his latest album. Other inhabitants of the town – many casually carried AK47 Kalaschnikovs over their shoulder – joined them to greet the star. Jimmy had flown in with a UN escort, but there was absolutely no question who was in command here. They smiled, shook his hand and slapped his shoulder, but their look spoke another language. The UN escort was very uncomfortable, for the tension was palpable, like a dark cloud that threatens to release a torrential downpour. A boy of about ten, dressed only in shorts and wearing several hand grenades on a shoe lace around his neck, came up to Jimmy. He sang a couple of lines from Jimmy's hit "Jika Jika", moving his arms like an American rapper. Jimmy thought of himself when he was the same age. His life had improved, but this child's life would most probably be extinguished by the war.

Jimmy was led to the house of the Commandant. When he entered he had to think of the family that had lived here before. What had become of them?

The Commandant greeted Jimmy like an old friend. "Jimmy B," he shouted and held out his arms. "Welcome to Makeni! You do your thing in Freetown fantastic. We always listen to your music."

He was a small man in a camouflage jacket and boots that were a couple of sizes too big for him. The effect was almost funny. But, only almost. Behind the exuberant greetings the soul of a hard man was plain to see. He was not a man with whom one spontaneously made friends. They discussed the reasons that had impelled Jimmy to come to them. The commandant pledged his support and that of his men too. In the long bloody history of the civil war this was unprecedented.

The plan was put into practice the following evening. At first glance it looked to be a concert like any other. Rap music with African sounding rhythms blared from the enormous loudspeakers on either side of the raised stage. The crowd broke into storms of applause when Jimmy B, with his baseball cap, in jeans and trainers grasped the microphone with his right hand, while his left arm moved in time with the music. His upbeat performance hid the fact that this time he was not bothered by stage fright, but by fear; fear of his indisputably unusual public. To be sure, they reacted euphorically to his entrance, but it took some getting used to that; this involved brandishing their weapons in the air.

In the course of the evening both UN representatives and rebels joined him on the stage, and the tense relations were temporarily forgotten. Everyone was carried away by the music. It was a party such as had not happened in this place for many years.

After the concert Jimmy stayed a few more days and spoke with the fighters. He wanted to know what their motivation was for making war against their sisters and brothers. Music and laughter had created trust, so that they opened up to him. According to them, mainly they merely carried out orders, they had no personal motivations. He found it sad when he heard that their life was empty, that all direction and all meaning had vanished. The longer he spoke with them, the more clearly Jimmy realised that these people, who had earned themselves a reputation as bloodthirsty murderers, were like lost children. They urgently needed parents who could show them the way.

In 2001, after the end of the war, citizens from all levels of society were selected for the most prestigious honour with which a Sierra Leonean can be recognised; with the order named for the largest river in the country, the Order of the Rokel. Jimmy was one of them. He was recognised for the benefits he had brought through the development of the national music sector.

As he sat at the beach and let all that pass in review through his memory, a worker from the nearby building site came over to him. His bare chest is covered with white cement dust.

"Yes sah," he said and assumed a respectful attitude. "Your visitor has arrived sir."

"Send him here," said Jimmy. A moment later a young man simply dressed in T-shirt and jeans appeared. They greeted each other like old friends.

"Are you ready?" asked the young man.

"Yes."

The young man is a script writer whom Jimmy has invited because he wants to talk to him about his idea for a film. He turned on a tape recorder and Jimmy described the current rivalry between two of the most fashionable hip-hop talents of Sierra Leone. Their feud has led to violent quarrels among their fans. In view of the mounting enmities that recalled the conflict in the 1990s between the US rappers Tupac and The Notorious B.I.G., Jimmy B was requested to play a part in the settlement of the dispute, since he is presumably the only person commanding respect who would be recognised by both superstars: the one personality that both would listen to. His proposal was to give both rappers leading roles in a locally produced film on the theme of freedom from violence. If anybody can get it right, he can.

The script writer has long been an admirer of Jimmy, ever since that time he experienced in a minibus how enthusiastically a group of chattering school girls listened to his music. Their paths actually had first crossed a couple of years earlier, at the time when Jimmy was planning a new career, this time in the world of the film maker.

In the course of the last year films produced in Nigeria and Ghana had driven American, Indian and Chinese films from the market in Sierra Leone. They were so popular that even Nigerian words, for example *igwe* (bicycle) or *okada* (motorcycle) were taken over into Sierra Leonean usage. However there were hardly any Sierra Leonean films.

Since his time as an extra in Hollywood Jimmy B had been a cinema fan, and so it was natural that he thought the time had come to get involved. First he produced *Aminata*, a film with low production costs about an underprivileged girl who successfully holds her own in the city, and subsequent to that, *Eagle Eyes*, a joint project with a Nigerian film company, to establish that it was possible to make a film in Sierra Leone. For her role in *Eagle Eyes* ten year old Celia Greenwood was the first Sierra Leonean to be nominated for an award at the African Movie Awards.

Encouraged by his success, more films followed; *Live and Let Live*, a story about the poverty of AIDS victims in Sierra Leone, the romantic dramas *The Forbidden, Only for Love, Paradise Island, For the Love of Money*, the action film *The Assassin* and the musical drama *Genesis*. The world paid attention to him. Some of his films were broadcast by Sky TV in London, by AITH in Nigeria, by DSTV's Africa Magic in South Africa and TV Africa in Ghana. But still more important, Sierra Leoneans paid attention to him.

The success of these films brought more Sierra Leonean filmmakers onto the scene. Nigerian film posters were gradually replaced by Sierra Leonean ones. On the streets the sellers promoted Sierra Leonean films and banished foreign films to the back rows.

The film revolution continued, and owing to the growing interest in Sierra Leone film, which we have one single man to thank for, the proportion of indigenous backers that invested in local productions increased, even though making films in Sierra Leone is still no simple matter.

Earlier, it was not usual for Sierra Leonean artists, whether musicians or filmmakers, to raise their voice and be heard, or to be perceived as symbol of the culture of their country. With Jimmy Bangura, however, nothing is usual. After all, he is the Godfather.

OLAUDAH EQUIANO (Nigeria/Great Britain)

THE FIRST BLACK ACTIVIST AGAINST THE SLAVE TRADE

BY KARFA SIRA DIALLO

On 25th March, 2012, I was invited by the city of Nantes to the dedication of a monument to the abolition of slavery. The monument, the first in Europe, referred to the fact that Nantes owed its prosperity to the slave trade. In the 18th century the city was the centre of the French slave trade; around 450,000 African men, women and children were shipped from its port to America. The monument was erected on the quay where once the slave ships lay. One goes through a passage, surrounded by the waters of the Loire, with historical quotations on its walls that bring home to the reader the centuries' long struggle against slavery and oppression. There I discovered a quotation that made me aware of Olaudah Equiano, who, himself a former slave, struggled for the prohibition of the slave trade.

It was absolutely inevitable that I should encounter Olaudah Equiano. During the first twenty-five years of my life, spent in Africa, I had certainly never heard of this African and his role in the struggle for freedom of the Blacks. However, since I was advocating for the commemoration of the slave trade in Bordeaux, which after Nantes was the second largest slave port in France, sooner or later I had to bump into this man, who had made an impression on the movement for the abolition of slavery. That movement in the 18th and 19th centuries, was of decisive importance in the struggle against the servitude of Blacks, for the assertion of the common humanity of Africans, and for the freedom and equality of all people.

Olaudah Equiano's life is truly remarkable. This unusual personality, who had been carried away from Africa and enslaved as a child, not only managed to adjust to a highly xenophobic British society that was in favour of slavery, but also became a major figure of the enlightenment. Olaudah Equiano was the first Black in modern times to speak out against slavery in a manner that became the best weapon in the fight of Africans against European oppression: through literature. His outcry was a milestone in the struggle for the abolition of slavery in Europe: a literary phenomenon, and a political one.

Thanks to an advance subscription by three hundred people, his book appeared in London in 1789, the year of the French Revolution, with the title :*The Life of Olaudah Equiano, or Gustavus Vassa, the African, Written by Himself*. The author, who had initially been carried off to the Antilles, was the first African to have published his autobiography. The story that portrays Olaudah's struggle for freedom alternates between travel journal and spiritual autobiography. Equiano above all not only pilloried the slave trade ("What is the slave trade but a war against the hearts of men?"), but also the living conditions of the slaves on the ships and on the plantations. He describes these from his own experiences and what he had seen and heard wherever he had been. His work is the first report that gives an insight into the life circumstances of Black slaves in Africa and America.

In the first three years after it appeared, the book was translated into Dutch, German and Russian. The English edition reached eight new editions in the author's life time, one of them in the USA. For at least five years Equiano criss-crossed the British Isles on reading tours, and so he gradually became one of the most influential spokesmen and a pioneer in the struggle for emancipation of the Blacks and their presence on the international stage.

Olaudah Equiano was born in 1745 in Iseke in what is today the Republic of Nigeria. He belonged to the Igbo ethnic group. At the age of eleven he was seized together with his sister, by African slave hunters;

soon afterwards the siblings were separated. For a hundred and seventy-two cowries he was sold to an artisan and within a few months was sold several times. Thus at first, he was a "house slave". He tells us of his first experience of suffering: "One day when our parents had gone to work as usual and my dear sister and I were looking after the house, two men and a woman jumped over the wall and ran us down. Before we could cry out or resist they gagged us and fled with us into the forest nearby. There they bound our hands and kept going farther, until it became dark... And I travelled further by land and waterways through different regions and countries until I reached the coast, some six or seven months after I was abducted."

Then he was loaded onto a slave ship for the "great crossing", probably at Bonny (Nigeria). The despair of the Blacks on board this ship was indescribable. Despite the nets that were supposed to prevent them jumping overboard, two men succeeded in killing themselves. The fright of the little Igbo boy was even greater when he saw how a white sailor of the English crew was beaten to death. He also thought of jumping to his death.

At Barbados the impression was no better. Old slaves came on board to assure them that they would not be eaten for "these Whites seem so primitive and behaved like wild beasts." They would be gripped by the fear of being eaten again during the long crossing to England, when the provisions were getting finished, as in the old song in which it is decided by lottery who would be eaten...

Olaudah had the good fortune to escape work on a plantation altogether, for he was mainly a slave of marine officers for whom he worked as a sailor, but he was a witness of the violence that the slaves had to suffer. During a stop in Virginia he was sold to the English marine lieutenant, Michael Henry Pascal for forty pounds, a good price for a twelve-year-old youth in the year 1757. The boy would discover England and snow, make friends with a white boy and become acquainted with "civilisation": "The realisation that the Whites did not sell those like themselves, as we do, pleased me very much," but a damper: they ate without washing their hands, which shocked the young man as did the discovery that "their women are much too thin". "Civilisation also meant the discovery of writing – of books that spoke – for women. Friends of his master sent him for a time to school and to church. He was baptised and received the name Gustavus Vassa – it was customary to name slaves for European monarchs. In the Seven Years War our hero found himself on an English ship in the Mediterranean. On the *Namur* he took part in a sea battle against the French and in the siege of the Breton island, Belle-Île, which was of strategic importance to the harbour entrance at Nantes.

He was sold again several times until he arrived at Montserrat in the English Antilles to a Quaker named Robert King, a merchant and ship owner. Olaudah became his trusted assistant and second in command. He worked for him on his ships that brought slaves ("living freight") to Philadelphia. Because of this, he was able to earn money of his own through small business transactions and buy his freedom for forty pounds. Back in London he worked for Dr. Irving, the pioneer in desalination of sea water. In 1773 he took part in the Phipps expedition to the arctic north of Spitzbergen, at 81 degrees north latitude. He was friendly with Thomas Hardy and became an active member of the London Corresponding Society founded by Hardy, an association of craftsmen and workers that advocated for parliamentary reform and universal suffrage. As an engaged opponent of slavery he was named as an authorised member of an English expedition that was to prepare for the settlement of freed slaves in Sierra Leone. Conflict with the other members of the expedition, whom Olaudah accused of corruption and who accused him of being biased in favour of the interests of the future settlers, led to his being dismissed, so that he remained in England and never saw Africa again. In 1791 he married Susannah Cullen, with whom he had two daughters. Olaudah Equiano died in 1797.

His heritage was acclaimed on many sides. His autobiography, which combines two popular genres of that time, travel journal and report on the life of a slave, is on the curriculum of universities in the United States as a witness to African-American literature. In Great Britain, where he is considered the first leading political figure from the African populations, Equiano was fully honoured on the occasion of the two hundredth anniversary of the abolition of the slave trade (slavery was later abolished in 1833). *The Interesting Narrative of the Life of Olaudah Equiano* is definitely an important document in the history of mentalities and a mirror of English society at the end of the 18ᵗʰ century. The modernity of the work lies perhaps in the fact that it speaks to us with the voice of a multi-culturally informed person in search of identity and authenticity.

It is always difficult to transplant oneself into the time period that gave rise to a work but Equiano brought ten thousand readers close to the tragic experience of slavery for the first time. In taking up a position in opposition to the established order and as a manifesto for the abolition of the slave trade, the *Interesting Narrative* also facilitated a new image of African people, counter to all the prejudices of the time and with the radical challenge to finally recognise equality among human beings. Equiano wrote as a spokesman for all Africans, who are still trapped in prejudice, degradation and discrimination.

In this way, the fortune of an individual took on a universal dimension and an exemplary character. Equiano knew that he shared his experiences with other Africans, who, just like him, had been taken from their homeland. With his book he did not address himself to them, (because the overwhelming majority of them could not read), but to the Europeans whom he sought to persuade that the slave trade must be abolished. He wrote to instruct, without any complaint or bitterness, and revealed truths that were unknown or little known to European readers. They should react with disgust at how cruelly the English slave owners – not all! – mistreated their African slaves, and they should recognise that people from Africa had a cultural identity and a history of their own, that they were closely bound to the customs of their peoples.

In a time in which the universality of human rights was being proclaimed, Equiano's literary and political work contributed by giving form to a reality that was little known on the European continent. The *Interesting Narrative* was the first text that made the humanity of Africans public and not least, it is a lesson on the tragic relations between Africa, Europe and America; the history of globalisation; the history of the will to live against the laws of death; the history of the inexplicable relations between peoples; the history of freedom, equality and the history of human rights.

Olaudah Equiano, the great African personality, one of the first to attain international fame and importance, also took up the struggle against slavery. That this struggle was eventually successful is also owed to him. Equiano thus initiated the long list of Africans who would influence the history of the world.

Bibliography
Olaudah Equiano, *The Interesting Narrative of the Life of Olaudah Equiano or Gustavus Vassa, the African, Written by Himself.* London 1789; Black Classics 1998.

LOUIS ANIABA (Ivory Coast)

A PIONEER IN THE CLUTCHES OF POWER

BY URBAIN N'DAKON

One early morning in May 1688, two months after it has left the Gold Coast, the *Saint-Louis* sails into the haven of La Rochelle, which is the most affluent city of the French kingdom, if not of the whole of Europe. Usually, a ship, which returns from Africa or America, raises high expectations and intense anticipation. The expectations are especially high in the case of the *Saint-Louis* because it is sailing on behalf of the royal trading company, Compagnie de Guinée (Guinea Company), which has just been founded, promising enormous profits, and it comes from Africa, from the Gold Coast! The land of gold, of noble wood and spices, beads and other treasures – not least slaves!

However, on this day, the talk is not about the load or the stories the seaman can tell about the adventurous journey and the hardships they had to cope with, but about one topic only: two young Africans are on board the *Saint Louis*! The people are very curious. "Where do they come from?" "What are they doing on board?" "Which language are they speaking?" Many of them offer to put them up.

Even so, the offer was not entirely unselfish. It is true that the French trade in West African slaves was just beginning. For the ladies at the royal court it was considered good taste to surround themselves with pageboys, who came from Africa. Therefore, the French seamen supplemented their income by meeting the demands of the rich families for "protecting" or "adopting" Africans, whose status proved to be ambiguous; not entirely slave, but also not entirely free.

Soon the word got around that both Africans would travel on to a rich patron in Paris. While the arrivals were overawed at the sight of the great crowd of people and the innumerable ships in the harbour, the rumour mill began to seethe. Some believe one can recognise a special noble kind of person in them due to their dignified bearing, their noble appearance and their grace.

Soon, first information from a trustworthy source is spread by Commander Compère, the captain of the *Saint-Louis* in person: The one who is more charming is called Aniaba, and he is the heir of a mighty king of the Gold Coast; the other one is called Banga, and he is also the son of a nobleman.

Aniaba himself cannot even say when exactly he was born. Because, unlike in Europe, for the Akan people, the birthday is the day of the week when one is born. Before the European system was adopted during the process of colonisation, everybody knew, on which day of the week he was born; and other births and formative events in the life of the community were used to determine the year of someone's birth. Thanks to historical findings, it is possible today to date Aniaba's birth around the year 1672. The young princes are therefore about sixteen years old.

Three days later, the Commander Compère arrived in Paris together with his protégés. After a long and tiring journey in a horse carriage, a restless night in a pension in Niort and several new impressions, the youngsters experience a cultural shock. Paris! An imposition for the African soul! The chaos on the streets, the deafening noise, the beggars, the loud insults of everybody against everybody! The young people believed that they had arrived in a nightmare, and that they had to fear for their lives.

Actually, the contrast with the world they were familiar with could not have been greater. Assinie, their home (today Ivory Coast) is located on the Atlantic Coast between the sea and a lagoon, and it is surrounded by coconut palms and mangrove forests. Their longing for the beloved fishing village overshadows the joy about the discovery of the foreign countries. The commander uses the long carriage ride to explain to them the reason why they have been chosen to travel to France – of course not without honouring his own role in the colonial undertaking. He explained to his fellow travellers that the French had actually been the first Europeans, who discovered the coast in the Gulf of Guinea, and they had undertaken first attempts to trade with the local inhabitants, and to teach them the gospel.

After that, they had unfortunately allowed the Dutch to overrun them but because the rulers along the coast had kept faith with the French, the Dutch had used furious violence against them. Thereupon, the French king had decided to help the Africans by building fortresses as trading posts along the entire Gold Coast from Komenda to Acara (Accra). He underlines that therefore, their mission is of great importance! This is because the King of Assinie, Nana Aniaba Zéna heard so many good things about King Louis XIV that he made Pater François of the Dominican Order come to his court in Assoko to submit a proposal, namely: As a gesture of goodwill, he intended to send two of his children to the king of the French to expand and consolidate the relationships between both countries. They were supposed to learn French, attend a commercial school, and work for the French after their return so that they could act as mediators between the two nations. Compère had received both princes from Commander Ducasse in Assinie with the request to take very good care of them and to accompany them on their journey to Paris. Aniaba and Banga listened anxiously to this verbiage, and they were sure that this man comes from a family of storytellers because, who else could talk about the good deeds of his king with so much enthusiasm and especially with so much perseverance?

In Paris, Monsieur Hyon was waiting for his protégés. He received the order from the Guinea Company to take care of the young people, and to educate them in every respect according to their position. Monsieur Hyon is a warm-hearted person. He knows Africa and is an expert in African beads. He owns a small shop with precious rarities from Africa in the Rue du Petit-Lion. Aniaba and Banga are lucky that he is taking care of them because he always seems to understand them - he is always friendly towards both of them and taking his task seriously. He is only worried about the question whether he can handle the religious education of the two young Africans because Catholicism was the state religion in France at the end of the 17th century. To educate somebody means to show him how to be a good Catholic, whatever that can mean. The king will only accept or even support the plan with the young African princes when their religious education is to his liking.

Both students reveal very fast why they have been chosen for the cultural exchange. They are learning so quickly that they skip parts of the catechism. Monsieur Hyon talks enthusiastically to a friend about them, "The youngsters are surprising me every day. The many smart questions they ask are a proof of their high intelligence. They will quickly pick up our culture." Aniaba contributes to the speed-up of the whole process with a spectacular experience. Six months after his arrival in Paris, he announces during a visit to *Notre-Dame* cathedral that he is having a religious revelation.

Claude Chastelain, a canon, reports in a letter to his friend Grandet about the "sudden emotion of the African visitor, who was accompanied by another, physically smaller African." The young man introduced himself as a Prince from the Gulf of Guinea, and he explained to the other visitors present in his own mixture of the French and Portuguese languages that a great light beam filled his spirit. Could this have not been the very special grace of God? The young man got really carried away and uttered the 'wish to be introduced to the religion of the Lord and to receive the sacrament of baptism as soon as possible'." Banga, his companion, expressed the same wish, although more moderately.

When Monsieur Hyon gets to know about this incident, he only shows mild surprise. He already had realised that both are especially blessed. Monsieur Hyon explains to the curious canon that his educational work has been made easier by the special characteristics of the young man. With this, they were living up to their noble origin.

"Their noble origin?" asks the canon, who is visibly impressed.

"Sure!" answers Monsieur Hyon complacently. "It is kind of a secret." he continues confidentially. "One of the young men is actually the son of a mighty king and will one day enter into the inheritance of his father. He will govern a rich country, a beautiful archipegalo at the other end of the world, where the trade in gold dust, spices and dark beads flourishes. His companion is the son of an aristocrat at the court of this country. The Guinea company plans to show them our way of life, and to bring them up to be eager ambassadors of Christianity ... and to be ambassadors for the trade with the royal company."

"Brilliant!" replies the canon. "What we are mostly interested in is that the grace of God has touched the two heathens. Also, our bishop is waiting to hear about their further development with great interest ..."

"We too!" Monsieur Hyon interrupts him. "An important person of

157

the Guinea-company also wants that every progress of both of them is reported to him. This very day, I will inform him about this miracle ..."

"But it is not a miracle, Monsieur Hyon. The grace of God is not a miracle!"

"Let's say ... about this occurrence. I assume that it will be a great pleasure for Monsieur de Lagny, the head of the authorised agents, advisor and secretary of the king to forward this message to the competent bodies at court."

Monsieur de Lagny persuaded without any effort Madame de Maintenon, the mistress of the king to welcome the young Africans, "who had just received the divine revelation at the court in Versailles". Like this, Aniaba and Banga are standing in the new palace of Louis XIV, the most powerful ruler of the world, who has conjured a town out of nothing for his court and his government, Versailles – an architectural miracle!

Madame de Maintenon, who replaced the eccentric, pompous fashion taste of her predecessors by a rigid code of conduct at court, falls very much for the graceful bearing and the intelligence of the young people. She proposes to grant them an audience with the king. This is what Monsieur de Lagny was hoping for in secret. Three days later, Aniaba and Banga are introduced to the king. They march in magnificent uniform, the sword in the scabbard, on the side of the head of the authorised agents into the reception hall, into the centre of a large, garrulous and loud crowd. Here at court, they do not seem to attract attention. The king has accustomed his court to people with different skin colours. He enjoys to gather the most exotic ambassadors and other representatives from foreign regions around him, because like this, he can present himself as the absolute ruler, whose power radiates throughout the whole world. They are getting to the door of the Royal salon and stand opposite the Swiss Guards. The general murmur gives way to sudden silence, which was induced by three strong blows. The call sounds, "Messieurs, le Roi!" both sides of the huge door open ... and Louis XIV appears.

"So that's him, the most powerful monarch of the world!" are the thoughts of both of them. "Him, who is called the *son of the sun*." He is standing there, in front of their eyes, in his whole splendour. However, to the young Africans, he appears quite small, exhausted and worried despite his high wig. He has come back from Holland, where the war drags on. On his way through the rows of visitors, he shortly stops at

Monsieur de Lagny and talks to him. After that, he looks in a friendly, nearly fatherly way at Aniaba and Banga. All eyes turn towards them. Monsieur de Lagny bows dutifully. After that, the king puts his hand lovingly on Aniaba's head and walks on, without saying a word. On the way back, Aniaba and Banga learn that His Majesty expressed the wish that Bishop Bossuet, court chaplain and famous priest in France should personally watch over their further education.

On the 1st of August, 1691, three years after his arrival, Aniaba is baptised. The ceremony is carried out by Bishop Bossuet, in accordance with the Royal wish. "Prince Aniaba from Assinie" receives his Christian name, "Louis" also in accordance with the Royal wish. A few days later, Aniaba solemnly receives the Holy Communion in the presence of Madame de Maintenon in Versailles from the hands of Cardinal de Noailles.

Soon, both African princes are adopted into the privileged class of the French society. Their portraits are produced by the court painter of the king to document their special position. These show two smiling, self-assured young people in festive clothes.

The pictures that are not preserved are taken to their family in Assinie by Commander Tibierge, together with letters from the two, and they are presented in court.

Tibierge's expedition in the year 1692 brings an unexpected turn in Aniaba's life. The king demands that the young people should return, when he gets to know about their development so that they could serve the interests of their people with their good education. Aniaba could even inherit the throne of Ehotilé. Commander Tibierge pricks up his ears. He does not use his time for commercial transactions but he asks around and he provides Monsieur de Lagny with detailed information about the conditions in Assinie, especially about the true origin of Aniaba and Banga.

Meanwhile, both are enjoying the advantages and privileges of Royal protégés. In official circles, they are considered as god-children of the king, and due to this, they are accepted in the French army at the beginning of 1692, as the first black officers. Monsieur de Lagny forwards this good message to them personally, "Each of you will receive a yearly pay in the amount of twelve thousand livres from the royal treasury!" This is the basis for a comfortable life. They could move into their own home and enjoy the sophisticated life of Paris. The two officers from Africa look so good, so exotic, they are so cheerful, so rich, and people envy them, especially because the king supports them. Their first discreet and not so discreet affairs with the Parisian ladies happen between hunting games, balls and other social gatherings. They also take part in gambling, and they create scandals in the army by doing so. Our officers from Assinie do not foresee that the life of the king's musketeer can also turn out differently.

In the midst of this enjoyable life, they receive an order: Captain Aniaba is detailed to a cavalry regiment in the Normandy and Captain Banga to a regiment to the northern border. As such, the carefree life of both Africans in Paris comes to an abrupt end. Exhausting exercises replace pleasant walks; instead of the nice conversation with Parisian young ladies; the shouting of the sergeants pierce their ears. Soon, Banga experiences loneliness and hostility. He falls into depression and alcoholism in the permanent fog of his new location. It is gets so serious that he has to be sent back home in 1695 when he is very ill and emaciated. Aniaba, who has no idea about Banga's fate, is not suffering this much, thanks to his open, spirited way and his higher position in the goodwill of the mighty. He is still treated as a protégé of the king by the colonel and the other officers of the regiment.

However, Aniaba is no longer as carefree as he was in the Parisian times. He is worried because of the stay of the Commander Tibierge in Assinie, who could find out the truth about his actual origin and could confirm his real chances to ascent to the throne because his biography contains some secrets. First of all, his real name is not Aniaba. Moreover, he is a prince, but he is not really entitled to the throne of Assinie.

The Ehotilé, Aniaba's people, had once generously welcomed the displaced people of the Efié. Eventually, they had established their domination over their hosts. Fifty years later, the Essouma came from the East and drove the Efié away from the region. The always hospitable Ehotilé granted their guests the privilege to make contact with the Europeans, whilst they restricted themselves to what they had always done, which is fishing in the sea and salt production from sea water. The Essouma were capable traders and soon became wealthy. With the help of their economic superiority, they imposed their rule on the Ehotilé. They took in several children of the ruling families of the Ehotilé hostages to prevent a revolt. That practice was widespread amongst the Akan people; Ehotilé, Efié, Essouma and others.

Aniaba came at age six years to the court of the Essouma, as son of an Ehotilé-princess, where he lived in a kind of cultivated captivity. It was not visible for outsiders because the pretty, intelligent child had conquered the heart of the childless first wife of Niamkey, the brother of the Essouma-king. As such, he was adopted by the couple, well cared for and pampered. He forgot his mother-tongue in the course of time and the court of Ehotilé. He had become "Aniaba", which was the name of his new parents. Over there, nobody knew anymore, what his original name had been. Therefore he did not have claims to the throne of the Essouma, the more so as the Akan are a matrilineal soceity; a son inherits his mother's brother (uncle). According to this practice, the natural son of a king cannot succeed his father, but only his maternal uncles. Even as a stepson, Aniaba could not hope for the throne of Assinie because his adoptive mother was neither a sister nor a cousin of the king. Aniaba was concerned that Commander Tibierge might find out about this situation.

How will the French king react, when Tibierge explained that Aniaba was not at all a son of the king of Assinie according to European understanding? That he was not the crown prince, whom they expected to count on in the power struggle in the Gold Coast? For the first time, he became aware of the impending danger. He came to understand that the rulers were only concerned about their own interests and their power. Equally shrewd, he found a way out. If the truth is exposed, then Monsieur de Lagny would also have to fear for his post as the head of the Guinea Company. One would never forgive the failure of the project, which would occur due to his false information. The close connection between his fate and that of the smart head of the authorised agents, advisor and secretary to the king, made Aniaba hopeful. In fact, behind the scenes, a new plan had developed.

In the "virtually inexhaustible sources of gold" in Assinie, they envisaged hope for the French economy, which was weakened by numerous wars. Tibierge noted in his report that the problem was that the Africans 'unfortunately' knew the value of the precious metal. Moreover, representatives of other European powers courted them in such a way that they acted more and more with self-confidence. France would have to establish an absolute rule over the local inhabitants to be able to get to the sources of gold for themselves. Aniaba was supposed to come into play at this point because they believed they could easily control him.

Not long after this, when he came back from his expedition in the Gold Coast, Chevalier d'Amon sent the message of the death of Aniaba's 'father', the king of Assinie. Aniaba read between the lines that the Guinea Ccompany was planning a coup in his favour. He quickly recognised the unique opportunity: He would be able to effect changes with the backing of the most powerful king of the world.

During the meeting, which was convened immediately, Aniaba made claims, which amazed his dialogue partners. He did not only insist on a hundred soldiers, canons, lots of gun powder but also on a considerable number of French servants. Furthermore, he demanded tributes of power according to European tradition, which meant the protection of the Holy Mary during an official ceremony, the foundation of an order of knights, which he wanted to name *Order of the Star of our Beloved Wife*, and ... the consent of the Pope! The Chevalier d'Amon had a lump in his throat but he was careful not to confront Aniaba because the king and Minister Colbert were informed about the project, and therefore it must not fail. Cardinal de Noailles, meanwhile Archbishop of Paris, handed over the insignia of the grandmaster of his order on 12th February, 1701 in *Notre-Dame*. Traditionally, the cathedral received a painting of this, which showed Louis XIV and the Bishop of Meaux, as they were introducing Aniaba to the Virgin Mary. This was not preserved.

On 19th April 1701, the *Poli* weighed anchor in La Rochelle. On board were Chevalier d'Amon, about fifty soldiers, who were still commanded by d'Amon against Aniaba's will: construction workers, craftsmen and two missionaries, Pater Villars from Quimper and Pater Godefroy Loyer from Rennes. D'Amon wrote a detailed travel report, which was published in 1714. The presents from Louis XIV for the 'King of Assinie' were also on board the *Poli*: precious crockery, dishes, chairs, armchairs and his gold medal with the picture of the donor.

Shortly before departure, disputes occurred between d'Amon and Aniaba. Whereas the Chevalier considered his opponent arrogant and excessive because he demanded too many French servants and the leadership over the expedition, the captain of the Musketeers was angry because d'Amon had radically reduced the number of his servants. He did not grant him an active role and he insisted that the king's presents should not be given to him personally; but impersonally, and addressed to the 'King of Assinie'. The prince disappeared in the next harbour. Four days later, the crew found him. He had also antagonised the two missionaries.

The information that he had spent the four days predominantly with ladies, was not commensurate with the expected image of the Catholic king of Assinie. He showed himself as completely non-compliant because he knew the real life in France much too well to accept a moral lecture. During the course of the journey, which took two months , the dispute intensified so that Aniaba retreated to the rear part of the vessel and kept persistently quiet.

When the *Poli* reached Assinie on 27th June 1701, Aniaba was only a normal passenger. The Chevalier d'Amon had already developed an alternative plan because it became clear to him that he could not control Aniaba. Therefore he tried to discredit Aniaba, but without success, in the eyes of the new king of Assinie and in the eyes of the general public. However, he soon gets to know that the king received Aniaba and that they seemed to be on good terms. So he urgently requested an audience to hand over the gifts of his French friend to King Akassigny, and he used this opportunity to let him know that his beloved nephew had his eyes on the throne. D'Amon was greatly pleased when he saw Akassigny's obvious consternation. After the welcome ceremony, the king ordered them to reconcile with a handshake. This however did not mean that the rivalries had ended. After many twists and alternating triumphs, Chevalier finally succeeded in isolating Aniaba. He could even win Ehotilé over by awarding the lucrative job to him to supply all timber for the construction of the first French military base at the lagoon.

In 1703, two years after his return, Aniaba left his home on board a Portuguese ship. There was no place anymore for him in Assinie. From then on, the traces of a man, who had been seen as a pioneer of a cultural exchange, werea lost. With him, the model for a partnership, which could have given a different direction to the relations between both geographical regions, failed. France's claim to power, which eventually became concrete in the later colonial occupation, spoke against it.

According to the report of Dutch traders, who reported on him in the highest possible terms, Aniaba is supposed to have been working in Queta (Kéta/Togo) under the name *Hannibal* as advisor to the king of this place. In present day Ivory Coast, Aniaba is only known by the Ehotilé, Essouma and Abouré, who in each case claim him for themselves.

Bibliography

Henriette Diabaté: *Aniaba, un Assinien à la cour de Louis XIV.* Paris 1975.

ABRAHAM P. HANNIBAL (Eritrea/Russia)

AGAINST ALL ODDS

BY ISSAYAS TESFAMARIAM

O n November the 28th, 2009, a monument was officially inaugurated in Asmara, the capital city of Eritrea, in memory of Alexander Sergeyvich Pushkin: Russia's uncontested greatest poet. In attendance were officials from Russia. The monument is Eritrea's symbolic way of welcoming home one of its lost children. The connection between Alexander S. Pushkin and Eritrea is through his maternal great grandfather, General Abraham Petrovich Hannibal/Gannibal. The story of an eight-year-old boy kidnapped from Eritrea in the 17th century and taken to Russia, where he became, against all odds, a military engineer, a general, an intellectual and protégé of Czar Peter the Great, is an inspiration to people of any age, place (especially Africa) and period, including that of his future great grandson, Alexander S. Pushkin. General Abraham P. Hannibal died at a ripe old age. However, his life was full of obstacles, due to his skin colour and palace intrigues, and also due to his loyalty to Czar Peter and his family. Even though his loyalty to the Romanov family was seen as a liability by his detractors, he remained true to his commitments and moral principles. He was exiled many times to different places due to various official commissions and assignments;

throughout, he kept his dignity and sanity intact. In the end, he proved that virtue, that is, human resilience and resolve, are more powerful than short term gains obtained by human vice. He is an example of a great African personality and mind.

In the summer of 2011, I gave three presentations in Asmara, the capital city of Eritrea. The title of the presentations was "Pushkin Me'as d'a Tegadilu?" ("When did Pushkin fight?"). Of course, this was a rhetorical question presented to a population where the word "gedli" (fight/struggle) or "tegadalai" (fighter) for Eritrean independence conjure a litany of nouns, adjectives, verbs and adverbs. I put it in that context because almost three years earlier a monument in honour of Alexander Sergeyvich Pushkin was officially inaugurated in Asmara, even though Pushkin had not physically fought for the independence of Eritrea. As a matter of fact, A.S. Pushkin lived in nineteenth century Russia whereas Eritrea got its independence from Ethiopia in 1991 after thirty years of armed struggle. According to Artem Efimov, Pushkin, in his famous novel, *Eugene Onegin*, states that he (Pushkin) will one day leave cold Russia to enjoy the warmth and sunshine "beneath the sky of my beloved Africa". The monument is significant because it is Eritrea's way of welcoming home one of its lost children. In his life, Pushkin never left Russia. However, a soil sample permanently placed at the foot of the monument from Pushkin's burial place at Svyatogorsk Monastery near Mikhailovskoye, Russia, fullfils Pushkin's dream of enjoying the warmth and sunshine "beneath the sky of his beloved Africa". Mikhailovskoye was one of the estates of his maternal great grandfather, a full-blooded African, Major-General Abraham Petrovich Hannibal (Gannibal in Russian). The real life-story of Abraham P. Hannibal (not to be confused with Hannibal: born 247 B.C., son of, Hamilcar Barca of Carthage) was so phenomenal that it makes fiction (which is obliged to stick to possibilities, according to Mark Twain) a child's game. It is unbelievably remarkable because he survived and thrived against all odds and lived to a ripe old age at a time and place where his colour was a mark of a designated slave, "a badge of hell", strangeness, backwardness and a circus curiosity. Who was Abraham P. Hannibal? Where was he born? What was his remarkable story? To get answers to the questions above and more, (especially the second question), it depends on who you ask.

At the onset, I must acknowledge that there are many gaps in Abraham Hannibal's story that we may never know; especially the first part of Abraham's life from Africa to Constantinople, in Turkey. There are also many gaps that have been recently filled, such as his life after Constantinople, Turkey, till his death in Russia, by various scholars and authors (Dieudonné Gnammankou, Hugh Barnes, Frances Somers Cocks, N. K. Teletova and others). Thanks to the works of Hugh Barnes and Frances Somers Cocks, English language readers can finally read, in detail, about this incredible historical figure. In *Gannibal: the Moor of Petersburg*, Hugh Barnes brings Abraham P. Hannibal out from the shadows of Alexander S. Pushkin, and projects him into a full blown biography on his own merit. Like a good eye surgeon, Barnes removes the cataract that had been obstructing us from seeing the complete life of Abraham P. Hannibal. Barnes succeeds in removing most of the cataract that had been the cause of the blurriness before. However, like a cataract that had not been fully removed and keeps recurring, in Barnes' *Gannibal,* the original birthplace argument still remains blurred. To be fair though, it is understandable that proving a birthplace is very difficult given the unavailability of original documents and strong evidence from 17th century Africa.

It is normal when countries tend to claim renowned personalities as their own. In Africa, the number of countries claiming A.P. Hannibal or A.S. Pushkin (through Hannibal) as their own is increasing. The latest addition to the fold is Cameroon. One thing should be clear, though. All of Africa should be proud of the extraordinary life and brilliant accomplishment of Abraham P. Hannibal because his story should not be confined to a particular place and time, but should be hailed as a triumph for the resilience and perseverance of the timeless human spirit. Having said that, the purpose of this essay is not to dwell on where Abraham was born but rather to write about his survival and excellence as a great African mind; but suffice it to say that I will point out the two main differing claimants (Eritrea and Cameroon) as the location of his birthplace and comment briefly on the subject before I proceed.

The search for Abraham's birthplace started with what he himself wrote. In a petition for nobility that he wrote in 1742 to Empress Elizabeth I of Russia, (1709-1762), Abraham stated that he was born in "Lagone" (*Lagon*). According to Hugh Barnes, the petition is the only surviving document in which Abraham G. (H)annibal refers to his ancestral background. According to Vladimir Nabokov, a renowned Russian novelist, the three biographies written nearest to Gannibal's time, Helbig (1787), the unknown author of the German biography (1785), and Batish-Kamenski (1836), are not in agreement. The German biography of Abraham was supposedly written by his son-in-law, Adam Karpovich Rotkirkh. The idea of "Abyssinia" as the birthplace of Abraham emerged from this biography. According to Frances Somers Cocks, Rotkirkh's view of Abraham's origin lay dormant for nearly a century and was picked up again by a Russian journalist named Dmitri Anuchin. Anuchin came to the conclusion that "L" town and district located on the right bank of the river Mareb in the province of Hamasen" (modern day Eritrea) was Abraham's birthplace. Frances Somers Cocks argues that Anuchin's aforementioned argument with Hannibal's 'Lagon' (*Lagone*) was simply on the grounds of the similarity of names and this had, as Anuchin saw it, tremendous advantage of making Pushkin's ancestor a pale-skinned aquiline featured 'Hamitic' or 'Semitic' type. Anuchin could not stomach the notion of him being a true Negro. According to Artem Efimov, in 1964, Vladimir Nabokov studied old maps of Africa, trying to find the exact birthplace of Pushkin's great grandfather, and one of his discoveries was that in the early 18th century the Arabic "Abyssinia" could refer not only to Ethiopia, but also to a considerable part of sub-Saharan Africa, spreading west as far as Lake Chad. Based on Nabokov's casual reference in (*Notes of Prosody Abraham Gannibal*) of the Lagona region of equatorial Africa, south of Lake Chad, Dieudonné Gnammankou shifted the " long held belief" of Abraham's birthplace from East to West Africa (Logone-Birni). I tend to agree with Frances Somers Cocks when she states that Gnammankou dismisses Anuchin's theory as fatally tainted by racism, and uses the similarity of the name 'Logone" (*Lagon*) to Hannibal's 'Lagon' (*Lagone)* as the foundation for a detailed claim that this is the true birthplace: he is just as passionate in his determination to make Hannibal a true Negro as Anuchin was to make him anything but!

Leaving racial semantics aside, as I've mentioned earlier, there are things that we might never know, but let's look at some of the circumstantial evidence to give us a clearer perspective. As Frances Somers Cocks states, the Abyssinian theory hangs on just two words: "Abyssinia" in Adam Rotkirkh's biography and "Logona" (*Lagon*) in Abraham's petition and the central African theory hangs on just the one word of Lagona/*Lagon* (I might also add the word "FUMMO"). The physical location in the "Abyssinian" theory is in modern day Eritrea, not in Ethiopia.

Let's look at Eritrea's case first. Eritrea has a 1000 mile Red Sea coastline and its proximity to the Middle East, Asia and the Indian Ocean was one of the main reasons that it had been colonised by various powers for many centuries. Also, because of its proximity to the origins of the world's major religions, Eritrea adopted Christianity and Islam early (4th and 7th centuries, respectively), therefore the use of such names as Abraham and Ibrahim in Eritrea have a very long tradition. Knowledge of the Ottomans' relationship with Africa is also important. In the case of Eritrea, the presence of the Ottoman Empire in Eritrea directly (the coastal areas, such as Massawa, which was the main port of exit for thousands of slaves who were shipped out over many centuries), and indirectly (the hinterland, target of many incursions and raids) lasted over 300 years. In fact, Ottoman rule was so vicious that Tigrigna, the main language spoken in Eritrea, has a word "Geza't Turki" (rule of Turkey), which is even used today to convey someone's mean-heartedness.

Eritrea has a long history of oral and written tradition with its own script. Many localities within Eritrea have their respective stories/ histories told to their offspring and others for posterity through oral and/or written culture. To cite just two examples: *Traditions de Tseazzega et Hazzega,* as told by locals to Johannes Kolmodin and published in 1912, and Enno Littman's stay with the Mensae of Eritrea and later Axum, Ethiopia produced four volumes entitled *Princeton Expedition to Abyssinia.* The work (especially dealing with the Mensae of Eritrea) would not have been a reality but for Eritrean oral historian, Naffa Wad Uthman, who in turn had learned the stories from his father. Reciting one's genealogy is part of Eritrea's culture. The most important reasons why many regions in Eritrea (as mainly an agrarian society) adhered to oral and written traditions were for land usage/distribution purposes, fairness and conflict resolution. The mechanisms that developed as arbitrators in the various areas and communities were their written customary laws. Therefore, in many localities in Eritrea, oral and written tradition as a proper venue of recordkeeping/accounting/genealogy of the community's activities and membership is of paramount importance.

The place within Eritrea on which researchers have focused is a place called Logo. Oral tradition within Eritrea mentions that there were/are at least seven Logos. (Logo Seraye, Logo Sarda, Logo Chewa, Logo Achemo, Logo Sikul, Adi Logo, etc.) Researchers including Frances Somers Cocks visited Logo Chewa and others. None of the places mentioned above ever claimed Abraham as their lost son, except a place called Lagwen, 12 miles from Asmara, which has an oral and written tradition that states that one of its sons called Abraham, son of Zerai, was kidnapped when he was eight years old and taken to Turkey from a place called Gobo (hill). Enda Mariam, his sister, drowned in the process of saving her younger brother. Therefore, researchers have been looking in the wrong place for a long time. In this version, there is no mention of Abraham as belonging to any of the nobility of the area nor that Abraham was a Muslim.

Now let's look at the case of Cameroon as the birth place of Abraham. Due to the physical distance between the Ottoman Empire and Lake Chad area (it is two or three times the distance from Eritrea to Turkey), the Ottomans did not have direct rule over the area as they did with Eritrea, but only through secondary and tertiary intermediaries.

Gnammankou's critique of the "Abyssinian" theory of Anuchin's as racist, as Frances Somers Cocks states, does not of itself mean that it could not have been Abraham's birth place. The other central African argument is that of the word "Logone" (*Lagon*). Logone-Birini is not the only name that has 'Logone' in it. But there are other similar sounding words as Logon that are located in other parts of West Africa. Legon in Ghana, Luango in Mali and others are some of the examples.

According to Hugh Barnes, who happens to lean towards the central African theory in his search for Abraham's birth place, he visited Logone-Birini and met the sultan, Muhammed Bahar Maruf. According to Barnes, the sultan had never heard of Pushkin and his great-grand father, Abraham, until a decade ago (he had become an expert since then), when he received a photocopy of a lecture by Gnammankou. In the case of Lagwen, every child had grown up hearing the story of Abraham.

"FUMMO" is another word that is one of the foundations for the central African theory. "FUMMO" is a word that is written on Abraham Hannibal's coat-of-arms. Barnes states that when he asked the sultan about the word "fummo", he was surprised to hear that it means "homeland". However, Frances Somers Cocks argues that when she discussed the word "fummo" with the same sultan, he explained it means "fighting" or "let's fight".

To understand Abraham's incredible story, it is important to know, first, that it's a human story and second, to put it in the context of the time he lived and died. Abraham was born in the late 17th century. When he was eight years old, he was kidnapped from Lagwen, Eritrea (according to *Twlde Lagwen:* Genealogy of Lagwen) and was taken to Constantinople. While Abraham was a slave in Constantinople, in a faraway Russia, Czar Peter I (1672-1725), at the age of 25 was trying to "modernize/westernize" "old/oriental" Russia. He wanted to make Imperial Russia equal to the royals of Western Europe. In order to learn from the capitals of Western Europe, Czar Peter travelled incognito with a large delegation and spent time working in various capacities as an apprentice. This opportunity led him to personally witness the advancement of various technological feats of the time. He also witnessed the cultural aspects of the various European empires. A sign of the times of haute couture and vogue, having a portrait taken by a famous artist of the time with the black pages of the respective royals was seen as hip. Back in Constantinople, in the summer of 1704, according to N. K. Teletova, Savva Lukich Vladislavich (Raguzinsky) received three blackamoor boys during a period when he was acting ambassador for P. A. Tolstoi. The three boys were sent overland to Moscow through the territories of Bulgaria and Wallachia (modern day Romania). One of the three boys was Abraham. In a recent archives discovery, according to N. K. Teletova, it was during this journey that Abraham was baptised. After a long journey, the African slaves arrived in Moscow on 13th November, 1704.

Joel A. Rogers in his *World's Great Men of Color (Vol.II)* states that history contains few figures more extraordinary than Abraham Hannibal. He continues by stating that stolen from his parents in Africa and sold into slavery, he became general-in-chief of one of the leading white empires of his day. Destiny was so kind to Hannibal, Rogers continues, from the beginning; *if he were* sent to America, he would have been at best a house servant. I would like to add that the meeting of two different individuals, one an emperor of an emerging white nation and the other a slave, was what Germans call "zeitgeist," the coming of history and destiny together. Their strangeness united them. The Petrine revolution, Barnes states, was a vast, utopian project in social engineering (which) was an attempt to reconstruct the Russian as a European. Barnes continues by stating that in some respects the life of Abraham Petrovich H(G)annibal served as its pilot scheme: an attempt to reconstruct the African as a Russian. Barnes argues that like Gannibal, Czar Peter was "a strange creature" (he was six foot seven inches tall) in many people's eyes. The "strangeness" in the eyes of their enemies was a constant mark of hatred and intrigue.

According to Barnes, Peter's zeal to introduce western habits met with incomprehension and fury among the doltish boyar nobles. Czar Peter I was so determined to modernise Russia. Rotkirkh, according to Barnes, argues that he (Czar Peter I) wished to make examples of them (Russians) and put them to shame by convincing them that out of every people and even among wild men such as "negroes", whom our civilized nations assign exclusively to the class of slave, there can be formed men who by dint of application can obtain knowledge and thus become helpful to the monarch."

Once in Russia, Abraham was discovered to be unusually bright for his age. He quickly picked up the Russian language and mathematics. The Czar, realizing Abraham's potential, put him under his wing. Over the years, Barnes writes, Abraham immersed himself in the study of mathematics under the guidance of the Ukrainian cleric, Feofan Prokopovich, who taught arithmetic, geometry and physics at the Kiev Academy. Abraham started to accompany Czar Peter I throughout Russia and foreign countries. In 1707, in Vilno (Vilnius, Lithuania), Abraham was baptised (re-baptised). On that day Abraham became Czar Peter I's godson. In 1717, when Czar Peter I was on one of his European trips, he took his godson to France and left him in Paris to study. While in France a war broke out between France and Spain which lasted a year. Abraham fought for France against Spain and was hit in the head at the fortress of Fuenterrabia in northern Spain. The injury had a lifelong impact. He became an invalid with a rank of a captain.

According to Frances Somers Cocks, it was France that set the seal on Abraham's promotion out of the servant class. It was in France, argues Hugh Barnes, that Abraham encountered the Parisian intellectuals (including Voltaire and Montesquieu who praised him as the "dark star of Russia's enlightenment"). Among Abraham's acquaintances, according to Barnes, was the scientist and man of letters, Bernard de Fontenelle, to whom Peter introduced Abraham during a visit to the Académie des Sciences. This visit put him in touch with a group of mathematicians, *philosophes* and natural scientists who operated in a narrow circle. Abraham's interest in mathematics and engineering led him to study at the best artillery schools in France. After six years in France, Abraham returned to Russia as one of the most educated people in Russia. He became a linguist (with an excellent command of French, Dutch, German and Italian) and a military engineer. His library, according to Frances Somers Cocks, became the eighth largest library in Russia, nearly four hundred volumes of geography, history, travel, literature as well as technical works relevant to his studies. After his return to Russia, Czar Peter I named Abraham to the post of 'principal translator of foreign books at the Imperial Court'. He was appointed an officer in the Perobrazhensky guard-regiment and also became an engineer-lieutenant in the bombardier-company of which the Czar was the captain. According to Barnes, Czar Peter lavished honours and gifts upon his godson. Barnes also states that in the hostile environment of the Russian court, the more G(H)annibal seemed to enjoy the Czar's favour, the more enemies he made. Among the many powerful enemies of Abraham were people such as Prince Menshikov and the Dolgorukys. What filled Abraham's enemies with envy and rage was that first, Abraham was black and second, he was educated. To top that, Abraham found himself in what Liza Knapp calls an anomalous position in the Russian power structure. According to Barnes, Abraham's influence over Czar Peter I on questions of defense and fortress building was absolute, and his influence went beyond the military into important projects of civil engineering. One of these civilian projects was the Lake Ladoga canal, which is still in existence today. Work on the canal, Barnes writes, had begun disastrously in 1718 under a Menshikov protégé. The failure, Barnes continues, complicated Menshikov's rage at H(G)annibal's success and the disappointed rival became neurotic and vicious. In the summer of 1723, according to N.K.Teletova, Abraham took part in the grandiose land works in Kronstadt. On the island of Kotlin, according to Barnes, near the head of the Gulf of Finland, Abraham constructed the fort of Kronstadt which guarded the approach to St. Petersburg.

According to N.K.Teletova, from late 1724 Abraham was busy with the fortress works in Riga (modern day Latvia), where the news of Czar Peter I's death reached him. The death of Czar Peter I came as a big blow to Abraham when his career seemed promising. Barnes writes that Abraham was so closely associated with his godfather that many Russians wondered if he could survive a change of regime. At first, Barnes continues, the succession was quickly settled in favour of Catherine and she renewed her dead husband's patronage to the Moor [Abraham] by employing him as a private tutor in mathematics and geometry to Czar Peter's son Alexei's 9-year-old son Peter. Even though the empress was Catherine, the main power lay with Prince Menshikov, who assumed the rank of 'generalissimo'. As tutor to a future Czar, Abraham's position became very precarious and as a result, Abraham became a liability in the eyes of his enemies. Abraham's precarious position within the context of his enemies became magnified because the two most powerful enemies, Menshikov and Dolgorky, were hoping that their daughter and their niece, respectively, be betrothed to young Peter (Czar Peter's grandson). Barnes argues that Peter, the young hereditary prince, soon fell under the African spell and here was the beginning of G(H)annibal's misfortune. It was during the reign of Catherine I that Abraham's two-volume work consisting of "*Géometrie practique*" and "*Fortification*" (Practical Geometry and Fortification*)* came into being and was presented to the empress. It was unfortunate that the Czar who had invested so much in his godson was not able to see the fruition of his "pilot project in social engineering".

On 6th May, according to Barnes, only two years and three months after her accession, Catherine died and the youngster was proclaimed Czar Peter II. By the order of Prince Menshikov, on May 8th 1727, in the name of Peter II, Abraham was ordered to Kazan (five hundred miles east of Moscow). This was the beginning of the many exiles that would test Abraham's resolve. While in Kazan, Abraham received another order to move to Toblosk (700 miles further east from Kazan in Siberia) and build a fortress there. In Siberia, Barnes writes, Abraham as an African and a keen naturalist drew up lists of hundreds of unique animal and plant species that live on Lake Baikal (the oldest lake located in Siberia). While Abraham was in exile in the eastern wilderness, the palace rivalry and factional intrigues continued unabated. The victim of this palace intrigue, this time, was none other than Prince Menshikov. With the fall from grace of Menshikov, the Dolgorukys came to prominence. The Dolgorukys feared Abraham's influence no less than Prince Menshikov. In January 1730, before Czar Peter II (at the age of fifteen) was to be married, he died of smallpox. As a result, Ann, Czar Peter I's niece, became empress. With the help of his friend, the German-Russian Count Münnich, Abraham was transferred to Pernau in Estonia.

In 1731 Abraham married Evdokia Dioper, a daughter of a young Greek captain. According to N.K.Teletova, this forced marriage was to bring the young couple nothing but sorrow. The marriage reached its disastrous climax when Evdokia Dioper gave birth to a white baby girl. Abraham started a divorce process which took twenty years with charges and counter charges. According to N.K.Teletova, at the conclusion of this lengthy process, Evdokia Dioper was installed in the Uspensky Staroladozhsky Convent and later the Vvedensky Convent in Tikhvin, where she died. While the divorce process was going on, Abraham married Christina von Schoberg, a daughter of a retired Swedish army captain. They would eventually have eleven children and stayed together for fifty years. The first born, Ivan, would have an illustrious military career (despite his father's firm objection), becoming admiral of the fleet of the Russian Navy, a hero of the battle of Navarino and Chesma and finally the founder of Kherson in Ukraine. His fifth child, Osip, would become the grandfather of Alexander Sergeveech Pushkin (A.S. Pushkin's descendants through his daughter, Natalia, would end up in various European royalties including the British Royal family). Through his last daughter, Sofia, the Gannibal family would subsequently forge ties with many prominent German-Swedish families including the Vrangels, whose direct descendants would include Lydia Dmitrievna Zinovieva-Annibal (author and dramatist) and General P. N. Vrangel, a Menshevik (white) General who fought the Bolsheviks. While the number of his household was increasing, after Pernau, Abraham was transferred to Reval (modern day Tallinn, Estonia). In January 1741, he was awarded the rank of lieutenant colonel of the Reval artillery garrison.

On November 25th, 1741, Czar Peter I's daughter Elizabeth became empress. Abraham's fortunes once again began to open up. According to Barnes, on the day of Empress Elizabeth's coronation he [Abraham] organised magnificent fireworks to display in the night sky over the garrison. Abraham's interest in fireworks, pyrotechnics and rocketry is described in detail in Hugh Barnes' book. With Elizabeth's ascendancy to the throne, Abraham was promoted to a major general, and was also appointed commander-in-chief of the Reval garrison. For his commitment and loyalty to Czar Peter I, he was granted various villages and estates such as Kobrino, Suida and Mikhailovskoye (which would have a tremendous role in Pushkin's life). With a stroke of Empress Elizabeth's pen, Abraham P. Hannibal instantly became a wealthy man. It had been a long journey! From an eight-year-old boy stolen from Eritrea to become, against all odds, a military and civil engineer, a general, an intellectual and protégé of Czar Peter the Great, is indeed an inspiration. All his enemies who had held him back were disgraced. For a long time his loyalty to the Romanov family was seen as a liability by his detractors, but he had remained true to his commitments and moral principles. As we have seen, he was exiled many times to different places due to various official commissions and assignments; but throughout, he indeed kept his dignity and sanity intact.

For the next ten years, according to Frances Somers Cocks, Abraham was assigned different tasks such as leading a delegation to fix the new Finnish-Russian border and directing fortification all over the empire. Abraham was also promoted to a full general and invested as a Knight of Order of Alexander Nevsky. After serving Russia for many decades, Abraham retired in the 1760s and lived to a ripe old age, right into Empress Catherine II's reign. He lived and served through eight Czars and Czarinas. Even in his retirement, he was asked for advice. Artem Efimov writes that Catherine II (1729-1796), impressed by the experience of King Frederick II of Prussia, who managed to prevent mass starvation by growing a lot of potatoes, asked Hannibal to test it in his mansion at Suida. It worked, so eventually potatoes became known as "another bread" in Russia. Also, Artem informs us that while in retirement Hannibal met a young nobleman named Alexander Suvorov, who desperately wanted to join the military, but his father did not want him to. After talking to the young man, Artem continues, Abraham persuaded the father to let the young man live his dreams. Alexander Suvorov went on to become one of the greatest generals in European history. It is appropriate to conclude by stating that this is no ordinary story. It beats any fiction. His descendants, in their own right, also became important in Russian and European history. Abraham is an important figure in the history of Russia. His indomitable spirit to survive and thrive in an age and a surrounding that is alien is absolutely remarkable and should be admired by people of any age and country. It is a story of human resilience. He was blessed with a noble and elevated character and 'incorruptible probity'. He died in Suida in 1781 a few months after his wife of fifty years had died.

Bibliography
Vladimir Nabokov; *Komemtar zu Eugen Onegin*. Frankfurt 2009
Hugh Barnes: Gannibal; *The Moor of Petersburg*. London. 2005:
Frances S.Cocks; *The Moor of Petersburg. In the Footsteps of a Black Russian*. London. 2005.

ANTON WILHELM AMO AFER   (Ghana)

AN AFRICAN PHILOSOPHER IN GERMANY DURING THE 18TH CENTURY

BY JOE DRAMIGA

In 1707, a small boy fell into the hands of Dutch human traffickers near the small village, Axim (in present-day Ghana). Whilst his parents were searching for him desperately, the four-year-old was brought to a ship and displaced to the Netherlands. Three years later, he was given as a "present" to the Duke Anton Ulrich of Braunschweig-Wolfenbüttel (1633-1714). He thereby shared the same destiny of many African children, who were used as status symbols of the European upper class at that time. To own a black pageboy, who was supposed to prove the cosmopolitan spirit and the wealth of the landlord like an exotic animal, was good form in this class, but it was a blessing in disguise for the small Amo: He was spared the fate of the grind on the plantations in America or the Caribbean. The duke probably recognised the intelligence of the child early and his defiant steeliness in his view and his posture. He probably thought of his relative Czar Peter the Great. A young African, Ibrahim Hannibal, was living in his court and the Czar accorded him an excellent education. The Duke Anton Ulrich, who was one of the most educated princes of his time, decided to do the same and support the boy.

Amo benefitted from a humanistic education instead of having to lead a life of a lackey: He learned Latin, Greek, Hebrew, Dutch and French and intended to push forward to the greatest heights of knowledge and to stand on his own feet one day.

The first impression of the duke was proved to be true, when the christening of the eight-year-old took place. Despite his young age and all odds, the boy insisted on keeping his African name. On the 29th of July, 1708, he was baptised with the name Anton Wilhelm Amo in the castle chapel of Wolfenbüttel; after the duke and the hereditary prince Wilhelm August (1662 – 1731), who was his godfather. Later, Amo expressed his self-assertion even more clearly by adding his ethnicity to his name: Afer, the Latin word for African. In this manner he signed with Antonius Guilielmus Amo Afer at the university.

Amo played a pioneering role in the history of the African diaspora with this explicit tribute paying to his home, because the identification with his own roots as a sign of self-determination played a decisive role in the African American civil rights movement more than two hundred years later. One of the most dazzling figures of the civil rights movement symbolically freed himself from the surname imposed on him, and called himself Malcom X to indicate the loss of the African names. Amo is also of great importance with regard to the struggle for civil rights for the slaved Africans.

On 9th June, 1727, he registered at the University of Halle for philosophy and legal studies. In the course of his studies, he decided to bring the dealings with Africans onto the academic agenda. He definitely knew about the scourge of his times in spite of his privileged situation. The young student called the societal conditions into question in his first disputation, which was an essay with public lecture and subsequent discussion. It corresponded with the present-day bachelor degree. Under the title De iure Maurorum in Europe (About the rights of the Moors), he examined the situation of the slaves in Europe, an undesirable development, nearly nobody was bothered by. A critical statement like this is the evidence of a spirit of contradiction and fearlessness at a time, when the social discrimination against broad segments of the European society was glorified as a divine order. The ruling class of the nobility and the clergy had common interests. A prominent example of such independent thinking is the "Religious community of the friends", which in 1671 denounced slavery as a grave violation of human dignity.

It protests against human trafficking in 1727, appealing for a more just order. That the writing was nicknamed "Quaker" reveals to what extent the attitude of this writing was in conflict with the spirit of the age.

Amo experienced at first hand the effects of a worldview, which described injustice as if it was wanted by God. He did not only reason philosophically but especially legally to illustrate the indefensibleness of the lack of rights of Africans. We know from a summary – unfortunately the disputation is lost, that he explained that the Europeans broke existing law because "in earlier times African kings like European kings were loyal to Rome. Through the slave trade, the Europeans disregarded the common heritage of Roman law, namely the principle that all Roman citizens including those living in Africa were free". He thus exposed the social practice as homemade deprivation of rights and a relapse below the standards of an earlier time.

One has to bring to one's mind the attitude of renowned scholars, who shaped the history of German philosophy decades after Amo's death, to appreciate the importance of his view. Africans were inhabitants of a "land for children, which is beyond the day of the self-confident history and it is wrapped in the black color of the night" for Hegel and Kant denied them any form of intelligence. Could these representatives of reason have known it better? Yes, because firstly, there were historical examples like Abraham Petrowitsch Hannibal, who was well known across Europe and even Amo, who refuted the theses of Kant, Hegel and other philosophers. Secondly, the research of the explorer, Peter Kolb (1675 – 1726), also has to be taken into account. He proved the groundlessness of the disparagements of Africans in his famous book "A journey to the forelands of Good Hope" (1719), which has been translated into many languages, and which was based on studies of several years in Southern Africa. The words of the dean of the University of Wittenberg, Johannes Gottfried Kraus, also showed that the great philosophers had to revise their judgements. He addressed the public on the occasion of Amo's thesis in the year 1734 with the words: "Africa's reputation was once great as well in view of the talents related to the scientific efforts and the church organisation".

It produced several quite extraordinary persons, whose brilliant studies established worldly wisdom and theology even more. At our time however, this part of the world is supposed to be fertile with things other than studies. However, the extremely famous Magister of Philosophy and the Free Arts, Anton Wilhelm Amo, an African from Guinea, may prove by his own example that the talents of Africa have not been exhausted."

What was behind the intellectual lapses of Hegel and Kant? An explanation may be found in the feverish search for the *missing link* between the human being and the ape, which was supposed to reinforce the theory about the system of nature. The African, who was treated like an animal anyway, was the *missing link* for most academics, because they were clinging to the prejudices of their time. In any case, this approach was unrighteous, and the titles of Kant's writings: *Critique of Pure Reason* and *Critique of Judgement* get an ironic sound against this background. Amo's work appears like an appeal for the literati, to check their unsustainable theses about non-European peoples. In his *Treatise about the Art to philosophize in a down-to-earth way,* which he presented 1738 in Halle, he did not only deal with intellectual obliqueness, dogmatism and prejudices, but he also made a classification of the different types of knowledge, which can absolutely be considered as a precursor of Kant's *Critique of Pure Reason,* which was published in 1781.

Amo did not do himself a favour with his critical attitude about the predominant way of thinking. He went on the offensive by declaring openly his belief in the progressive ideas of the early Enlightenment, which meant that he saw the dogmatic theories in a critical way, because he belonged to the rationalists, who were enthusiastic about scientific findings and who started to weaken the power of the church. The quarrel between the rationalistic view of the world and the orthodox pietistic theology had the dimensions of a cultural war. The way of dealing with the leading rationalistic philosopher, Christian Wolff (1679-1754) shows how fiercely it was fought. Wolff received the order from the Prussian king *"to leave the town of Halle and all of the states belonging to the king within forty-eight hours after receipt of this order or be hanged",* after he had declared that ethical behaviour does not depend on Christian belief. He declared that atheists can also behave in an ethical way and therefore good does not happen because of God's will.

The promulgation of his writings was forbidden "under threat of a lifelong prison sentence". Amo also left Halle like other representatives of the early Enlightenment. In the following years he had to change universities more than once.

Despite the powerful opponents, Amo remained true to his

conviction that the feudal ruling structures and an uncritical attitude towards dogmas are in contradiction to progress. His unyielding stance is expressed in one of his lectures, which he temporarily gave again in Halle about Wolff, who was forbidden over there, and especially in his main work, the *Treatise about the Art to philosophize in a down-to-earth way*, with which he revealed himself as a representative of Wolff's philosophy. He was aware of the possible consequences, which can be seen in his sarcastic reference towards how important adaptation is for success: "The one who knows about the necessity to adopt, is wise and aware of divine things".

Amo experienced only a short relatively carefree time. On the 10th of May, 1733, his appearance as a person responsible for the solemn reception of the university for August III, Elector of Saxony and newly crowned King of Poland on the occasion of his visit in Wittenberg, belongs without doubt to the highlights of Amo's life. This social event, which was described in detail in the journal *Hamburg Reports about Academic Matters*, is a proof of his high standing in those years. It is possible, but there is no evidence that he was appointed Court Counsellor in Berlin. It was getting more and more difficult for the African scholar after the decline of Wolff's philosophy and the death of his friends and long-time patrons. He felt that the rising discrimination did not leave any further career prospects for him at the university and consequently he lived in extreme poverty.

More and more often he thought about returning to his African home, which was no home anymore. How should he have lived in a country he had had no connection with since he was four years of age? A country, where he would not have been able to talk with the people: German, Latin, Greek, Hebrew, Dutch and French would not have gotten him anywhere. He was not sure whether he still had a family in the Gold Coast, his country of origin.. He decided to persevere.

In the year 1747, a notable event happened. The fifty-year-old had fallen in love with a woman and he proposed marriage to her. This revelation of his feelings to her proved to be a serious mistake because she obviously passed the letters on. On 23rd October, 1747, an advertisement for poems was published in the journal *Halle Weekly Advertisements*, and later a book was published with excerpts from the exchange of letters between him and this woman. Amo was exposed to public mockery. Prominent points from the woman's answer could be found in the advertisement. Amo was not only rejected but also subjected to severe racist insults. It read in allusion to his education: "Nothing can obscure the fact that you belong to a wild race!"

Amo, who was now isolated, without means and subject to public mockery, realised that there was no place for him in Germany. He turned to the Dutch-West-Indian Company with the request to make his return journey possible. In the same year, he embarked at Rotterdam and travelled to the country of his parents. Only the father and one sister were still alive. He found out that his brother had been kidnapped and taken to Surinam. Amo led the life of a hermit because he could not speak the local language. Europe learned about his last years only in 1782 through a Swiss ship's doctor, who worked for a Dutch shipping company. David-Henri Gallandat talked about the miserable life of the philosopher whom he met in the year 1752 in the then Gold Coast, now Ghana. He said that he had the "reputation of a fortune teller among his own". Amo probably died in 1759 in the Dutch fort Shama. Maybe his stay in the castle was not voluntary: The human traffickers could have seen him as a danger and could have arrested him in the light of the revolts against the Dutch slave traders in Surinam.

In the year 1965, the University of Halle dedicated a Bronze statue to him. "In memory of Anton Wilhelm Amo from Axim in Ghana, the first African student and lecturer of the University of Halle, Wittenberg and Jena 1727 – 1747" is written underneath the statue, which portrays an African couple – for what reason so ever. Strangely enough, the male statue was created with a naked upper body and a long wrap skirt. The *Anton-Wilhelm-Amo-Award* is opposed to the stereotypical picture of the statue. Since 1994, the University of Halle honours special scientific works with this award every year.

Amo's extraordinary and tragic career in Germany appears like a warning. His fate shows how integration can fail because of prejudice, despite best intentions.

Bibliography
Jacob Emmanuel Mabe: *Anton Wilhelm Amo read interculturally.* Nordhausen 2007;
Peter Martin: *Black Devils, Noble Moors. Africans in the consciousness of the German people.* Hamburg 1993.

YENNENGA (Burkina Faso)

THE REBELLIOUS PRINCESS

BY MONIQUE ILBOUDO

This evening, Riaré – *the one who eats everything* – returned without prey. This had happened for the first time since he had arrived in this savanna, which was so rich in game. Three months before, he had pitched camp here, far away from his home because he was hoping for an even more successful hunt. In the past hunting season, he had been chosen as the best elephant hunter of his country. This year, in the absence of the grey giants, he would have been content with smaller game, as the saying goes: "In the absence of the mother's breast, one gladly feeds on the breast of the grandmother". On this day, his disappointment was immeasurable. He was even more frustrated because he had planned to break camp before the beginning of the rainy season. The first clouds had already started to pass by in the sky, and soon the first raindrops would splash on the thirsty savanna. He sat, saddened, in front of the fire which he had lit to warm himself in the chilly evening hours and to grill the guinea fowl, which got trapped near his hunting lodge. It was a silent night. A gentle breeze blew and spread the scent of the roast in the area. "Hopefully, I will not get unwanted guests tonight," he grumbled as hyenas were constantly creeping around his camp.

Suddenly, he heard the neighing of a horse close behind him and he jumped. He turned round and nearly screamed in terror; he, the king of the bush, who did not fear any living creature on earth, as it is said in the songs of the griots of his home. No warrior, no wild animal could frighten him. The griots were not wrong in their songs. However, the appearance in this night was somehow supernatural: a young woman of breathtaking beauty sat high on a horse right behind him. She held a spear in one hand and a rein in the other. Riaré jumped up at once and took one step back from the beautiful appearance. This is surely a forest spirit, he thought. How else could she have surprised him; him, who is called wildcat. His keen ear had saved his life many times, and his ability to stalk his prey soundlessly was legendary.

He asked, "Who are you?"

The answer to this question took the whole night; the horse rider literally uncoiled the thread of her whole life, as if she wanted to gain clarity herself.

"I am called *Yennenga*" – *the slim*. My father, Ndega is the most powerful king of Gambaga (in present day Ghana). My mother, Napoko is the most beautiful woman in the whole country. My father saw her at a feast when he was still a prince and he fell head over heels in love with her. However, he had to wait for three years because she was only fourteen. He married her shortly before he inherited the throne from his deceased father. After that, he had to wait again because my mother did not get pregnant. Other girls were recommended to him again and again because of my mother's failure to conceive. He however hung on to his love. Eventually I was born. As a single child, I was pampered by my mother until my father decided to introduce me to warfare. I was not even ten years old when I was snatched from my mother and confined to the educators – two men and two women, who were under the control of the head of the cavalry.

Tipoko introduced me into the secrets of the plants, whereas Niinda made me understand the basics of culinary art. I learned warfare and horsemanship from both men. At the age of fourteen, I participated in my father's campaigns at first, only in the reserve but soon Gandaogo took me under his wing: he had realised that I could handle spear and lance much better than a spoon and a ladle.

Three years later, when my peers got married, I led my father's cavalry. Gandaogo was fatally injured during one of my father's frequent campaigns against the Malinke: predatory bands who attacked us often because of the wealth in Gambaga."

Riaré flinched inwardly when he heard these words, but he did not let it show. He himself had heard already about King Nedega and his wealthy kingdom. Once, mercenaries had nearly succeeded in recruiting him, to hunt for the treasures of Gambaga. However, he desisted from this adventure and preferred to continue hunting elephants as a hermit in the savanna. The story of the invisible King of Gambaga was known everywhere, but no warrior would have admitted that his troop was put to rout by this delicate young woman. She was so slim that one had to be worried about her any time she made a jerky movement with her arms. Riaré put more wood on the fire to cover up his embarrassment.

The young woman seemed to be exhausted, but she remained on her guard; her hand remained on the lance, which she had put down on Riaré's request. Riaré offered a piece of guinea fowl to her, which she had not touched at all. He had been fascinated so much by her story, and she was not used to eating anything which had been prepared with so little care. Even though she was a warrior, she was still a princess, and she had pages around her in the camps, who served her selected meals.

She thought, "This warrior is still *uncooked*." and smiled imperceptibly about the ambiguity of the expression. In her language, one called single men "uncooked": In the eyes of the Dagomba, it is the woman, who brings the fire into the house, so she civilises the man and transforms his house into a comfortable and hospitable home.

Riaré asked curiously, "How did you come here?"

Yennenga hissed, "I have had enough!"

The hunter did not make any noise, but his body posture said, "But of what?"

The princess said, "At first, I spoke with my mother about it. But in the beginning, she did not really understand my despair. She thought that I would be happy with the life my father determined for me. And in a certain sense, I had been very happy. Though I envied my friends when they got married, I was grateful to my father for sparing me that fate, which was contrary to my dreams; for three years after her marriage, I saw Kibsa, my childhood friend.

She was very worn out and when she had to take care of her first child, she was already pregnant with a second one. Her husband belonged to the comrades, who got carried away after victorious battles and plundered and raped. My father punished such abuses severely. The unit leaders however, tolerated them as an outlet to keep up the morale of the troop. The longer I was in my father's army, the more conscious I became that this kind of life would not satisfy me permanently. Therefore, my mother suggested that I sow *gombo* - okra. This would attract the attention of my father.

"You sow it directly at the entrance of the palace, and you do not harvest it, even when every stalk dries up. One day, it will catch your father's eye, and he will want to know, who had done such a senseless thing." I followed my mother's advice. One morning, my father sent for me.

He asked, "Why did you let your gombo dry up?" My mother had prepared me with a fitting answer to this question.

So I said, "Father, you are right. Gombo has to be eaten fresh; this one here is inedible now. It is like a young girl, who was not allowed to get married, and grew old in the house of her parents. My father thought for a moment, while his gaze wandered over the roofs of the palace and the trees. After that, he left without a word and sighed. I could not read this sigh. I was not surprised that he had not reacted at once because the king never spoke without having thought for a long time. He used to say, "A word is like water.When it has been spilled, it cannot be collected anymore." I waited for a word or just a hint from my father about my gombo field for days, weeks, months. However, nothing came from him. After that, we had to fight against the Malinke again. My father sent me out with troops, which were more than ready to go because they were not used to long lulls in combat. Two weeks before, I had returned victoriously from this campaign."

A dreadful giggle out of the darkness brought the princess to a halt. Both of them knew that it was just a hyena but it made them shudder. The fire flickered and revealed the profile of the young woman. She was really beautiful. This tender skin, this small, trembling nose, this anxious mouth!

Everything in this profile awakened an irrepressible desire in him to pull the princess towards him, to hug her, to protect her. However, he did not dare to do so. Who would dare to take Nedega's daughter into his arms without his permission? Riaré's heart raced and it was hammering in his temples like on a war drum. "So beautiful and yet so rebellious!" he thought and took his eyes off her. "A bit clumsy..." thought Yennenga,

185

who now for her part looked closely at the face of the hunter.

"However, he gives me the impression that he is honest. His eyes were big, but not completely open; his thick lips indicated a small smile, which made them gentle. Only the big snub nose was in discordant note in the quite sympathetic face." They were both quiet now and lost in their thoughts.

Why did she bring her horse in a wild gallop exactly here? Was this the hand of fate? Yennenga remembered Tipoko's words that morning. This woman, who introduced her into the secrets of plants, knew even darker secrets she did not like to reveal. Tipoko could talk to the ancestors, and see the souls of humans, which were still cheerfully eating and laughing. She could foretell attacks against the kingdom as well as the future of everybody whose hand she shook. Therefore, everybody knew that one did not extend their hand to the old woman unless she did it herself. Some would even refuse to shake her hand when she offered it, but their fear that she would lay a curse on them was greater. The king was the only one who was looking for Tipoko's handshake. In this case, the old woman indicated the usual formal curtsey, to kiss the feet of the ruler for her part, as all other subjects did. The king however always lifted her up before she bent her knees, which were stiff because of rheumatism. Then Tipoko whispered in his ears what would happen in the near future. The king's face however did not reveal whether it was something pleasant or unpleasant.

"At that time, Tipoko took my hands at every opportunity but she did not reveal anything to me. This annoyed me extremely, but I soon understood that my father's decisions regarding me were based on her advice and her predictions. I kept out of Tipoko's way when I had to think day and night about marriage. I did not want her to take my hands and tell me straight that my dreams would never be fulfilled."

Riaré admired the long *lampé* made out of black and white woven cotton fabric, black shorts and a top, which covered the delicate breasts, shimmering beneath. He was sure that this was no battle dress, even though he had never seen a uniform for a woman: where he came from - no woman would have ever dared to get involved in combat! Yennenga was so lost in her thoughts that he gave a little cough to bring her back. When she turned to him to continue with her story, her gaze was caught by the amulets, which covered part of his arms and filled the hunter with joy.

"This morning," the princess continued," before Tipoko burst into my room, I knew that it was the right day because Timoaga, the visionary, gave my mother a hint. She had asked him for advice because Tipoko wrapped herself in silence. He had said that I should leave the palace to find the answers to my questions. He said I should saddle Ouédraogo very early, as I always did and I should let the stallion guide me. It would take me to the answers I was looking for. After getting up, I was supposed to ride in the direction of the sunrise. The first person I would meet would have the answer to my questions. Therefore, Tipoko came to me this morning and gave me an amulet, which was different from those I received before actions from her; then she said only one sentence, before she left the still dusky room as fast as she had entered, 'Do not worry, the spirits of our ancestors will lead the steps of your horse.' Why did she say 'the steps of your horse' and not 'your steps'? Is a horse independent of the one who holds the reins?

Silence fell across both of them while she thought about this question again. Riaré wanted to suggest that the princess could stay overnight in his hunting lodge. The thought of the rustic furnishing though and the lack of communication made him hesitate. After mulling over this for a long time, he did not see any other possibility. Therefore, he dared to ask, "May I prepare the mat in my hut for you?" and he hastened to add, "I will sleep outside."

Yennenga looked at him, but her eyelids had become so heavy that he did not fear her disagreement and went inside his hut to clear up.

The next morning, the princess, who came back from her morning ride, woke Riaré up. How could she have untied a horse without him noticing it? His pride was hurt once again. Now he knew how the young woman could surprise whole armies and rout them. He helped her to get down, slightly embarrassed and tied the horse to the Néré tree, which was some metres further away. The princess had not come back empty-handed. Berries and leaves were hanging on one side of her *Lampé*. The hunter would not have considered them edible despite his familiarity with the plants. She sparked off the fire again with Riaré's only bowl. In her shoulder bag she found flour inside and ingredients, with which she prepared a tasty breakfast.

After any unsuccessful hunt the previous day, before sunrise on the following day before sunrise, Riaré always went to the big pond, where it was easy for him to catch something. He did not like to do this because he preferred the real hunt where the hunter and the prey had the same chances; but he liked even less the feeling of failure. This morning, when his life as an hermit had been disturbed in such a pleasant way, he did not feel the need to compensate for yesterday's disappointing experience at all. Actually, the princess was so impressed by the trophies that he could not withstand the temptation to tell her at length about his numerous hunting adventures.

The nightfall surprised them and they sat at the fireplace again. However, this time, the cooking pot on the fire received a new task. The princess showed the other side of her education and to his great joy, the ascetic hunter realised that she did not only master the arts of war.

For three nights, Riaré watched over the sleep of the princess. He stayed awake for so long as his eyes would stay open. After this he would wake up when Yennenga returned from her morning ride. On the fourth night, the princess came out and proposed that he should sleep in the hut. The howling of the hyenas, which sounded closer, served her as a welcome excuse. Riaré could not refuse such a beautiful offer. They both knew that they would not be able to sleep like brother and sister beside each other because the conversations of the past days had brought them closer together. After the first night together, both were convinced that they belonged together. Nine months later, they had a son. They named him Ouédraogo in honor of the stallion who guided Yennenga to the crossroads of both of their lives.

Meanwhile, the king and his court had given up the search for the princess. Some urged the king to conduct the funeral service, but he could not bring himself to declare his beloved daughter dead, especially not after what he had learned from Tipoko. Seeing the king's despair, the clairvoyant had told the king a few days later that his daughter was not dead but that she wanted to go her own way. The king had besieged Tipoko with questions but she did not want to give away more. In his desperation, he let his followers look for the apple of his eye in the whole area. They looked everywhere in the range of a day's ride, but in vain. The king became more and more mournful and his kingdom was more and more in danger.

At some point, the queen forced her husband to marry her niece, who had just turned seventeen. The wedding celebration lasted a whole week but the king did not celebrate whole-heartedly because the queen was the motivating force. Her generous proposal however was soon an effective therapy. Before the end of the forty days, which the bridal couple traditionally spends together, Nedega's unique laughter could be heard again. The whole of Gambaga heaved a sigh of relief, and nearly everything was like before. From time to time, the king's face darkened, and then it seemed as if he would not realise anything anymore. Even when he received guests, it happened that he all of a sudden seemed absent-minded, and then, as swiftly as this condition occurred, he would suddenly come back to his senses and continue with the conversation, as if nothing had happened. The situation improved when the young bride gave birth to a boy, who was followed by three brothers and two sisters. Even the queen flourished slowly again, having gotten very lean after her daughter had gone away. She took such great care of her niece's children that the fertility gods honoured themselves once again: To the great joy of the king, who never neglected his companion of his younger years, she gave birth to two boys.

A few years later, late in the night, a couple with a ten-year-old boy arrived in Gambaga and asked for shelter for the night in the first house. The next morning, the father of the family, a veteran of the king's army, came to the strangers and recognised the lost princess. He informed the chamberlain immediately, who assured himself personally, before passing on the message to the king. Nedega was very impatient to see his daughter again, but he had to control his feelings and he had to comply with the regulations

After all, Yennenga had committed a serious offence, when she turned her back on the community. A ram and several chickens had to be sacrificed for the return of the lost daughter to appease the ancestors. Since Tipoko now belonged to the ancestors, whose consent had to be obtained, her competitor Timoaga had to conduct the ceremony. In the evening, he brought the good news to the king. It was not until the next day that a royal delegation could come for the princess and her family, the host family, who were now Riare's family, belonged to them. The inhabitants of Gambaga welcomed the princess befittingly. Many tears flowed in the royal family. The queen Napoko cried so much that her two small sons desperately tried to comfort her. Only the king managed to keep his eyes dry. However, a revealing teardrop escaped him when he embraced his daughter.

For a whole year, the princess stayed in Gambaga. Her father allowed an even bigger wedding celebration to take place than when he got married to Napoko's niece. He overwhelmed her with royal gifts, gave her an army with the offer to allow her to return to the location of her first meeting with Riaré and establish a new kingdom. This is how the *Mogho-nation,the people of the savanna,* emerged; the descendants of a capable hunter and a rebellious princess: the Mossi!

Ouédraogo became a feared warrior. He inherited the throne from his mother and expanded the *Tenkodogo, motherland, country of origin,* by many areas. With Yennenga's support, he established a functioning administration in the upper regions. His son, Zoungrana, continued with the expansion of the empire and improved the political and social organisation so that his descendants were in a position to rule over a stable and prosperous kingdom. Oubri (1182 – 1244), the son of Zoungrana and Poutoènga, the bearded woman, became a great reformer. After the cry for help of the Nyonyonse and the Teng-bissi, his territory also included other regions: among others, Kudugu and Wagadugu, the capital of present day Burkina Faso. The typical scars, which served as distinctive marks, stem from Oubri. They saved the Mossi from being trafficked by the Europeans (because they were considered as damaged goods).

One after the other, Yennenga's descendants built an empire, to which the best political and social organization in Africa belonged. Yennenga's story is the founding myth of the Mossi and furthermore a symbol for the pride of a nation, Burkina Faso. Thus, the award of the film festival of the FESPACO (Pan African film festival of Wagadugu) shows her stallion. In the collective memory, Yennenga stands for resistance against obedience, which is demanded from the women of the former Mossi Empire until today.

MBUYA NEHANDA   (Zimbabwe)

SPIRIT MEDIUM OF THE SHONA
BY TENDAI HUCHU

There is a grainy, old, black and white photograph in which Mbuya Nehanda stands next to Sekuru Kaguvi, their shadows striking a mud brick wall against which they are standing. The camera takes their photograph from an angle at the side, almost as though fearful of confronting them head on. Nehanda's dress is a simple length of cloth wrapped round her body, knotted at the shoulder. She is barefooted and her sole adornment is a simple chain of beads around her neck. Her fingers are interlocked, her hands placed around her navel, as she looks into the distance, serene. The only indication of her discomfort is the slight knitting of her brow, which may just be because she is facing the sun. Kaguvi beside her, is a tall, slender man, his feet slightly apart, wearing a waist cloth wrapped round him, staring defiantly into the distance.

This is one of those interesting photographs in which what you see inside the photograph is perhaps as interesting as what lies in the margins, outside of the shot. No doubt around these two figures was an army of white men, the British, with their guns and weapons of conquest and destruction, the full might of the empire brought down against these two people.

On 12th, September, 1890, the British planted their flag in Fort Salisbury, (now known as Harare), and the process of colonisation, at least as far as they were concerned, was complete. The British, who had gained a foothold in South Africa by smashing the Zulu Empire, now pushed up across the Limpopo, tricking the Ndebele king, Lobengula, in the south, into signing the Rudd Concession which they used to legitimise their colonial enterprise. The main column on this enterprise was driven by promises of claims of gold which was said to be plentiful on the new country's plateau.

The first rebellion against the new order was by the Ndebele people in 1893. King Lobengula had launched a punitive raid, to extract tribute, against a Shona chief, who now lived in a British controlled area. Sensing this as a threat to their control of the area, the whites retaliated, arguing that they were protecting the 'peaceful' Shona tribe from the 'warlike' Ndebele tribe, and though the whites were greatly outnumbered by Lobengula's Impis, their superior weaponry, especially the Maxim machine gun, proved decisive. They destroyed Lobengula's capital, Bulawayo, but failed to capture Lobengula who they pursued for months. Though they failed to capture him, Lobengula died of small pox in January 1894 which paved way for his senior Indunas (Military Commanders) to negotiate a peace treaty, and the terms of their subjugation under the British.

The country was officially named Rhodesia because of the work done by Cecil John Rhodes to facilitate its colonisation. Within months of the Ndebele defeat, work was already underway to build telegraph poles and railway lines with the ultimate aim of linking Cape Town and Cairo.

During this earlier period, Nehanda was supportive of good relations between the white pioneers and the Shona people in the north. The Shona, who had had large empires wealthy on trade in the past, such as the Great Zimbabwe Empire and the Munhumutapa Empire, assumed that the initial modest influx was of white people were traders coming to the country and would leave with time. There is evidence that these early white settlements were not resisted.

Nehanda was a *svikiro*, spirit medium, for the Shona people, living in the Mazowe hills, twenty five miles outside of Harare, an area under the chiefs Wata and Chidamba. Traditional Shona states had a separation of powers between the chiefs on one hand, who dealt with civil, political matters, and on the other, spirit mediums who dealt with religious matters and advised the chiefs on important matters. This was a system of checks and balances that ultimately helped to moderate the powers of the chiefs and reduce the risk of despotism. The Shona believed that the land and everything in it belonged to the ancestors, who allowed their descendants to use it, but only insofar as traditional values were maintained through elaborate rituals that linked the living to the dead. Thus under this system, land could never be owned by any individual, only the right to use it could be granted by the chiefs who were acting as the living representatives and the embodiment of the authority of the ancestors. Within this cosmology, it was important for the mediums, who were the direct link between the living and the dead, to instruct the chiefs and to warn them should they overstep the boundaries set by the ancestors. There was also a secondary system of elders who sat in the *dare* to advise each chief.

Shona religion believed that there was one God called Mwari, who was the owner of everything. He was also known by the titles Musikavanhu – The Creator of Man and Nyadenga – He of the skies, among others. To communicate with Mwari, it was essential to go through the ancestors, a chain that linked the youngest, most recently deceased, to the next ancestor up, through a long, timeless chain leading to the first man. For a supplicant to go directly to Mwari would have been grossly disrespectful and blasphemous since he was all powerful and remote. The link between the living and these ancestors were the mediums, though ceremonies could still be held for the ancestors without them.

Nehanda would have begun her life as an ordinary child in a traditional Shona family. As she grew up, she would have had no idea that she was going to become a medium. This was because the gift of being a *svikiro* was bestowed by the ancestors on whomever they chose. It was not passed down in a set family or lineage. As a child, Nehanda would have suffered unexplained illnesses and misfortunes, until she was seen by another medium to confirm she had the gift. Most mediums in Shona religion are minor mediums in that they communicate with lesser spirits, ancestors recently deceased and so their powers are limited and their recognition is only tied to their particular village or chieftainship under which they practise. Nehanda was specifically a *mhondoro*, that is, a spirit descended from royal lineage, the lion spirit, which means that her influence would have been nationwide.

The 1840-1898 *mhondoro* was a later incarnation of an earlier

Nehanda. Her own identity was obliterated and subsumed under that of the Nehanda spirit. This spirit was first recognised in the Mutapa Empire which ruled most of modern Zimbabwe and huge chunks of modern Mozambique between 1430 and 1760. This empire was the direct successor of the Great Zimbabwe Empire, and was connected to it both politically and culturally. The Mutapa Empire was also a trading empire, trading gold and ivory along the coast which ultimately was trade between the Mutapa Empire and India.

The first Nehanda, originally called Nyamhika, was the daughter of Nyatsimba Mutota who was the first ruler of the Mutapa Empire. It is said that Mutota ordered his son, Matope, to commit incest with his half-sister Nyamhika to increase the power of his clan. This incest is said to have increased the power of Matope and the size of his empire, so much so that he handed a sizable portion of his empire to Nehanda to govern as his co-ruler, thus formalising the duality between the medium and the king. Nehanda became a powerful spirit that endured in many different human incarnations over a five-hundred-year span. The mediums performed ceremonies to ensure that the rains fell and for good harvests, they were also required to make oracular pronouncements. They also served as oral historians, recording the names and deeds of past kings, thus establishing themselves as a crucial link between the people and their past. The empire expanded and increased its influence on the Zimbabwean plateau, until it collapsed because of infighting and succession disputes. By the 1700s, the Portuguese had a firm foothold on the Mozambican coast and because various principalities vying for power in the Mutapa kingdom hired Portuguese mercenaries to fight on their behalf, this had a destabilising effect on the empire, especially as the Portuguese used these arrangements to increase their own influence, and interfere with the lucrative Mutapa-Indian trade. By 1760, because of these constant civil wars, the empire finally collapsed, leaving the Shona people with no real centralised state, but a patchwork of chiefdoms who were not united enough to be able to resist foreign domination, as evidenced by the success of the Ndebele in capturing the south of the country, and of course the movement of the white people into the country that shortly followed.

Nehanda, in the early 1890s was initially supportive of the white settlers, encouraging her people to trade with them and to even give them welcoming gifts. The white people of course misinterpreted this goodwill as a sign that the Shona were grateful to them for having subdued the Ndebele, and thus the Shona would be content to live under white domination. This was a misinterpretation of the relationship between the Shona and Ndebele at the time. While the Ndebele did launch regular raids into Mashonaland to capture cattle and produce, in certain areas there was co-operation, and some Southern Shona groups were absorbed into the Ndebele tribe. The Ndebele also accepted the Shona Religion and consulted with Shona mediums, in particular the Matonjeni shrine in the Matopos, which had been the seat of an earlier Shona empire, the Rozvi. Therefore while it offered the colonialists some moral justification for their conquest, the truth was that the relationships between these two tribes were complex and evolving.

As white settlers began to increase on the land, and their confidence grew, following the defeat of the Ndebele, they began to impose taxes, and began taking people for forced labour. They also began expelling the Shona from their ancestral lands and forcing them to relocate into harsh, dry parts of the country, ill-suited to their agricultural economy. The tension was not helped by the drought, locusts and rinderpest that devastated the country.

In March 1896, Mlimo, the Ndebele spiritual leader convinced the Ndebele that these problems were a sign that the white settlers should no longer be tolerated. The Ndebele had already lost a great herd of cattle after the first rebellion, cattle being the main form of wealth in this part of the country. This war was initially called by some sources as the Second Matebele War, which was inaccurate, as the Shonas, particularly in the south, also heeded Mlimo's call. This shocked the British, who came up with the excuse that the 'peaceful' Shona only joined in the war fearful of Ndebele reprisals should the Ndebele win. Again they failed to see the link between their occupation and the resistance.

In the first week of this war, now more accurately termed the first Chimurenga, over two hundred settlers in both Matebeleland and Mashonaland were killed. Their homes, mines and businesses were burnt and destroyed. The aim of the resistance was not genocide, Mlimo asked that the Mangwe Pass west of the Matopos be kept open so that the settlers who wanted to flee would be free to do so. The structures set up by the colonialists quickly began to disintegrate, and the Native policemen they had hired deserted in droves.

The Ndebele in the south besieged Bulawayo, which by then had become a large settler town. It is important to note that in the absence of a king, since none had been chosen since Lobengula died, both the Ndebele and Shona accepted the leadership of Mlimo, the medium. This goes to demonstrate just how important the mediums were in these African states. Crucially though, the Ndebele neglected to cut the telegraphs from Bulawayo. This allowed the besieged town to call for outside help which duly came through the Mangwe Pass which they had kept open, and so the Ndebele were forced back by a superior force from South Africa. The turning point for the war in the south came when a Zulu informant told the whites of Mlimo's whereabouts and two men, Burnham and Armstrong, successfully assassinated him in his sacred cave while he was doing his sacred dance. With their spiritual leader dead, Rhodes had no difficulty in convincing the remaining Ndebele Indunas to lay down their arms.

In Mashonaland, in the North, the war was not settled so quickly. In June 1896, Mazowe Native Commissioner Pollard was captured and his death ordered by Nehanda Nyekasikana. Again, as in the south, in the absence of a strong central ruler, Nehanda stepped in to fill the role of military leader of the Shona people. In this she was joined by the male medium, Kaguvi. Their joint voices were accepted by the Shona as the voice of Mwari. Their call to arms was taken up by chiefs Gwabayana, Makoni, Mapondera, Mangwende and Seke, most prominent among many others. With the Ndebele defeated in the south, the white settlers could now concentrate their forces and lead them north to fight the strong Shona holdfasts.

The Shona resistance was not as centrally organised as the Ndebele resistance, which enabled the settlers with their superior weaponry to suppress the Shona chiefs one by one, where they had not united their military strength. Although the British deaths in the war were numerically less, they represented one tenth of their population. A warrant for Nehanda's arrest was issued in 1897 and she managed to evade arrest for a year, until she was captured and brought to trial for the murder of Native Commissioner Pollard. Kaguvi was also brought to trial, and condemned for his role in the resistance. When Nehanda was sentenced to death by hanging, her last words were, "My bones will rise again". This was a prediction for the Second Chimurenga, and the whites did not understand that they were killing a single incarnation of a spiritual entity that would always endure.

The legacy of this Nehanda Nyekasikana was in that she provided inspiration for future generations to resist white domination. The gospel of resistance did not die with her, and in actual effect, her death served only to martyr her. For the next seventy years, the British consolidated their rule in the country. They took on more forced labour of the indigenous people. They imposed more taxes, there was a hut tax, cattle tax, dog tax, bicycle tax. These were all measures to destroy indigenous wealth and to reduce the people to a life of servitude, where they had to work for the whites in order to pay for their taxes. In this time, the British annexed greater parts of the country taking fertile lands and pushing the black people into dry, arid lands ill-suited for farming. This was the main grievance of the people, and for one hundred years, remained one of the key causes for dispute in the nation.

As a larger black population settled in the cities as labour for the white regime, the loci of resistance shifted from the chiefs in the rural areas to a young, educated leadership in the city. The powers of the chiefs were limited, and their ability to act compromised because their authority, which was traditionally derived from the ancestors, now rested with the Rhodesian state. Thus as they were co-opted as agents of the state, it was difficult for them to act against it. This position also helped the Rhodesians to resist the voices of the young resistance leadership by arguing that they were not the authentic voice of the black people, but that this role belonged to the chiefs.

After the Second World War it was becoming increasingly untenable for the British to hold most of their colonies in Africa. When Ghana became independent, this increased calls in Rhodesia for independence and democracy, which meant giving the vote to the disenfranchised blacks. These calls were resisted by the white government which instead, wanted to follow the path of 'separate development' very similar to apartheid in South Africa. While there are indications that Britain was amenable to the eventual self-determination of its colony, and desegregation of its racist power structures, the whites in Rhodesia, under Ian Smith, pre-empted any moves towards this direction by a unilateral declaration of their independence. This aggressive scenario left no real options for the black leadership to negotiate a peaceful transition to majority rule, especially since the white leadership became more aggressive in their efforts to eradicate opposition by arresting the nationalist leadership and banning political parties.

On 28th April, 1966 the Battle of Chinhoyi signalled the beginning of the Second Chimurenga, nearly seventy years after the death of Nehanda. Nehanda again found prominence as an inspiration behind the struggle and this war was seen as a continuation of her efforts, and the fulfilment of her prophecy that her bones would rise again. The war was a long and bitter struggle, with many losses on both sides. In 1972, the spirit of Nehanda found a new medium in an elderly woman who was whisked to safety by the liberation forces. This incarnation, known as Nehanda of Dande is credited with giving guerrillas who passed through the Zambezi region instructions on how to navigate its forests, what food to eat in the area, which parts of the forest were safe to rest in and which parts were safe to fight from, and also, how to interpret the various signs that the forest would yield. She was consulted on military strategy, and took on an important religious, cultural role, further cementing the legitimacy of the armed struggle. Her prophecies also played an important role in the independence movement's decisions. This incarnation of Nehanda died in 1973. The war was to rage on for another seven years, until the victory of the black, nationalist forces, and a negotiated settlement which led to the end of white minority rule, and the establishment of the modern state of Zimbabwe.

Nehanda's memory is now a key part of Zimbabwe's historical discourse, and this memory of a female leader in a patriarchal society is very important to Zimbabwean women. Modern Zimbabwe remembers Nehanda today, and honours her with streets named after her, through visual arts, and literature. She remains one of the most important historical figures in the nation, representing a link between past and present. Today the government of Zimbabwe recognises an incarnation of Nehanda called the Karoi Nehanda but her popularity is waning due to another spirit claiming to be 'real' spirit of Nehanda. It is very difficult to truly legitimise any such claims today, and so there is no real agreement of who the true Nehanda is. Be that as it may, her history, which now serves as a unifying force for the nation, especially in her 1840-1898 manifestation, is likely to be the most important, and most relevant for Zimbabweans today.

Bibliography
Yvonne Vera; *Nehanda*. Roman; Triesen 2000.

KINJIKITILE NGWALE   (Tanzania)

FROM THE POWER OF WATER

BY ABEDNEGO KESHOMSHAHARA

In July 1905, the Maji-Maji war began in present day Tanzania, at that time, German East Africa. It was one of the last large rebellions against the colonial expansion in Africa. It was also one of the most exceptional because it was based on the spiritual persuasion of the prophet Kinjikitile Ngwale ("It has answered me"). He united several peoples in the fight against the German colonial rule with recourse to the traditional religion, and he fought for the right of the Africans for self-determination and for their land. Although he could call the population in the South of Tanzania to resistance only for one month, the war continued for more than two years after his death and it ultimately led to a reformation of the colonial administration, which kept the suppression down in at least some areas.

Several uprisings against the colonial conquerors proceeded without success; in the Maji -Maji war between 1891 and 1897 alone, the German "protection force" carried out sixty-one so-called punitive expeditions to "pacify" the area. Forced labour was the trigger for the intensive opposition, as well as a rigorous fiscal policy and the fact that the part of German East Africa, which is Tanzania today, was a colony, where Europeans settled. These were blatant breaches of law in the eyes of the indigenous people. Plantations were created at places where the soils seemed arable. Moreover, the Africans were forcibly recruited to work on the cotton plantations and carry out assistance services in the colonial army and the administration for very low pay. The indigenous people had to pay head tax and the so-called shack duty unlike the German settlers, who received support from the colonial administration.

The arrogant behaviour of representatives of the German East African Company, which was since 1884, entrusted with the security of the German sovereignty, led to the uprising of the coastal community, which means the Arabs and Swahili in the towns of Bagamoyo, Tanga, Mikindani, Pangani and Kilwa, even before the colonial rule had been officially established. The uprising was suppressed by the Germans with the help of soldiers from Zululand, Somalia, Sudan and Turkey, as well as by a British naval blockade.

At the beginning of 1891, after the fall of the German East African Trading Company and an alignment of interests with Great Britain, the colony of German East Africa was founded, and at the same time the second big war against the colonial power took place.

On 17 th August, 1891, the protection force battalion, Zelewski, which was much better armed, suffered a crashing defeat near Lugola (near today's Iringa) by Mkwawa, the Chief of the Hehe, with his army of two thousand men. Only the rest of the battalion was able to flee and report. Mkwawa intervened because the battalion had set villages and farmsteads on fire in the course of advancement from the coast to the interior. In the following year, Mkwawa fought a fierce guerilla war against the troop. The Germans replied with the tactic of scorched earth. In 1894, Mkwawa escaped the attack on the town. However, he shot himself in 1898, in order not to fall into the hands of his enemies.

The Germans had even antagonized the Wamatumbi with this terror. These neighbouring peoples of the Hehe had always gotten along well with them for more than a decade. They beat every German, who they met with sticks because they were enraged about the forced labour, which was imposed on them. In 1896, the colonial administration forbade the Wamatumbi to carry sticks with them. Thereupon, the Wamatumbi changed their tactic: they started the *ngondo ya mayawa*, the "war of the pumpkins." Whenever they met a German, they threw pumpkins at him or beat him.

Detentions and executions followed. The protests died down

thereupon and the Wamatumbi gave up in recognition of their defeat. A healer with the name Kinjikitile Ngwale appeared in this hopeless situation, who would free the Wamatumbi and other ethnic groups, who had been suppressed by the Germans. He was reputed to be able to tame wild animals such as snakes and lions. Until June/July 1904, he was an unobtrusive man from Ngarambe in the territory of the Matumbi, where he lived off agriculture like everybody else with his wives and children. One day, according to the oral tradition, he was possessed by a spirit, and he crawled into the river Rujiji, where he disappeared. Two days later, he emerged from the water with medicine from plant roots, which could reputedly weaken the force of the bullets, and could turn them into water. According to another tradition, he came back three days later with a message from the ancestors. They had shown compassion for their descendants, who were being tortured continuously by the Germans, and they had revealed a remedy to him, which could defeat them - it would transform bullets into water. The message spread amongst the Wamatumbi orally. It said that the ancestors were alive, were with god, and Kinjikitile was used by them as a medium between them and the population. In this message, the healer did neither refer to Christian religion, which was spread by the missionaries, nor did he refer to the religion of the Arabians, who had enslaved the Africans for centuries, but he referred to the traditional African religion.

The people came from far away to see him in his village Ngatambe. He encouraged the different ethnicities in a festive ceremony to unite because they could only defeat the Germans as a unit. He also spoke to them of the power of the *maji*. When the rainy season began and the way to Ngarambe became inaccessible, Kinjikitile sent out messengers to bring the *maji* to the surrounding ethnic groups. In the course of the year 1905, the message reached nearly the whole south of present-day Tanzania and spread into the north of river Rujiji, even up to the southern shore of Lake Victoria. About twenty ethnicities joined the movement.

Kinjikitile's prophetic message strengthened the determination of the people to put up a fight against the Germans. The Wamatumbi vented their anger by plucking out the cotton sprouts, by burning the fields and by refusing to pick the cotton. The actual war began on 31st July, 1905, when followers of Kinjikitile killed the German planter, Hopfer, with an axe. On his part, he had shot four Wamatumbi in the fight.

The war against the Germans continued, though it was clear now that the *maji* did not work. Kinjikitile explained that the dead persons must have made a mistake. Either they must have applied the *maji* in a wrong-way or they must have had too little trust in its effect. The belief in the power of the magic water actually remained so great that it furthermore mobilised thousands of people against an all-powerful enemy.

The Germans learnt from the experience with Mkwawa and did not tolerate another powerful leader and they avoided another long war. In a month, at the end of August 1905, they had caught the prophet and hanged him. In the same week, the biggest battle of the Maji-Maji war took place near Mahenge. Several thousand warriors attacked the German station, which defended itself with machine guns. The heavy casualties on the side of the Africans had far-reaching consequences: The unity of the insurgents broke down; the tactic of war changed on both sides. The Africans switched to a guerilla warfare, and the Germans' response to that was again the tactic of the scorched earth.

A new awareness was the result of Kinjikitile's call, and this political spirit carried the rise far beyond the grave of the healer. At first, the colonial power could not defeat the rebels. The Germans had to request support from the motherland and they needed help from the British who sent soldiers from their colonies Kenya and South Africa, and from other Tanzanian peoples, who took sides with the Germans. The Maji-Maji war still lasted two years longer despite this large military contingent. In July 1908, the last leaders were executed.

The consequences of the war were devastating. Approximately 120, 000 Africans died; some died during the fighting; others of hunger and and of diseases. The systematic destruction of the farmsteads and settlements, the burning down of the fields and the forests did not only lead to famine but it also destroyed seeds and crops for years to come. Fields remained uncultivated because many men did not return from the war and the agricultural area turned to steppe.

Hunger, diseases and the loss of younger men caused the dropping of the birth rate by one quarter. Not until after the independence of Tanzania in 1961 was the same density of population before the Maji-Maji war reached. The devastation in the war zone impeded the continuation of planned infrastructural measures such as the building of roads and the construction of railways, which even today slow down a comparable development in the North of Tanzania.

The colonial policy changed under governor von Rechenberg (1906-

1912). His administrative reform led to the possibility of indigenous people becoming village leaders. They could control their villages themselves and were no longer restricted by non-local Africans or Arabians. The training opportunities were improved; trained Africans replaced the traditional chiefs more and more and they were also more often employed as civil servants in the German colonial administration. In 1907, the forced labour was restricted to national building projects and remuneration was paid. The farmers were encouraged to cultivate their own fields instead of working on plantations. The heavy leather whip made from hippopotamus or rhinoceros skin was forbidden. Rechenberg believed that content colonial subjects, who could bring their products to the market at fair prices, would increase the agricultural production. Moreover, Africans with money preferred being consumers of industrial products made in Germany.

In any case, the Maji-Maji war was an identity-creating event in the development of the Tanzanian society. Indeed, the people in the south of Tanzania could not continue the war against the Germans with weapons, but after the defeat, they realised that only education, a constitution and the dialogue with the Europeans could achieve freedom. Kinjikitile's encouragement to organise joint resistance was in this respect a milestone on the long way to Tanzania's independence.

Bibliography
Felicitas Becker / Jigal Beez (editors): *The Maji-Maji War in German East Africa 1905-1907*. Berlin 2005;
Jigal Beez: *Bullets to Water Drops. Socio-religious aspects of the Maji-Maji War in German East Africa*.Cologne 2003.

NTEMI MIRAMBO   (Tanzania)

THE "AFRICAN BONAPARTE"

BY MSAFIRI MBILU

King Mirambo from the people of the Nyamwesi is a myth, a symbol for the resistance against the foreign rule, a great historical name in the countries of East Africa, especially in Tanzania. President Julius Nyerere put his audience in the mood for his speech in 1962 in Tabora after the liberation from the colonial rule with a well-known battle-song: *Uhuu! Chumu chabela mitwe!* Oh, iron broke their heads! Of course, he had converted the text, so that it suited his Party, TANU.

However, during Mirambo's lifetime, his name created fear and terror amongst some of his contemporaries: neighbouring nations, which felt threatened by him, Arab traders, caravan guides, European travellers, missionaries and researchers. In their notes, he was given the derogatory names "former load carrier" of the Arabians, who had gained the dignity of a ruler with violence, robber, murderer, burner and despot. At the same time, a kind of respect for him resonates, and when Stanley described his martial fame in the bestseller: *How I found Livingstone*, Mirambo was the talk of the town in Europe. Stanley met the ruler in person during his second trip to Africa in 1876. "A beautiful man with regular facial features, a mild voice, gentle language, with a conduct, that one could call nearly gentle and humble, and at the same time noble and generous".

That is how he describes him. "I had expected to see something like the Mutesa-type; a man, whose outer appearance would reveal his lifestyle, his rank; but this modest man with his steady eyes, with his quiet, in no way flashy, nearly humble appearance and a calm being, which avoids all gestures, presented to the eye nothing of this Napoleonic genius, which he had unfolded for five years in the heart of Unyamwesi, when he harmed the Arabians and their trade and when he doubled the price for ivory. "Obviously, there is more to 'the African Bonaparte', Stanley called him, "than just a mighty warrior".

Mirambo's father was Ntemi (king) of Uyowa, a mini kingdom of Tabora, which belonged to the territory of the Nyamwesi people. Kasanda – that was his father's name – and Nyakasi, his mother, gave him the name Mbula Mtelya, traditionally in honour of his grandfathers. Mbula Mtelya was born approximately in 1840 in the neighbouring Ukune, the home of his mother. It was only later that one of his military leaders called him Mirambo, which means as much as "corpse". What is meant is, "The man, who leaves dead bodies behind him". Such and similar meaningful names were common in those days, as well as even later to motivate one's own people and to threaten one's enemies.

It is not known how Mirambo became Ntemi after his father's death (about 1858); actually, the matrilineal succession applied. Possibly, no nephews existed, and Mirambo was the designated king or he conquered the throne by force. Shortly thereafter, he was even more supported by the army and became king of the nearby Ulyankulu as well. Both tiny countries, in which Nyamwesi, Sukuma and members of small nations lived, overall about ten thousand persons, were soon called Urambo, land of Mirambo.

During the height of his power, Mirambo's territory included a vast area around Tabora in the west of the present-day Tanzania between Lake Victoria and Lake Tanganyika.. The powerful Nyamwesi-empire evolved from the mini kingdom of Uyowa under Mirambo's rule. It was comparable to the kingdom of Buganda, its northern neighbour, in terms of its profile and relevance.

In the 19th century, East Africa was the location of major social changes. The island Zanzibar became the seat of government of the Sultan of Oman, and Arabian trade centre. Plantations for the cultivation of spices and coconut palms were developed on Zanzibar and the East

African coastline. The growing need for workers led to a rapid increase of the slave trade. The net of trade routes from the coastline to the interior of East Africa grew, commercial settlements were founded; the number and size of caravans, which transported slaves and ivory to the coast, as well as weapons and other European goods in the interior, increased constantly. Because of their more powerful weapons, Arabian traders took over the caravan trade virtually completely, which had been in the hands of African traders before. The enforced concentration on slaves and firearms led to an escalation of violence, which had not been known hitherto. At the same time, new working possibilities and horizons of experience arose for the local population with the caravans, which transported large amounts of goods. Also more and more European travellers came to the inland of East Africa, amongst them "discoverers", traders and not least, missionaries, who wanted to stop the slave trade.

The land of the Nyamwesi was inhabited by a large number of tribes, which were connected with each other by socio-cultural and economic relations, but they were politically independent from each other and they fought from time to time, when Mirambo assumed his reign. The trade route passed through this area from the coast to South-Katanga (in present-day Congo). The population lived on agriculture, craft, local trade and on the caravans. The Nyamwesi had a good reputation as carriers; about one-third of the men worked in the caravan trade at the time of Mirambo's death.

It was clear to Mirambo that he needed military strength, if he wanted to assert himself with his small kingdom in the war-torn region. He had probably fallen into the captivity of the Ngoni as a young man. Mirambo learned from the Ngoni, who escaped from the king of the Zulus, Shaka, the English and the Boers from South Africa, and moved the tactics of warfare northwards and started using short spears and clubs, which were introduced as effective weapons by Shaka. He made a pact with them and took the Ngoni and Massai as mercenary soldiers in his army, who became known under the name Ruga-Ruga.

Within three days, Mirambo mobilised ten thousand warriors. The few firearms at first were fired off for the purpose of deterrence in an attack. After that, the Ruga-Ruga pounced on their opponents with piercing screams, in frightening war clothes, cutting and thrusting weapons in their hands.

Mirambo managed to increase his power with this mobile, forceful army. He demanded duty from the caravans, which moved through his territory; he attacked the slave and ivory caravans of the Arabians, which moved to the coast. He divided freed slaves and prisoners of war amongst the Ruga-Ruga and their leaders. They were integrated and had to work as soldiers or in agriculture. After the rainy season, the sowing period, and when the path network was passable, he went to war against neighbouring kingdoms. Once defeated, they were obliged to pay tribute and charges to Mirambo and they received him as Ntemi, a ruler, to whom they were loyal. That is how he created the kingdom of Nyamwesi, a large federation of small kingdoms. Its capital, Isela Magazi, consisted of a fort, residence of ten thousand people and another five thousand citizens settled in the periphery.

His next step was to exercise control over the trade of the Arabians. The headquarters of the Arabians was in Tabora, not far from Urambo. The first "wicked deed" of Mirambo was, as reported by Stanley, "to stop a caravan on the way to Ujiji and to demand from the caravan five barrels of gunpowder, five rifles and five bales of cloth. This exceptional demand was paid for after one day had been spent in the wildest quarrel. He however forced them to turn around and let them know that no Arabian caravan would move to Ujiji (at Lake Tanganyika) as long as he lived. The consequence was a war, which lasted from 1871 to 1876. Even Stanley was included in the war events. The about fifty Arabian traders in Tabora mobilised one thousand two hundred slaves, eight hundred Nyambesi warriors from other local Ntemis. One thousand five hundred of them carried firearms. Their march off to fight Mirambo's residence turned into a foray. Mirambo dodged them with his Ruga-Ruga, so that they dragged off everything they found, ivory, women and children. Mirambo's trap snapped shut on their way back. He burst out of his hiding place and his Ruga-Ruga subdued the enemies, who were hindered by the loads, with great difficulty. The survivors abandoned their prey and returned on detours to Tabora. "Mirambo smashed the Arabs to bits. The rest of their people are running to Tabora", reported the servant, Selim, to Stanley, who had been laid low.

It was the beginning of the end of the time, when the Arabians controlled the trade routes in East Africa.

Even Stanley got so scared of an encounter with the "African Bonaparte" that he accepted a detour of six hundred kilometres and a delay of two months, to get to Ujiji with his caravan, where he was hoping to find David Livingstone. Mirambo advanced with two thousand Ruga-Ruga against Tabora and set fire to the town. After a few days, he withdrew again, because it was not in his interest to drive the Arabian traders away permanently because he believed, that he needed them as a connection to the economic and political centres of Zanzibar and the coast.

The Arabian traders turned to the Sultan. He sent an army of a thousand soldiers from Zanzibar to Tabora. In 1875, they left without having achieved anything because a stalemate had developed. Mirambo never again attacked the Arabians militarily. He pursued completely different strategies in the following ten years preceding his death. He sent his own ivory caravans to the coast but he soon realised that he was lacking the necessary know-how for the marketing of his goods. He therefore searched for a contact to European traders, who were supposed to transact business. They, however, did not justify the confidence he had placed in them. The influence of the Europeans on East Africa, which became more and more noticeable, made him finally understand that he had to get acquainted with European knowledge and techniques, if he wanted to develop the Nyamwesi-Kingdom to a powerful trading empire. The British, the French, Germans and the International African Association of the Belgium, of King Leopold II, competed for colonial pretensions in the East Africa of those years. The most influential European was the British Consul, John Kirk, who served as the advisor of the Sultan of Zanzibar and who made an effort to establish British trade patterns on the mainland. Mirambo turned to Kirk and the Sultan with the help of a trader and offered to bring peace to the caravan routes and to allow the settlement of Europeans in his territory. He judged the balance of power correctly and sent ten ivory tusks to Kirk and only six to the Sultan. He hoped that he would enlarge his political prestige and would get direct access to European goods, especially to rifles, ammunition and fabrics by means of good relations with the British.

The Sultan feared that Mirambo's intention could call the predominance of the Arabian traders into question. Kirk however saw a possible ally for the extension of the British influence on the mainland in the powerful Ntemi; and the London Missionary Society actually founded a station in Urambo. Without knowing it, Mirambo had been made so famous by Stanley's books that more and more Europeans visited him, and he was able to expand his level of knowledge about Europe.

Ebenezer Southon, missionary and doctor of the London Missionary Society, established the missionary station. He lived from 1879 up to his death in 1882, close to Mirambo's residence, and became a friend of the Ntemi. Mirambo instructed Southon with the writings to Kirk and the Sultan, with the establishment of a school and the building of a health centre, where more than a thousand patients were treated annually. To the suggestion to teach the Christian religion to him, he answered however that he would like to continue with his belief. The considerations about how the European techniques could be used for the good of the population were still at the initial stages, when the promising connection with the British Consul suffered a setback in 1880. The British men were killed during a military expedition of Mirambo, and Kirk blamed him for it. The Ntemi undertook several attempts to get the negotiations underway again and explained, "I would like to open my country, to learn from Europeans, to trade honourably with everybody and to maintain peaceful relations with my neighbors." It did not help.

Tippu Tip, an Arabian from Zanzibar had founded a mighty empire, which was based on the trade with slaves and ivory, in the west of Urambo, in the region Maniema in present-day Congo. He was infamous as a cruel hunter and slave trader in the whole of East and Central Africa. According to word of mouth, Tippu Tip's grandfather is supposed to have made Mirambo's grandfather, the Ntemi of Uyowa.

In 1882, Tippu Tip planned to guide a caravan of three thousand men from the Congo to Zanzibar. They handed over slave girls and ivory as presents and offered to care for the safe conduct of the caravan. Mirambo had heard the rumour that Arabians from Tabora would prepare a war against him and he intended to ask Tippu Tip to put in a good word for him to the Sultan. The pact was made during a visit of Zefu bin Mohammed, Tippu Tip's son in Mirambo's capital. Tippu Tip visited Mirambo on his way back. He did not achieve anything on Zanzibar. Kirk remained rigid, the Sultan did not undertake anything against the trading settlement in Tabora. Tippu Tip confirmed to carrying on supporting Mirambo's interests but only polite writings came from Zanzibar.

Several Nyamwesi-vassals fell away from Mirambo. This could already be seen during his last military campaigns, particularly when he was weakened in his conduct of war because of a serious laryngeal illness. He asked the Europeans for medicine but nobody could help him. Mirambo died on 2nd December, 1884. His big empire disintegrated. It had not been a state, but a federation of small kingdoms, which were held together by Mirambo's charisma. Mirambo failed in establishing central administrative structures. The Nyamwesi could not develop a "national consciousness" in the few decades of his rule.

It is tragic that Mirambo died so early, at the age of about forty-five years. He did not have enough time to complete his life journey; no time to draw new conclusions from his political experiences; to give his empire lasting structures and to focus on the future of the Nyamwesi. Had he not died so young, he could have completed this task, which the tradition assigns to the ruler: The Ntemi was the ritual guarantor for the wellbeing of the country and the people. As it is, he remained an unfinished leader. It is also tragic that the Berlin Africa Conference which started the division of Africa amongst the European powers, took place at the time of his death. The German Empire took over the dominion of East Africa on the 20th of November, 1890.

Mirambo stands out because of his vision of political unity in a time of social upheaval. With all his strengths and weaknesses, he remains a personality of Tanzania, who is remembered as a warrior, politician, diplomat and innovative thinker.

Bibliography

Norman Robert Bennett: *Mirambo of Tanzania 1840? – 1884*. New York 1971;

J.B. Kabeya: *King Mirambo. One of the Heroes of Tanzania*. Kampala 1976;

Henry M. Stanley: *How I found Livingstone*. Wiesbaden 1871; *Through the dark part of the world*. Leipzig 1878.

SAMORY TOURÉ (Guinea)

The Lion Of Bissandugu

BY CHEIKH BÂ

Father and son had set off in the early morning hours. It was a special day. For the first time, the eighteen-year-old Samory would close a deal on his own because a Diula could not be introduced early enough to the art of bargaining and negotiating; and the boy's negotiating skills were supposed to spare Laafiya Touré from further business trips. The father gave final instructions and advice during the trip of several hours. With particular emphasis he warned his son to hastily conclude transactions and he reminded him of the most relevant commandment; "An agreement is sacred!" he said emphatically.

A disaster was brewing near their home village Mamyambalandugu (in present day Guinea). A troop of the Cissé prepared themselves for a raid. The Cissé, who were resident in that region interpreted Islam in a fanatical way and had developed an abysmal aversion against the followers of traditional African religions, to which the relatives of Samory's mother belonged. The Cissé bought themselves weapons with what they had captured in the raids. These arms were used in the power struggle against the clan of the Béréré, who were less radical. Not least the Diula traders, who lived dispersed in the respective areas suffered from these feuds between the ruling dynasties. The political reorganisation of the disintegrated great empire of Mali had thrown West Africa into a destructive power struggle.

Samory was put to a tough test on the wholesale market. After he had won through the first traders, who lunged at him in expectation of a favourable bargain, but who, however, had to realise their mistake, he was treated by others like an equal business partner. He had enthused even the most experienced trader with proverbs, which he sprinkled in his speech and with a lot of humour.

The elderly man said on parting, "I do not know, who assigned such a young man with a transaction like this, but somebody knows what he did." Samory accepted the compliment like a certificate and smiled. Father and son set off on their return journey in a good mood.

The sky broke down on them when they arrived in their home village. The events had stirred up everybody. Samory's mother, Soghoma Camara had been abducted by the Cissé. The eighteen-year-old saddled his horse foaming with rage, but also full of worries and galloped to Madina, to the home of the kidnappers. His only weapon was the assurance of the trader, who knew that his offer was compelling and that nobody would turn it down. He let himself be led to the king. "Release my mother and take me captive," he said, confidently but a bit defiant. The king looked surprised at the tall young man and fought against a smile, which was about to appear on his face, due to the unusual daring, which he respected in secret. After a short break, he said with nearly fatherly kindness, "I will make another proposal to you: Both of you will stay here. In return you will not be treated like slaves, and you are allowed to fight in my army." Nobody had to explain to the baffled guest that this was not a proposal, but an order.

Samory learned the art of warfare with great zeal and, studied the Koran and the theoretical writings. His bravery and his interest in the sciences caused the king to be more and more favourably inclined towards him, whereas the king's brother, who was responsible for the raid, let him feel his everlasting hostility. Samory used the state of shock of the court and escaped with his mother, when the king had died after seven years of this strange confinement. The officer, who was now twenty-five years old, knew that only one safe place for him existed: at the arch-enemies of the Cissé, the Bérété. After two years of military service with the Bérété, their leader was killed by a rival, and Samory decided to leave. A high ranking officer like this, who stayed outside of his area of influence, presented a risk for the new ruler. That is why he had Samory arrested under the pretext that he had defrauded payments of tribute and he pilloried him. A friend was able to free him secretly. The second experience with the arbitrariness of rulers finally convinced Samory that something had to be done.

Discontent with the power structures and with their own political insignificance increased strongly amongst the Diula, Samory's people.

In 1861, the representatives accepted Samory's invitation and came together at a conspiratorial meeting. The host followed the unwritten rule of the African rhetoric when he began his speech with a proverb: "One can inflict unscrupulously on an adult, what he permits." He had appealed to the spirit of resistance of each individual with this saying, "Each one of us knows what is going on in our countries" he continued. "It is about time to do something about this". He saw unconditional consent accompanied by deep bewilderment on the faces of his audience. To clear their doubts, he gave a knowledgeable speech about the weaknesses of both dominant armies. In a solemn ritual, Samory was appointed *Kélétigi,* warlord and took the oath, "to protect the Diula against the Cissé and the Bérété." He however, had a far greater project on his mind: a comprehensive political reorganisation of West-Africa.

The treaty of 1861 was an exceptional process: citizens without any political influence and power had decided to take their fate into their own hands and to found a new state. Their confidence is expressed in the hymn of the Wassulu Empire, which owes this revolution its origin. The hymn is a reminder to the ruler; it is an expressive declaration of belief in the basic values of this society instead of a customary homage. So it says:

Turn to more capable men, if you are not capable to lead the land of your fathers'.
Turn to more courageous men, if you are not capable to say the truth anytime and anywhere.
Leave the throne to more just men, if you are not able to be unbiased.
Hand over your sword to the women, and they will show you the way to honor, if you are not able to protect your people and to fight against their enemies.
Let griots speak, if you are not able to express your thoughts without fear.
Ruler, your people trust you, because you embody these words."

Samory's strategical abilities as well as his style of leadership convinced his followers. He turned into an advantage the fact that the

Diula lived scattered throughout various countries, which used to be their weakness, by using the travelling traders as perfect cover, and like this set up an information network, which had never existed before. The foundation of a troop of professional soldiers, the *Sofa*, showed to be even more convincing because they became legendary by means of their physical performance and their defiance of death. Within the shortest time, Samory conquered one place after the other and received the next titles: *Murutigi* – Master of the Sword – and finally *Fama*- Ruler. His successes were based on his leadership style in the first place: the fearlessness of the *Sofa* in the fight was based on the fact that Samory assured them that their families would be taken care of. Samory ensured injured people were cared for; and he went ahead of everybody when danger approached, which made him receive numerous wounds. The *Sofa* experienced a leader who was not thinking about his own well-being, and who was undemanding and modest. During celebrations, he did not wait for others to entertain him, he was rather at the top of the dancing crowd.

Samory wanted to occupy Komodugu without unnecessary fight, just by the mere appearance of his troops, like he had done with many places before. The leader however refused to accept his invitation to the drinking of *Dege*. He who drinks *Dege,* a drink consisting of rice or millet and sour milk with a leader, recognizes the leader's superiority with this act. Samory managed to invade unnoticed, on a rainy night, thanks to the soundscape and the corruptibility of a guard. He sat in the market place with his troops when the inhabitants woke up the next day and there was a good deal of gunpowder and ammunition spread behind them. He explained to the angered residents that he just wanted to dry his powder, and he asked for an audience with the ruler. The *Sofa* fired shots in the air, as discussed. After the impressing volley, he turned to his counterpart and said, unmistakably, "The gunpowder seems to be dry by now. Should we not drink *Dege* now? What do you think?" He conquered Komodugu in this way without shedding one drop of blood.

Samory had to face another challenge in Gboodu.

Though the ruler had explained his willingness to carry out the ritual of the drinking of *Dege,* when he saw the mighty army; he did not want to host the public festival associated with it. He even offended Samory's brother, Keme Brema, who in his fury, thereupon hit his skull with the knob of his sword.

Samory saw his opportunity when he was told about the incident. Immediately he went to the injured man and threw himself dramatically in front of him, on the floor, as if he was performing on a stage. "I apologise for the blood, which was shed by my brother," said the conqueror, who regularly had plays performed. Samory said with acted relief, "We have to celebrate this reconciliation!" When the confused leader spoke to accept the apology, the festive entry into the village still took place, although the leader over there did not agree at first.

Samory's nickname *"The Lion of Bissandugu"* reveals that he was able to strike forcefully.. With a single blow, he had permanently freed the British, who were stationed in the neighbouring country, Sierra Leone, from their desire to invade his territory. The French also had to sufferthis same humiliation: After the first battle with the French in 1882, which he won, despite his military inferiority;, and after further victories over the colonial troops, one of his French opponents called him the "Bonaparte of the Sudan".

The French came at the wrong time for Samory, for he saw that his life's work was in danger. Only in 1880, after the victory over the Cissé and the Bérété, did he tackle his long-term plan to unite West Africa in one great empire. This project was challenged by the military conflicts with the colonial troops. Samory wrote a letter to the kings of Segu and Kenedugu, "The time has come for us to move together to be able to face the common enemy. We can only permanently force back the white invaders and maintain our liberty, when we use our combined forces."

Unfortunately, the addressees recognised the danger only when it was too late.

Samory was engaged in a structural reorganisation in the empire of Wassulu, which he had in mind for the whole of West Africa, and which would have facilitated an autonomous development. The empire was tightly organised despite its spatial extent. Samory achieved this with the division of hundred and sixty-two districts in ten provinces.

He replaced the arbitrariness of the old regime, which he had painfully experienced, by a functioning tax and judicial system. He included representatives of the common people and the lower castes in his council. That he supported agriculture, which was a foreign economic sector for his people, the Diula, was part of this modernisation project too. He purposefully acquired modern weapons, which he had recreated partly to save costs, bearing in mind the expansion of colonialism and the military superiority of the Europeans. So the *Sofa* had taken a canon from the English, which served as a model. He also strategically formed an army of 40,000 *Sofa*, to which a cavalry consisting of three thousand men belonged.

However, the size of his empire of Wassulu proved to be his downfall. There was no strong foundation in the huge project, no connecting idea, which would have strengthened the solidarity of the different tribes. The French turned the weakness of a multi-ethnic state to their own advantage. They incited the several small rulers against Samory, and Samory realised too late that the Europeans only made agreements with him to gain time and to be able to defeat him more easily.

At the end of 1880, Samory had to fight on several fronts. The English overcame their rivalry with the French and blocked amicably the respective arms shipments, whereas the African rulers realised only ten years later that only a mutual rebellion against the colonial powers could have led to success. Samory's brother, the army chief, and one of his sons, who belonged to the leading officers' corps died during the war years. Samory kept his oath against all odds and produced something unique: a wandering empire.

He made the advance of the French troops more difficult with the tactic of the "scorched earth", and he relocated the whole empire eastwards. In 1896, he ruled over an area, which was completely outside the borders of the first empire. Even the French enemies acknowledged this achievement.

On 29th September, 1898, Samory was surprised by a squad of the French colonial troops during his morning reading in Gélému (in present-day Ivory Coast). It was easy for his opponents to find out his whereabouts, where his campaign of conquest set the inhabitants against him. The coup worked out so surprisingly that the sixty-eight-year old did not have any opportunity anymore to shoot himself. Like many resistance fighters, he was banished to Gabon, where Cheikh Ahmadou Bamba was in captivity for three years. It is said that the two men, who were knowledgeable in Islam, and who walked on contrary paths, met only once. Samory died on the 2nd of June, 1900, reportedly of pneumonia, what it was often called in comparable cases.

With the arrest of Samory, the way was cleared for the colonisation of the region. He was declared a bloodthirsty tyrant and slave trader in the schools which were founded by the colonial power. The positive example, which he represented for the generations of students in those times, was supposed to be smothered at the the root; but this effort did not succeed. Up to the present day, despite all disparagement, the population in his homeland associates his name with resistance against foreign opression and the vision of the unity of West Africa. The renowned historian, Joseph Ki-Zerbo from Burkina Faso, says about him, "This man was inspired by the willingness to accomplish something great with energy and nobility"

Biliography
Joseph Ki-Zerbo: *The history of Black Africa*. Wuppertal 1979.

BABEMBA TRAORÉ (Mali)

THE LAST KING OF KENEDUGU

BY DJIBRIL DIALLO FALÉMÉ

A ugust 1969.
I had just turned 10 years. After I had successfully completed the fourth grade of my primary school in Kolondiéby, my father wanted me to spend my holiday with my elder sister. She had just moved to Sikasso. That is how I came to this historic city, which was the last capital of the Kenedugu-empire, which withstood every attack until the death of the last king Babemba Traoré on 1st May, 1898.

Sikasso, Kenedugu, Babemba! This was the triad, which stimulated my imagination during the 225-kilometre trip. I had learned a lot about these three names.

Sikasso

Capital of the third economic region of Mali, three hundred and eighty kilometres southeast from the capital of the country, Bamako; one hundred kilometres from the border to Ivory Coast in the South; and forty-five kilometres away from Burkina Faso in the East; junction of the other regions of Mali and of both countries mentioned above, as well as Togo, Benin and Ghana; granary of the country, thanks to the subtropical climate – up to three hundred millimetres rain in August. It was built by Mansa Daoula Traoré, Babemba's father and founder of the

Traoré dynasty. It was famous as an impenetrable fortress. It withstood a sixteen-month long siege by Samory Touré's mighty army.

Kenedugu

The Senufo Empire. It was founded in the 19th century by Mansa Daoula Traoré, who reigned from 1845 to 1860. His son, Tiéba Traoré, reigned after him, from 1866 to 1893. He shifted the capital to Sikasso, and in 1887 he built the Tata, a fortification wall, which was nine kilometres long and six metres high.

Babemba Traoré

He was born in 1855 and he died on 1st May, 1898 in Sikasso. He was one of the most serious opponents of the colonisation of West Africa by the French. He was known for his remark, "The French will never enter Sikasso as long as I live."

On 15h August, I arrived in Sikasso. Soon, I became friends with some children, and we roamed around in the streets of the city. No quarter was left out by our daily inspections, no matter how far apart they were from each other. One day, we passed by the city hall on the way from Mankurani to Wayèrèma I, our place of residence. This was a magnificent edifice at the end of the street, which led to the headquarters of the governor. I, however, was interested in the hill, which towered over the town. There was a building on top of it, which seemed to be hidden deliberately by high trees. My friends told me that it was the Marmelon Fortress, the palace, in which Babemba had been killed seventy-one years before. He died, because he preferred to die instead of seeing his people being conquered by the French.

The blood froze in my veins. What a lecture on patriotism! When my friends told me that it was once in a year, that the palace was open to the public again, I suggested that we should visit it. We climbed the hill, and after one strenuous half hour, I stood on the second floor on the terrace. The town of Sikasso was underneath me!

I stood, touched, on top at the palace of Babemba, the great fighter for the African cause, and I strongly intended to honour the achievements of this man. In 2009, forty years later, I published the drama *Les derniers jours de Bolibana* (The last days of Bolibana), which is a reminder of his struggle for the unity amongst Africans.

On the 29th of April, 1898, a man, who came riding in hellish speed, knocked on the gate of the fortress. The guards suspected that the final hour had struck. "They are coming! They are coming!" the man shouted very excited. Babemba showed himself on the terrace. He knew that the French would drop their masks then. Since he succeeded his brother to the throne, a tense relationship with the foreigners had prevailed. He had cancelled the convention which was concluded between them and his brother. Latest, by 1885, he had decided that the African kings should fight together against the invaders from Europe. At that time, he faced his greatest challenge as chief commander of the army: Sikasso was besieged by twelve thousand *Sofa* (soldiers). By doing so, the great military commander responded to a friendship pact, which Tiéba Traoré had concluded with the French, because Samory knew from his own personal experience, what the strangers were up to. They concluded friendship pacts and non-aggression pacts with the African rulers,which gave them the opportunity to concentrate on one front at a time. After the conquest of one territory, they were ready to attack the next contractual partner. Samory wanted to frustrate this tactic with the conquest of Sikasso. He however did not succeed in conquering the town, despite a siege of sixteen months. Babemba was made to think in view of the confrontation with Samory; and he decided in the future, to look for alliances with other rulers to be able to defend against attackers.

Before that fateful 29th of April, colonel Andéoud suggested to him to establish a French garrison in Sikasso. Babemba informed him, "I will not fall for your words, which are as sweet as honey, anymore."

After this rejection, the French commander set a deadline for him. Babemba's short response was, "I am not afraid of you because one dies only once."

After the alarm, the Fama (king) found out for himself, how the preparations were proceeding. Then in front of his soldiers, he renewed his oath, "As long as I live, the French will not enter this palace."

On 30th April, the colonial army stood in front of the town walls. Babemba's soldiers resisted valiantly, despite the superiority of the enemies. An unequal fight raged the whole day. Babemba's soldiers did not have anything they could set against the canons. Nevertheless, the attackers could not conquer the defendants of Sikasso. The next day, a soldier came running inside the king's camp. He disclosed to Babemba whilst the gunfire was getting more and more threatening, what he already knew: Sikasso would fall. The decline of the kingdom of Kenedugu was close. The desperate soldier however was not alone, a shooter from the enemy ranks, who had been caught, was with him. When Babemba got to know that this man was a Bambara, which meant a member of the largest ethnic group of Mali, he was even more sad because of this disclosure than about the certain defeat.

"Are you a Bambara, you, who preferred servitude over death?! The whites cannot do any harm to a united people. We however cannot defeat them as long as blacks exist, who eat the whites' rice and meat and betray their black brothers. If Sikasso will be defeated, it is not because the defenders lacked courage, but it is because of traitors of your kind, who preferred to fight together with the whites against their brothers. They fed you because they need you, but you do not mean more to them than their pigs and cows which they feed, before they slaughter them. You have also been dead for a long time because you obey them for fear of your life. And that is exactly what is awaiting our people, when Sikasso will be conquered." After that, the king went to the reception hall followed by Tiécuru, his closest confidante and commander of the royal guard.

Babemba and Tiécuru are standing opposite each other alone in the hall.

Babemba: Tiécuru, my faithful companion! The hour of the decision has come!

Tiécuru: Yes, Fama, the hour of decision...

Babemba: Today, the Kenedugu Empire will open the most glorious page of its history for posterity.

Tiécuru: The entire history of Kenedugu is glorious.

Babemba: Yes. Today however, something will happen that has never happened before. (*He walks to the throne with small steps and sits down*).

I am sitting on the throne of my forefathers for the last time.

He stares into the distance, lost in thoughts.

"Tiécuru!"

Tiécuru *rushes to the throne and kneels down:* "Fama!

Babemba: He who is lying on his back and wants to piss in the air, should have two spines, in order not to get the urine on his chest.

Tiécuru: That is true, Traoré!

Babemba: Is it not so that the testicles of the swimmer are in god's hand?

Tiécuru: That is, what one calls a true word!

Babemba *excited:* Six years ago... Alas, cruel memories! At that time, Amadu Seku from Segu sent a message to my brother Tiéba. In it, he requested to end the fraternal war against the Almami Samory Touré, so that we could jointly raise an army of three hundred thousand Tondjon, and destroy the white invaders. That was the voice of reason, which brooked no delay. At that time however we, the black kings and princes, were only anxious to expand our power, and we did not realise that only our mutual enemy benefited from our disunity. At that time, I agreed to the proposal of Fulaké from Segu...

Tiécuru: That is true, Fama. I can remember this well...

Babemba: At that time, a rebellion of the Bobo in Kong was a more pressing task for us, and when I followed my brother to the throne, it was clear to me; I had to terminate the insincere friendship of the whites, and I had to extend my hand to the Almami Samory Touré. That is what I did, when his brother Kémé Birama visited us here in Sikasso. It was too late, however. My arm did not reach the hand of the Almami because the enemy raced him further and further away in the forests of the South.

Silence. Babemba listens to the gunfire, which comes closer and closer, and announces the advance of the whites towards the palace.

Now, that everything seemed lost, only one honourable decision was left for me: I could die as honourable Senufo instead of experiencing powerlessly, the subjugation of my people. Tiécuru, do not let me fall into the hands of my enemies.

Tiécuru *looks at him bewildered:* No, Fama!

Babemba *gets up, takes the rifle and approaches Tiécuru with it, he hands the rifle over to him:*

"This is a command Tiécuru. A command from your king. Rather death than disgrace."

Tiécuru takes the rifle, Babemba sits down on the throne again.

"Shoot! Shoot, Tiécuru, if you feel compassion!"

Tiécuru *closes his eyes:* "The one, who has always loved you, takes your life away from you today." *He shoots.* "Oh, god!"

Babemba *badly hurt, leaps up, pulls the rifle out of his hand and presses the rifle barrel against his chest.* "Yes, rather death than shame." *He shoots and falls on the ground.*

Tiécuru *walks slowly to Babemba's lifeless body, kneels in front of his head and kisses him on his forehead.* "A great man has passed away." *He straightens up and presses the barrel on his right temple.* "Then we will all die."

He shoots and falls on the ground.

On this first May, 1898, the reign of a man who embodied the dignity of a whole continent ended. The French troops went plundering and murdering through the town. Babemba's death and the conquest of Sikasso marked the end of Mali's resistance against the French conquerors. In his short life – he was only forty-three when he died – Babemba brought to the fore a sense of honour, fraternity and reliability, values, which should be foremost to us Africans as we build a united Africa. It is on this alone that the sound future of our children can be grounded.

Bibliography
Djibril Diallo Falémé: *Les derniers jours de bolibana. Bolibana-la-course-est-finie.* Dakar 2009;
Djibril Tamsir Niane: *Sikasso ou la dernière citadelle.* Paris 1971.

CHEIKH ANTA DIOP (Senegal)

THE RETURN OF THE PHARAOH

BY M. MOUSTAPHS DIALLO

❝So we have a job to do for Europe. We have to help Europe to let go of the bad habits it has acquired during colonialism. Europe alone is too weak and it needs help to build up." Long lasting applause broke out in the overcrowded hall, when these words were said. The speaker had hit the nerve of a whole generation. He perceived the longing for renewal as well as happiness about the self-confidence, which was expressed in the appeal, when the students, who were usually rather sceptical, applauded frenetically. They were freed from an oppressive burden in this moment; the burden of those who are eternally inferior and in need of help.

Everybody knew that the appeal to help Europe was no sensational phrasing because the creator of this quote, in whose honour the students had gathered spontaneously on this 7th February, 1986, was the most famous scientist of the country, even though only very few of them knew what he had been dealing with. The previous speaker had captivated even the unaware with another quotation, "The black person does not know that his ancestors, who had adapted to the natural conditions at the River Nile, are the oldest guides of humanity on their way to civilisation. That they are those who invented art, religion (especially monotheism), literature, the first philosophical systems, writing, the exact sciences (physics, mathematics, mechanics, astronomy, calendar ...), medicine, architecture, etc., when the other inhabitants of the earth were still in the state of Barbarism." Most of them pretended they were not surprised. Every African intellectual should know about Cheikh Anta Diop! They were confused and many of them asked themselves the same questions: What is Africa's help for Europe supposed to look like? Do we not have enough to do for ourselves? Moreover, who actually was the man called "The last pharaoh?" Why did they not know anything about his work?

On 29th December, 1923, the "last pharaoh" was born in the small village Caytu in Senegal. He grew up at his uncle's residence, Cheikh Anta Mbacké, a younger brother of Cheikh Ahmadou Bamba, the revolutionary founder of the Murid-brotherhood, whose father died shortly after his birth. The young Cheikh Anta attended the Koran school, and was shaped by Bamba's vision of an autonomous society, in the care of the highly regarded Islamic scholar, who is called the "lion" due to his rebellion against the colonial dictatorship. His attendance of the French school exposed him to the colonial conception of the world, which would determine his career. The French teachers claimed that the Africans were ignorant, uncivilised and immoral.

He understands, thanks to the explanations of a mentor, how this caricature picture occurs. However, in the grammar school, he is uncertain about how one sees his hero. Like many of his peers, he admires Samory Touré, the greatest opponent of the French colonial power. The memory of this resistance fighter has a great influence on the adolescents, and this is seen as a threat by the colonial administration. That is why they make every effort to destroy the aura of this national figure. In the history lessons, they put him down as a ruthless criminal. Cheikh Anta's mistrust of the curricula grew. Faced with such teaching content, he developed the desire to schedule his own experience of African history .

The desire is kept awake by a contradiction in the following years, which attracts the adolescent's attention in several disciplines: He is again and again told about Greek academics, founding fathers of European sciences, who visited Egypt. For example, Thales is supposed to have derived the famous formula, the "theorem of Thales" at the site of the pyramids and their shadows. The doubting student does not want to believe in this miraculous enlightenment. Could he not have found out the same in Greece? And what were the famous thinkers actually looking for in Egypt? He had been gripped by these questions.

After his high-school graduation in the Natural Sciences and in Philosophy, in the spring of 1946, he boarded a ship to France. During the passage, he dreamt about becoming an aviation engineer and to solve the Greek puzzle in the libraries. In accordance with the principles of the Murid Movement, he would like to play a part in the community of the African students because he was dreaming of a great Pan-African state like his hero, Samory Touré. The colonial era would end one day, and then Africa would need a lot of people, who had received as broad an education as possible. "We cannot restrict ourselves to one field, if we want to be independent later, when we are having only a few people with a school education." This is what he told a friend, who accompanied him on the journey. Several months after his arrival in France, he formed the *Association des É tudiants Africains* (Association of African Students). He earned degrees in physics, nuclear physics, chemistry, applied and nuclear chemistry as well as in linguistics, philosophy and history with the same determination.

Cheikh Anta Diop joined the *Rassemblement Démocratique Africain* (African Democratic Assembly), an umbrella organisation of several parties from the French colonies in Africa, when France in 1950 perpetrated a massacre of the population in Dimbokro (in today's Ivory Coast), which was in revolt. Already in 1948, he had developed the vision of an African Renaissance in one of his numerous articles. He derived this Renaissance from his discoveries in African history. The brutal suppression of the struggle for emancipation in Dimbokro made it clear how crucial it was to unite against colonial rule. It also showed Cheikh Anta, how closely linked his researches were with politics: "The political liberation of Africa cannot be achieved without intellectual decolonisation, and a mental emancipation arises out of the knowledge of one's own history and culture." From now on, the project of African Renaissance became the main task in his life. He decided against aviation, which was his childhood dream and turned to history. As he was searching for an explanation for Thales' theorem, he realised that the Greek did not really make this discovery, but that he used Egyptian knowledge. Meanwhile, he was also convinced of the fact that he could unmask the overpowering colonial ideology. The Ghana Empire, which was created in the third century before Christ, served as an indication for him: "How were 'primitives' able to maintain such a political structure with the size of Europe for about 1250 years? And how could such a structure develop with different languages and religions emerging out of the 'cultural nothing'? Even more has been distorted in this connection."

He could not confront the prevailing doctrine without sufficient historical sources, even more so, because he was a young student from Africa. That is why he decided to make his findings known to the public only after he had studied the historical sources intensively. At this time, this was a Herculean task; a time in which Africans were regarded as "sub-humans" for centuries, an unknown student prepared himself to turn the generally accepted conception of the world upside down that: "The black people civilised Europe!"

One has to bring to one's mind the outraged reaction of the scientific world to Darwin's assumption in 1871 that humans originated from Africa, to imagine the brilliance of this thesis. The idea alone that white people and black people could have a common origin was so unbearable in those days that Charles Dawson, who was Darwin's fellow countryman, composed a contrary theory in 1912, which remained accepted until 1954. At that time, another Englishman, K.P. Oakley, proved that Dawson's alleged European progenitor consisted of the skull of an English farmer and the jawbone of an orangutan. It was only in 1964, with the finding of the *Homo habilis* in Tanzania, was the fact accepted that the origin of humankind lies in Africa.

The whole colonial world was turned upside down by the topic, which Cheikh Anta Diop chose for his doctoral thesis in 1949. It is an incredible story. It was clear to him that he had to expect passionate disagreement. He could already hear his opponents say, " Fantasies of a frustrated African," and accordingly prepared meticulously for the defence of his doctoral thesis in confrontation with the established professors. He composed the main thesis of his work: *The future of the African thinking* under the aegis of the famous philosopher Gaston Bachelard. The explosive was planted in the secondary thesis, which he formulated under the aegis of Marcel Griaule, the famous researcher of the Dogon culture (Mali): *Who were the ancient Egyptians?* His answer was: Black Africans. These words hit the people of that time like a bomb, because of the open racism in those times.

This statement was more than a hypothesis. It was rather distilled out of the report of those who travelled the country and whose writings were the basis for the history of ancient times: Herodotus, who is said

227

to be the father of the writing of history, or Diodor, Strabon, Plinius, and Tacitus, (all Greek and Roman contemporaries of the ancient Egyptians, describe them as black people, namely "like the Ethiopians and other Africans". Cheikh Anta Diop finds the same description even from Champollion-le-Jeune, who was the first to decipher hieroglyphic characters in the middle of the colonial epoch, and who is said to be the father of Egyptology. It was incredible for him, why this was not present in science. He received the following answer, when he continued with his research: Even Champollion-Figeac called the findings of his younger brother and colleague "scandalous", without being able to refute them. Other researchers do not feel embarrassed to use grotesque names like "whites with red skin" or even "whites with black skin". And not least, the word "black" is replaced by "brown".

"If the Egyptians were black, why then are there no traces of this civilisation to be found in other African societies, like traces of the Greeks in Europe?" Cheikh Anta Diop studied the African languages, the first names, the surnames, names for places, the African art, the religious customs, and the social and political structures just as the agricultural practices to counter this possible objection. As further support, he used physical anthropology. In the relationship between the nations, the Egyptian Copts included, he did not only see a supporting argument for his theory, but above all also, a basis for overcoming the fragmentation, which had made the colonial suppression possible.

The candidate did not expect the smart move of his opponents. They refused to listen to the jury, instead of dealing with his work, so that the examination could not take place. The reaction of the Africans however was nearly worse than this trick: Aimé Césaire, the co-founder of Négritude, a movement for the cultural self-assertion of black people, called for financial support in Paris from Africans and progressive French people, so that Diop's research results could be made public, but in vain. The Senegalese publisher, Alioune Diop, joined in the unequal fight of a small group of fearless anti-colonial intellectuals against the colonial academic life, and took care of the printing of Cheikh Anta Diop's findings. The book triggered 'an earthquake,' when it was published in 1954 in Alioune Diop's pragmatic publishing house *Présence Africaine* (African presence) in 1954. A French newspaper for example used the title, "Two hundred- year-old doctrine queried. A young historian from Senegal claims: 'The Western civilisation is the heiress of a black African civilisation at the River Nile.' A public radio debate between Cheikh Anta Diop and Jean Sainte-Fare Garnot, one of the leading French Egyptologists, followed right away.

In the writings of reputable European scholars, one could re-read what nearly everybody refused to believe. This applies to Herodotus, who called Pythagoras a plagiarist, and for Champollion-le-Jeune, who characterised the "whole Greek philosophy" as "studies about Egypt". The list of plagiarisms, which are proved by Diop, is a *Who is Who* of the ancient Greek intelligence: Plato, Aristotle, Archimedes, Hippocrates, Heraclitus, Eudoxo, Eunopides... stand beside Thales, who was miraculously enlightened and Plato. Beyond these foundations of the European sciences, Diop also talked of Osiris, who was said to be a Saviour three thousand years before Christ. Like Christ, he did not only rise from the dead but also rose to his father, the god Ra, but also to save humanity. Diop also points out that the concept of Trinity – Osiris-Isis-Horus or Ra in the morning, at noon and in the evening – already shaped the ancient Egyptian religion. One can easily imagine, how such discoveries would have sounded in the ears of the Europeans. Up to today, these and other achievements of black African peoples are hardly known.

In 1956, Diop challenged the scientists again, this time with the application to habilitate. "You know that everybody will pounce on you", That is how his professor warned him. Diop answered confidently, "This time they cannot escape the debate", because it was impossible to ignore him after his publications and his presence in the media. On 9th January, 1960, the long awaited confrontation with the representatives of the prevailing opinion took place. The welcoming address of the Chairman of the Board of Examiners alone revealed that a lot was at stake, "The importance of the work we will discuss today goes far beyond the boundaries of our town. The exceptional attendance is an unmistakable sign for ..." Africans from all parts of France arrived to witness the decision in the fight between David and Goliath, live; even international journalists were present to transmit the result to African radio stations on time. The duration of the examination was also exceptional: the defenders of the prevalent conception of the world tried for six hours to refute Cheikh Anta Diop's findings, but in vain. In spite of this, he was awarded only a second class degree. In this way, he was denied holding a university chair because only somebody with a first class degree is entitled to this. The candidate had proven that he could challenge the academics, and this was a first victory for him.

Cheick Anta Diop's response to the request, to contribute as a member of the scientific council to the UNESCO-major project *The history of Africa* shows that he emphasised the power of arguments. He wanted three requirements to be fulfilled: 1. The world's leading specialists had to be invited to a conference with the topics: *Population of the ancient Egypt* and *Deciphering of the Meroitic writing*, hieroglyphics. 2. The participants had to get enough time, at least one year to be able to prepare themselves properly. 3. Somebody else had to write the final report, and not his Congolese student Théophile Obenga or he himself. The French historian, Jean Devisse, one of his sharpest critics, took over this role. Diop, Obenga and the Sudanese Abdalla were facing seventeen specialists, five observers and two representatives of UNESCO from fourteen countries in total as the only representatives of black Africa when the decisive conference took place from 28th January to 3rd February, 1974 in Cairo. In the final report, Devisse wrote that he was disappointed because of the great imbalance between Diop's and Obenga's diverse arguments on the one hand, and the scarce counterarguments from the others. Twelve years later, Devisse thanked Diop, because the results of his research made it possible for him to overcome his old prejudices, and he said this about his opponent::"Only a few historians overturned so many old-fashioned ideas, overturned so many perspectives, and opened so many new ways to research."

In the time between the first victory at the Sorbonne in Paris and his greatest in Cairo, Diop had to deal with a more persistent opponent. His first statement after the habilitation in Paris had already made his counterpart prick up his ears. Diop replied when a journalist asked him about what he was up to: "I will return to Africa, because a lot of work is waiting for us. The coming generations might not be able to achieve decolonisation, if our generation cannot succeed in doing so. After five hundred years of foreign rule, Africa has to build a new future with confidence; it has to unite and bring to the fore its own cultures." The newly appointed "Father of the African historiography" is again on a confrontational course, because Senegal's president, Senghor, was just establishing himself, with the support of France, and he had totally different aims.

In the following period, Diop gave lectures about the topic *Introduction of a common language for Africa.* He translated classics of European literature and philosophy, and Einstein's relativity theory into his mother tongue, Wolof, against the common opinion that African languages were not suitable for getting across complex contents and modern sciences. He travelled to the villages, where the elite only go for electoral purposes, to raise awareness for reorientation. He talked with the farmers about the relationship between the peoples and its importance for the reawakening of Africa. He told them about democracy, the perspective of a Pan-African state and modernisation ... The activities of the popular scientist were watched in the palace of the president with suspicion. The democratic mask slipped from the president's face, when he established the *Bloc des Masses Sénégalaises* (Unit of the broad masses of Senegal).

The politically suspect intellectual was arrested in the middle of July 1962. He was released after one month of futile search for a reason for the arrest. In 1963, Senghor offered him five ministerial posts and a quarter of the parliamentary seats for his party, and Diop replied, "It is about ideas in politics and not about posts". After this rebuff, the president dissolved the party of his opponent and passed a law, which forbade the founding of new parties. Diop was not allowed to teach at the university during Senghor's twenty-year-long period of government. The president imposed a travel ban on him, when he was awarded the title *Most important African author of the 20th century* during the *First World Festival of African Arts* in 1966, and he was more and more frequently invited to lectures in other African countries and to Europe. Why this persecution? The reason can be found in the completely different model of society, which was embodied by his enemy..

In 1956, Senghor still declared, "Whoever is demanding independence, is looking at the world from upside down and is holding a phoney debate". Cheikh Anta Diop on the contrary, was already in the fight against colonial rule as far back as 1940. It is even more ironic that he became the first president of independent Senegal four years later. Diop stood up for an autonomous federal state and promoted the African languages; Senghor advocated for the maintenance of French as the official language, and for the spreading of Greek and Latin with unrivalled passion. The subject combination French/Latin was the only one, which ensured a governmental scholarship. Moreover, in the same way as Diop was famous for his modest appearance, the president carried his elitist behaviour to the extreme by insisting guests wore tailcoats at

231

his receptions. The people started calling these meetings "Show of the penguins". It was about the fight of the two different ideologies between the two men: "African Renaissance" versus "Europeanisation of Africa."

At the spontaneous gathering on 7th February, 1986, it became clear, which model the Senegalese would have chosen even though the students had gained only first insights into Diop's work. Anger mingled with sorrow. The reason for this gathering only a few hours after his death because especially the man, who had dedicated his life to a real reconstruction had been fought against and ostracised. What they heard about him now, sounded like a list of missed opportunities in their ears. They especially mourned the future-oriented *Plan for the industrialisation of Africa*, which was drawn up by Diop at the beginning of the 1970s. The realisation of this concept would have made the answer to the economic problems of the continent possible, and would have gotten Africa a much different position in the international context.

This plan also shows what Africa's help for Europe could look like. Beside the promotion of renewable energies, which is stipulated in the draft, and which would have shown the rest of the world the way in an ecological development, an independent Africa could force Europe to change its policy. It would halt Europe's habit of laying claim to the riches of other countries, and to waste resources, which are not at their own disposal. Europe would have to change its views, when Africa would take a resolute stand, and would contribute for the sake of its own interest to the creation of a world, where solidarity exists. Diop remarks in this context that also racism in the USA could be eradicated by the civil rights movement, and not because the dominant group had changed for the better. The help for Europe has its origin in the vision of a humanitarian design of world society, "The question is how we can educate ourselves to a perception of the human, which frees itself from apparent differences, and which takes the human into account without ethnic co-ordinates."

A man rushed to the podium shortly before the end of the commemoration. It was visible that he was glad about his task, took the microphone and declared, " I have just received a message from the palace of the president ..." He hurried to raise his voice against the emerging grumbling about the originator of this message, "The institute, where Professor Diop worked, will be named after him." Obviously, the new president wanted to use the mood in the auditorium to ingratiate himself to the rebellious students. The man using the microphone did not finish the last word of what he wanted to say, when a deafening noise created by whistles and booing filled the auditorium. As if by agreement, it resounded from all corners, "The whole university! The whole university!" A few days later, the university bore the name Cheikh Anta Diop, as well as the street, which goes past.

Cheikh Anta Diop would have been happier about other not opportunistic honours, for example about the fact that his portrait hangs in the famous Afro-American Morehouse College in Atlanta, and that the 4th of April, 1985 was declared *Dr.-Cheikh-Anta-Diop-Day*, in memory of his visit.

The words of the representative of the Egyptian delegation during the official memorial service would have also surely moved him: "Cheikh Anta Diop will always be in our hearts and in our heads.

Only God lasts forever. However, he who dedicates his life to the people, will forever remain in their memory."

Bibliography

Cheikh Anta Diop: *Nations nègres et culture. De l'antiquité nègre égyptienne aux problèmes de l'Afrique noire d'aujourd'hui.* Paris 1954;
Civilisation ou barbarisme. Anthropologie sans complaisance. Paris 1981;
Cheikh Mbacké Diop: *Cheickh Anta Diop. L'homme et lœuvre.* Paris 2003;
Leonhard Harding / Brigitte Reinwald (publisher): *Africa – mother and model of the European civilisation. The rehabilitation of the black continent by Cheikh Anta Diop.* Berlin 1990.

VALDIODIO N'DIAYE (Senegal)

THE DREAM OF JUSTICE

BY AMINA N'DIAYE-LECLERC

On 19th March, 1923, a man travels in French West Africa from Kaolack to the town of Rufisque. What he is about to do will be called document fraud, if it is detected. He had rather not think about, what the authorities would do to him, if this happens. Society would not accept him anymore. However, he is very sure about what he is going to do, "It is right to break this law. I am obliged to bypass this law because I am a caring father. I want the best for my son, and this means that I have to keep it a secret that the baby was born in Kaolack." His wife also meant, "At all costs!"

Several years earlier, the French parliament had passed the 'Four-commune-law', which separated the population of the colony of Senegal into two groups: into French citizens and subjects. Citizens with all rights and duties were those who were born in the old capital Saint-Louis, in Dakar, the new capital, in Rufisque, and on Gorée, an island off the coast. The other Senegalese had no right of vote, they were simple subjects, had to pay tax, and had to do compulsory labour.

The discrimination of the large majority of Senegalese had seemed especially absurd to the traveller because he is Samba-Langar N'Diaye, the prince of Saloum, descendant of a dynasty, which existed for eight centuries. Lingeer Adiaratou Sira M'Bodj, his wife, is also a dependent of the aristocracy of Sine and Saloum. The first president of Senegal, Léopold Sédar Senghor, whose father had to pay the tithe to the prince Samba-Langar, comes from this region too. So it is not understandable for the prince why other children should be higher up the hierarchy than his own, and that is why he travels to Rufisque to register his son there. Surely, he could have sent somebody else. However, this matter was too important to him. Who knows whether this person would not have opened his mouth too wide and revealed the secret. "The fate of one's own children should not be put into the hand of strangers."

On his way, he thinks of all kinds of questions, so he will be able to answer them as credibly as possible. He especially memorises the name of the town, which is foreign to him. This town means the future, and he is not on any account allowed to mention the place of his descent, which is like a second name for him.

That is why, a strange feeling gives him pain, a sense of guilt, which makes this matter difficult for him. The exchange of the names seems like a betrayal to him. There is a thought in his head, "You are hiding your home as if you are ashamed of it!" He curses the colonial administration, which forces him to use this trick, and he swears to let his son know his real place of birth as soon as possible and to teach him to be proud of his home.

The name Valdiodio N'Diaye is registered at the registry office in such a short time, that he is angry about the easiness in which they decide about the future of a person. He thinks, "Pure arbitrariness! Weal and woe are in the hands of a bored civil servant!" With silent gratitude to his ancestors, he starts his way back. The certainty that his father gave him their blessings inspired and motivated him.

Ten years later, his family was struck by misfortune. Valdiodio's elder brother Biram dies. Valdiodio loses his brother, his role model, and his best friend at only ten years of age. His pain is even greater as he has to follow an inhuman rule: He is not allowed to weep. Biram's soul – he should not be saddened. No tear, no grief of a person, whom he loved is supposed to weigh him down during his transition to a happier world because humans only suffer on earth. The boy clings to his mother's hand with the feeling that his heart will burst in his chest because of his grief. He is fighting against the upcoming tears and an oppressive dizziness, when slight agitation develops behind him.

The crowd slowly parted to give way to a tall and slim man. He was an undisputed authority: Whoever was desperate asked for his advice. He wore white like everybody, the colour of grief. Valdiodio's mother let his hand go and held out both hands to receive the prayers of the wise man, as soon as she turned around and recognised him. He also held out his hands, and recited *surah* from the Koran in a low voice when he stood opposite her. The crowd was silent. After he had finished his prayer, the man looked at Valdiodio for a long time and said finally, "Lingeer Sira Mbodj! The child here at your side will bring you a sack of gold. This is what I swear by god!" The man held the amulet tight, which he wore around his neck, whilst he said this. Afterwards, he continued to look at the boy for a while and added, "My amulet reveals all the secrets of the world to me. Nobody should believe anything I say anymore, in case my prediction does not become true."

These words left a profound impression especially on the ten-year-old. It was clear to him that it was a metaphor. Was he supposed to be rich one day? Or would he accomplish something special later? What could this be? The prediction had had an effect on him, without him realising it; it had gotten stuck in his head, and it took away some of the weight off the suppressing thoughts about his deceased brother.

In school, everything seemed to confirm the prediction. The small Valdiodio learned everything with such an ease that it surprised his classmates, and he passed the entrance examination, which afforded students from the French colonies in Africa the opportunity to attend the grammar school, Faidherbe, in Saint-Louis. Cheikh Anta Diop, who proved the black African origin of the ancient Egyptian civilisation, Cheikh Fall, director of the airline *Air Afrique*, and Birago Diop, who achieved fame across the borders of the continent with his collection of African fairy tales, belonged to the friends Valdiodio found in this grammar school.

In this French school, young people learned that African societies did not create any civilisations, and that they did not have any history. That these were falsifications of historical connections was even more obvious for Valdiodio, since he was very familiar with the songs of the griots since his childhood, who talked about the centuries of history of his family. Like his friends, he realised the contradictions of a regime, which says about itself that it has developed the African colonies, and at the same time, took the riches of these colonies to Europe. His interest in political questions arose from this recognition. One year before the school leaving examination, he was dismissed from school because he criticised the Vichy government, which collaborated with the Nazis, the occupying power. He decided to prepare for the Abitur by himself, by borrowing the exercise books from his friends.

At this time, he came down with hepatitis. He lost every hope to recover when after weeks there was no sign of recovery. When he was ill in bed, his uncle came to him full of concern, and whispered into his ear, "You did not fulfill your task yet. Do you remember the prediction?" This reminder did not miss its aim. Soon however, he doubted the prophecy again. He was barely healthy, when a new setback followed. Contrary to his former classmates, the "exempted" Valdiodio could not take his Abitur examinations: His application, to be able to do his military service at a later time had been rejected. He was recruited, and he remained in the army as a driver until the end of the Second World War.

At the end of the war, he had only one aim: he wanted to become a lawyer to put an end to the colonial arbitrariness. His main priorities in this matter were to act against injustice he had experienced himself, as well as to fight against the structural violence, which was directed against every colonised person. In 1946, he passed the Abitur as best student of the year. Now, the director of his school had to ask him for help so that a good character reference would be issued for him. This request filled him with satisfaction. It took the shadows of the past away from him, and he was able to look forward to his law studies. His dream, to speak for those who do not have a voice came within reach.

For obvious reasons, local lawyers were a thorn in the side of the colonial power. It is for this reason that in 1947, he was awarded a scholarship to study dental medicine. At the University of Montpellier, he additionally enrolled at the law faculty and the philosophy faculty. Three years later, he was solely dedicated to law studies, which he completed after one year with doctoral thesis. The topic of his thesis was citizenship in the French colonial empire, which he himself could only acquire at the cost of disguising his place of birth. He felt that with his brilliant analysis of the discriminating admission requirements to citizenship, he had footed the bill of his father with the colonial regime, and that with it, he had risen to speak for all of his fellow countrymen, who did not have the privilege of French citizenship. Despite the grade "very good", and the advocacy of his professors, he was not awarded a scholarship for

237

a postgraduate course, which he could have completed with the highest title, *Professeur agrégé*. Conspicuous here was the fact that his fellow countryman Senghor, at that time one of the few delegates from the colonies, did not support him in any way. Actually, the nearly twenty years younger Valdiodio N'Diaye would have outshone him, since his title in Law was of a higher value than Senghor's title in Grammar. Against the background of the events from 1951, this suspicion does not seem to be too far-fetched.

Valdiodio did not suspect anything of the turbulence, which he would blunder into, when he in 1951, returned to Senegal to open a law office in his hometown Kaolack. In the registry office of Kaolack, he married his fellow student Claire Onrazat, a lawyer with a PhD, who fought for the Resistance in the Second World War. Mamadou Dia, Senegalese member in the French Senate, asked him with a view to the oncoming end of the colonial era, and considering the lack of local executives, to participate in politics. In 1952, Valdiodio was elected into the local council, and in 1957 – in the course of the *Loi Cadre*, which gave the colonies a certain amount of autonomy – he was elected Minister of the Interior of the first Senegalese government, which was formed by Mamadou Dia. In 1960, in the year of the independence of Senegal, he became mayor of Kaolack after his engaged electoral campaign.

Despite his aristocratic origin, he initiated the abolition of the traditional power structures. For this purpose, he undertook a restructuring of the country, which guaranteed equal rights for every community, and which removed the borders of the old kingdoms. As mayor, he extended the poor infrastructure of the region, and he devoted particular attention to the partnership with European cities. In these partnerships, he on the one hand, saw the possibility to make use of European knowledge for the necessary modernisation, and on the other hand, he saw the chance for a cultural opening, which was coherent with his vision of a global society. In this way, Kaolack became a partner city with Narbonne (France), Aosta (Italy), Gelsenkirchen (Germany), Haifa (Israel), and Le Loche (Switzerland). However, the name Valdiodio N'Diaye is not connected with these reforms in the collective memory of the Senegalese, but with the referendum of 1958, which led to independence, and to the events of 1962, which ended with the detention of N'Diaye.

In August 1958, the French president Charles de Gaulle undertook a journey to Africa, which was supposed to decide the future of the French colonial empire. Under the impression of the lost Indochina war in Dien Bien Phu in 1954, and the liberation war in Algeria, which broke out in the same year, the general decided to take the bull by the horns, before further front lines could develop. With a referendum, the colonies were supposed to speak in favour or against the model of a French community, so to say for or against a "colonialism light". Behind the scenes, it was made clear that no co-operation with France would exist anymore in case of a "No". The vast majority of the political leaders around Mamadou Dia and Léopold S. Senghor pleaded for the neo-colonial community, only N'Diaye and a few others declared themselves in favour of independence. The advocates for the "No" were not even given the opportunity to speak in the meeting, in which a decision would be taken, and formulated as a recommendation for the general public. N'Diaye expressed his disappointment in the words, "Democracy is a choir, in which all notes have their place, even those, which sound wrong. This is one of the most beautiful sides of political justice."

On 26th August, 1958, a preliminary decision about the future of the country was supposed to be taken. The political leadership was asked to announce their decision in a public demonstration in the presence of General de Gaulle. For weeks, the people awaited this historical moment, which would herald a new era. In several demonstrations, they had unmistakably expressed their demand: no sovereignty in pretence under French leadership; instead complete independence. Because of this, the political leadership found itself caught in a dilemma. The "Yes" to the French community, as they had decided unilaterally, would throw the population into turmoil. The incidents which took place, when Guinea said 'no' to French colonialism, made this even clearer. One day before the demonstration in Senegal, Sékou Touré, who became president of Guinea a few months later, had challenged General de Gaulle with his legendary speech in such a way that de Gaulle left the meeting inflamed with rage, and forgot his hat on the stand.

In the afternoon of August the 26th, the centre of Dakar was full of people. Already in the morning, the crowds, which had come from everywhere, filled the central square. Everybody wanted to experience the hour of birth of the republic, and because the government had not officially expressed itself, it was necessary to be visible. The message of the population could be seen on oversized posters: INDEPENDENCE.

Behind the scenes, unbelievable things happened. The political leadership abandoned their responsibility in the conflict between the will of the population and the claim of General de Gaulle. Immediately preceding the historical day, the head of the government, Mamadou Dia, travelled to Switzerland for medical treatment. Senghor, the second most important man of the state, travelled to France all of a sudden, where he had to deal with "family matters". Nobody amongst the other supporters of the "Yes" were willing to speak at the demonstration.

Valdiodio N'Diaye accepted responsibility in this situation. There was a tense silence when the thirty-five-year old took the microphone and directed his greetings to the official guests and the crowd. The listeners waited impatiently for the decisive sentence. It was surprising for his political opponents that N'Diaye shared the vote of the population, which corresponded with his conviction. He demanded independence also for the other African nations, after the loud, long lasting jubilation had reduced. With this explosive speech, he became the hero for the independence of Senegal. General de Gaulle in his anger, avoided looking at the young man, who taught him with quotations from French literature about the indefensibleness of the neocolonial claim, and he exclaimed angrily towards the crowd, "You want independence, so take independence!"

On this day, Valdiodio understood the mysterious prophecy of the wise man. He also remembered the dream of his youth, "to speak for those who do not have a voice".

Valdiodio N'Diaye explained in the midst of the cold war in public that the young Republic of Senegal did not want to become a plaything of the major powers, and that is why the country had relations with countries of the Western as well as those of the Eastern bloc. Domestic Politics aimed at radical change of neocolonial structures, and the fight against social differences, which fuelled the discontent of the former colonial power. The new leadership counted on an agriculture, which was oriented towards their own consumption. Accordingly, co-operatives were supported to help the small farmers.

In January 1959, Senegal and Mali joined forces in the Mali federation, which however collapsed in August 1960, due to differences between Léopold S. Senghor and Modibo Keita, president of Mali. A confederation was dissolved with this, which could have become a model for the whole continent.

In the night of 17th December, 1962, N'Diaye was rung from bed by Colonel Alfred Diallo. The colonel informed him by phone that a confrontation between army and police was imminent, and he begged him to mediate to prevent a bloodbath. The national crises developed into a dramatic power struggle. For some time now, a number of members of parliament had tried to overthrow Mamadou Dia, head of government, and supreme commander of the army, together with his cabinet. Two days before 17th December, 1962, Dia had received a call from General Fall, the Chief of the armed forces, who informed him what he had learned from the commander of the paratroopers: President Senghor had instructed him to hold himself with his troop in readiness, and to wait for a signal. The commander now considered it as correct to inform his superior, General Fall. Dia consulted with his closest friends. N'Diaye believed that an escalation could be prevented by deploying soldiers for Senghor's protection. His justification was that the president seemed to be worried about the smoldering conflict in parliament.

When Senghor saw the guards, he understood that the general knew what was going on. He arbitrarily appointed Colonel Alfred Diallo as the new Chief of the armed forces, and closed down the parliament building. After this affront, Mamadou Dia commanded that the police had to be mobilised. At this time, the police had been better equipped than the army. In this power struggle, Valdiodio N'Diaye as former minister of the interior and minister of defense and current minister of finance was able to convince his opponents that the matter had to be sorted out at the round table by civilians. Senghor ordered that Mamadou Dia should be arrested, whilst the army and the police withdrew. A few hours later, Valdiodio N'Diaye was also arrested. A flagrant breach with any rule of law followed.

After a first hearing, the state prosecutor did not see a reason to press charges. It even got worse for Senghor, for whom his international reputation was very important: The renowned French newspaper *Le Monde* headlined, "The charges against Valdiodio N'Diaye have been melting like snow in the sun." After that, a jury was made up of the parliamentarians, who wanted to overthrow Dia's government. But this matter is even unpleasant for these declared opponents, so that they appear with sunglasses on the day of the pronouncement of judgment. Mamadou Dia is sentenced to life imprisonment, Valdiodio N'Diaye to twenty years, Alioune Fall, Joseph Mbaye and Ibrahima Sarr to ten years each.. *Le Monde* writes, "Today, people were sentenced, who committed no crime". President Senghor does not only change the constitution, he also establishes a single party regime, and suppresses any critical press.

The grudge of the president is especially directed against N'Diaye. On Christmas Eve 1962, one week after his arrest, his wife was taken out of the hospital in her nightdress, and she was expelled from the country with her children, although all of them hold Senegalese nationality. They were sent to Europe in winter time in a cloak-and-dagger operation without papers and without warm clothes. The deportation took place in such a hasty manner that the officials had forgotten the plane ticket for the youngest son, and the six-year-old had to remain in Dakar for several days alone.

The hero of 26th August was supposed to be erased from the collective memory because his sight fatally reminded people how the president had run away from his responsibility. That is why the prisoners were taken to the Senegalese "Siberia", six hundred kilometres away from the capital, and a synonym for heat and abandonment in the vernacular. N'Diaye could not be seen any more on the pictures of the famous demonstration from 26th August, 1958. The original photos were kept under military secrecy by the French Ministry of Defence. The Senegalese fell back on their oral tradition to fight against this historical misrepresentation. The teachers ignored the mandatory contents in their history classes, and told their students about a man, who stood up to General de Gaulle, and who expressed the wish of the people. In prison, the banished man even received appreciation by the guards.

Officially, the detention is called "house arrest", but an absolute communication ban between the prisoners was imposed; they were even not allowed to go out into the yard. The children were not permitted to visit N'Diaye for ten years; his wife Claire could only see him once a year for one hour, and she had to specifically travel from France to Senegal. Doctor's visits were only permissible in case of illness, when the patient was at risk of death. N'Diaye had to wait for seven months for medical treatment because of this.

The prisoners were always told that they would be released soon, to pacify them. In 1966, a lawyer, with the offer to sign a plea for mercy, visited them. N'Diaye rejected the suggestion indignantly, "I do not have to ask for mercy because I am innocent." In 1971, a press campaign took place; however without a concrete result. In 1973, he once again went on the offensive. Valdiodio declared in a letter to his wife, "Senghor intends to keep us in prison until he does not reign over the country anymore. Only a well-planned public campaign can make him open the doors of his prisons. In this case he would fear that his image as a noble, democratic head of state would be destroyed, and this is how he wants to be seen by foreign countries."

Due to the support by numerous personalities, for example by Aimeé Césaire, Senghor's fellow campaigner in the négritude movement, Pope John XXIII, President Houphouët-Boigny of Côte d'Ivoire, the late president François Mitterrand, as well as the Nobel Prize winner René Cassin, and François Mauriac, the campaign was successful. Valdiodio N'Diaye and Mamadou Dia were released in 1974.

The international support made once again clear how bitter it feels, when a normal rule of law is missing. Valdiodio had pointed to this fact on the eve of decolonisation, "Nkrumah said, 'Take independence, and you will get everything else in addition'. Justice is not included in this.One has to work for it with one's mind, one's conscience and with one's heart. In addition, justice is no national matter, due to its political reference, but it is a matter for the whole of humanity." After his release, N'Diaye only worked as a lawyer. He was weakened by the conditions of his detention, and died on 5th May, 1984 at the age of sixty-one.

Valdiodio N'Diaye's vision of justice and African unity fell into oblivion extensively, but many Senegalese still know him as the hero of independence. The biggest grammar school of his home town Kaolack bears his name, and since 4th April, 2010, the fiftieth anniversary of the independence of Senegal, the big 'Independence Square' in the capital Dakar, where he gave his historic speech, is called 'Valdiodio-N'Diaye-Square'.

Bibliography
Amina N'Diaye-Leclerc /Eric Cloué: *Valdiodio N'Diaye. Independence of Senegal.* Documentary movie on DVD. Paris 2005.

KWAME NKRUMAH (Ghana)

OSAGYEFO THE VICTORIOUS HERO

By Benard Akoi-Jackson

"May your journey be rough..."
"Wiε!"
Kwame!
Shall I say it so? That it has come upon me to weave this tale out of yarns, much too delicate and maybe too precious, as they have long been left untouched? Then again, who am I? Who would I be? Who might I become? To assume the role of a scribe, yeah, a sage even, at such an age...one that is yet crawling? My hope will be not to throw out the baby, when in the process of chucking out the bath-water. We have so often done this and now, look at us today.

To presume to have the bowels enough, with which to stomach all that it takes, and lend the body as medium to the muses so they speak through me? I do not comprehend. None comprehends. The world indeed, needs not comprehend....but it is rumoured: ...and so the legend commences...
Kwame!
It is said, he had foretold his own birth before he was born. And Kwame, knowing what might have transpired thereafter, chose to delay his arrival...the whole clan waited. Indeed, all the world; the entire universe heaved a sigh when finally, he arrived, uncrying and yet pensive. But pensive? Why? And for one so little and yet innocent of cares?

Well they say the little ones are old and knowing. And knowing so much, they only opt wisely to hold their tongue, having just arrived from the sages beyond.

So Kwame kept his resolve and came uncrying.

And so Nyaniba, she who lay writhing in the pangs of labour, bore it all: her strength was unflinching; her spirit, even more so.

And we, we all did not even quail a bit when, at the child's blessing, on the eighth day, the quivering-lipped elder had dipped his thumb and index finger into the gourd of harvested rain water and sprinkled its cool droplets onto the tiny guest's forehead and wished him many days of trouble, turmoil and turbulence:

"Hm!"

"You, who have come, we see you intend to stay. You have lived beyond the threshold and though we are still intrigued by your uncrying silence, we bid you welcome."

"Wiɛ!"

"May your journey be rough," he had said.

"Wiɛ!" we had all intoned, wishing for the baby, all the strength it would take to walk this rough journey.

"May your path be rocky, slippery and parched."

"Wiɛ!" we knew these were not curses, but good wishes of fortitude and fortune, for how might one have grown up to become known as *the* Black Star, if one had not toiled to rise to the heights?...that was at the beginning, or really, just a little before...now at his death, none could tell if he really did have an inkling of its coming or not...suddenly, he was out of here before we all knew it.

Some knew though. We heard some knew. It is rumoured they had indeed aided in brewing the dose that did the deed. And when it was done, it was done.

And we, we just sat here stunned. What could we have done? What could we have told his mother?

She who outlived the gift she had and had shared with us and the world.

But her agony. It was profound. When she grimaced in wailing for one she had so dearly loved, we were left with this image; as haunting and enigmatic as the life for which she groaned and lamented.

She grieved.

And we sighed.

Kwame!

To relay his story, yea, to relate his tale, is to assume a responsibility that bears great gravity.

The story of how Busia was induced to ignore all intelligence advice and make Acheampong, the Commanding Officer of the regiments in charge of Accra, and thereby head of the most sensitive military installations in Ghana, has not been fully told.

And it is rather too early in our journey, to tell it I guess.

Yet, these are words and thoughts of an entire horde upon the book of a contemporary visage. Words and thoughts that have been traded, indeed, mongered from one to another, then to another and yet another, till their very verity either become challenged or rather suspect. But we are a generation that has inherited many tales, whether divined in oracles or mongered over waves.

The Bright one says:

Suffice it to say that the long arms of the Soviets were and have been ignored for much too long. Their Cuban proxies (the Chinese, on the other hand, often used the North Koreans) have rarely been placed where they belong, close to the security breaches that have defined our politics for 6 decades.

Hear Kwame when he was asked to look into the mirror and point his intended direction:

We neither face East nor West, we face forward!

Thinking aloud and thinking silently, we come to these. After all, it is a legend! Some might be true, but others will remain conjecture; rumour; rancour; even slander. But those who kept and still keep faith and hope alive, will tell it somehow lightly and gently, the tale of one who lived and left long before...

Hear the Bright one again:

They - the Soviets and the Cubans - have no "declassified files" to guide us. But that was in the past. Going forward, all those interested in a fairly accurate historical record must stop the complacency and become critical. Public scholarship in Ghana deserves no less.

And then the scribe would have to agree, if he is permitted.

"You couldn't have said it any louder! Are we not tired of this all the time? Oh, so you're African...Oh, so you're into recycling waste...Oh, so your work must surely have been embedded in your dead forbears' tribal rites and rituals."

The Bright one speaks again:

China's growing influence greatly threatened Soviet domination of the third world. Meanwhile, Osagyefo (for that is how Kwame came to be known by those who knew and loved him), was already considered unreliable by Moscow because of his unorthodox ideas about spirituality and trade unionism...Oh, your work is so rooted to the earth..." or so they want you to be. As if we all do not come from the earth anyway."

When considering Kwame and the onset of his demise, we should ask ourselves:

Which foreign power had the easiest access to Ghana's security services? Which of them had the most sophisticated motive? And what motifs had been and still are being repeatedly used over time to kill our prophets, while we stand aside and look? Having now examined the declassified FBI files (a treasure vault usually ignored by those to whom knowledge should belong, those for whom slumber has been an option even though the rainbow stopped being enough millennia ago...) We should be of the belief that those now grasping these thoughts will pause and gasp. You see, for we should have reason to believe the Soviet Union was the cardinal force behind the subversion that removed Osagyefo.

Was it not said of him, Kwame, that he was courting the red star? When we all knew his was the way of the black star? I can hear you gasp, but wait for it...

When it comes to Ghana, Nigeria, Senegal, Kenya and the myriad states that Africa has been forced to bear, indeed, stack up as if we were all stuck in some sort of quagmire; a lethargic doze or soporific maze. We are all made to group up. To those who really think Africa is one looming country, I guess it's only some Geography gone bad...But it is also for us, the severally, labelled Africans to either subscribe to those labels or not.

Kwame!

He always was a kind of seer. Some would consider, mystic. He was all in all, enigmatic.

Now consider the events after Osagyefo's overthrow. According to the Bright one, who in one rather young life-time has been audienced by nearly the entirety of this earth's nobility, Shirley Graham du Bois, was kicked out of Ghana, as soon as Kwame's chair was whisked from beneath him; (he must even have been in mid-air), when Shirley was thrown out.

The only security agent abused by the new junta was the intelligence station officer in Accra who was put in a cage and paraded through the streets. (Boye Moses). Not as a curiosity, but as one deserving of such.

For overtly lazy reasons, Soviet, Czech and East German intelligence officers remained put. The only iron curtain advisors sent packing were technical advisors to factory and scientific projects that had already collapsed anyway. The core of Soviet interests were left untouched.

Some would want to pander to Pan-Africanism and claim that, we are all Africans (and indeed, we are)... But, granted that Osagyefo was not the most ideal of allies, why would the Soviets remove him and allow a relatively pro-Western, even if also anti-Chinese, government to take his place?

Strategy, dear friends, strategy. These are words of the Bright one, as I said earlier. The one whose sash bears the colour of Kwame's star.

It was a mere interlude. Their long-term strategy paid off when Colonel Acheampong removed Prof. Busia a few years later and re-instituted a pro-Soviet regime in Accra. But would this simplistic reduction be what Nkrumah intended? Kwame? Most definitely not!

Over the years the subject of Osagyefo Kwame Nkrumah's overthrow has been treated with complacency by political historians. And Africa has indeed remained several shades (no pun intended) more complex than the complexion the world can ever comprehend. The world indeed, needn't comprehend...none has ever sought to comprehend America or even France. Neither has anyone sought to comprehend the UK. And we, ancient as we are, who would seek to comprehend the vastness of this vastness?

By 1966, she had become a major thorn in the flesh of the USSR's assigns in Africa and America. But who was she? An enigma, a presence, a manifestation? Who?

The Communist Party of USA, for instance, was deeply worried about her influence over Osagyefo. Together with Moscow, they were mounting constant protests about the damage her work was doing to Soviet interests in Ghana, and by extension elsewhere in Africa. She was a key Chinese agent in Ghana, and this was the time USSR-Chinese competition in Africa was heating up. You see, the principalities, when they have a unanimous mischief as intent, work together...

(Some readers may recall that in the 80s it went to a head in Zimbabwe where the Chinese-backed Mugabean revolutionaries, defeated the mainstream Soviet-backed Nkomo/ZAPU, and all Soviet advisors were kicked out). Have you noticed how we tend to just deal with the mess that is thrown at us...that is what we have done all this while. And this is what Kwame decried. You see, he came uncrying, but was made to leave decrying several misdeeds against a folk so ancient and wisdomed into self-mistrust.

So to have looted all of Tanganyika's coffee, Eldoret's tea, Bassam's tusks, Edina's gold, Addis-Ababa's Ark, U-Simba's pride and Kemet's soul unacknowledged, then TURN around and throw pittances towards the harnessing of the cultures of the cradle is a venture in futility. Kwame would turn in his grave if his offspring now take this TURN.

Citing declassified CIA documents that appear to suggest that the CIA had foreknowledge of the coup, these historians have simplified the narrative. The Ghanaian military high command that removed Osagyefo MUST have been induced by the CIA, they argue, though one wonders why CIA's help would be needed if the entire general corps of a country decides to remove an absent Head of State from power.

What's more, is it one Land in Europe's frozen centre that is going to spearhead the renaissance of an entire source? I have always known that by the mid-60s Osagyefo's Congo policies were deeply worrying to the Soviets (Congo was the justification given by the Junta that overthrew Osagyefo, by the way), who now saw his pan-African activities as potentially unruly.

But, hear the Bright one speak: I was drawn to this conclusion that their involvement in the affairs of February 1966 was much deeper than usually supposed by studying the FBI files on Shirley Graham du Bois, W.E.B du Bois' much younger spouse who remained in Ghana after the death of her husband.

These questions need not be answered. Who are we? Why are we? Where are we? What will we?

And by the way, which country was the first to acknowledge the Ankrah-led junta, even while Osagyefo was ironically still in China in the middle of his fruitless Vietnam peace mission? The USSR! They only need to be pondered, for answers to them may be rather obvious and super-fluous.

It is entirely possible though that the CIA may have worked to agitate the minds of senior officers against Osagyefo. After all, psychological operations form a major component of espionage. It is in that regard however that I believe our political historians to have been rather remiss in examining the record.

Kwame!

It is said, he had foretold his own birth before he was born. And Kwame, knowing what might have transpired thereafter, chose to delay his arrival...now at his death, could anyone tell if he really did have an inkling of its coming or not...?

Kwame Nkrumah was born in 1909 in the British colony of the Gold Coast, now Ghana, the son of a merchant and a goldsmith. He attended the Catholic Mission School, later the prestigious Achimota School in Accra. From 1935 he studied in the U.S.A. at Lincoln University, then the only black university and engaged in an African-American anticolonial fraternity. In 1945 he went to Britain and organised the Pan African Congress in Manchester together with the African-American civil rights activist, W.E. du Bois, who later followed him as his political advisor to Ghana. As a leading member of the Pan-African movement, convinced that Africa must be liberated and united to overcome colonialism and imperialism, he returned to his homeland in 1947 and fought for the liberation of the country from colonial rule. Ten years later, Ghana became the first African state to become independent again. In 1964, Nkrumah converted Ghana into a socialist one-party state with him as president for life. As Foreign policy, he strove for the merger of all African states. The "United Nations of Africa", however, remained a dream. Nkrumah's authoritarian style of governance increasingly encountered resistance. In 1966 he was deposed by a military coup and died in 1972 in exile.

Bibliography
Kwame Nkrumah; *The Autobiography of Kwame Nkrumah* Repr. London; 2001
Africa Must Unite, London. 1963.

PATRICE ÉMÉRY LUMUMBA (D.R. Congo)

A CONGOLESE TRAGEDY

BY JOSÉPHINE T. MULUMBA

Generally it is said, "If somebody embodies the history of the decolonisation of Africa, then it is Patrice Lumumba". Indeed, hardly an African personality combines the experience of colonial arbitrariness, the will to emancipation, and the intrigues of the cold war in his biography, as the first head of the government of the independent Democratic Republic of the Congo. Outside of Africa, one associates the name Lumumba more with an alcoholic beverage or a desert from the range of products of a big German company, than with one of the greatest scandals of the decolonisation.

On 2nd July, 1925, the story begins in the small village Onalua, where Isaie Tasumbu Tawosa was born. The young Isaie grew up under the most difficult conditions in this part of Congo, which was occupied by Belgium. Because the traumatisation of a whole country came along with the colonial occupation, the traumas went down in history as the Congo horrors, and their long-term effects can still be observed today. In their hunt for the immeasurable riches of the Congo, the Belgian colonial administration acted with such a brutality against the population that the other colonial powers and the USA intervened.

251

Reliable estimates show that at least five million humans became victims of the Belgian terror, which means forty per cent of the total population.

Isaie's father, a poor farmer, put all his hope in Isaie, who was already seen as curious and bold when he was very young. He did not want the boy to suffer the fate of colonial slavery, which was imposed on him by being forced to grow cotton, but he was supposed to become a religion leader - a profession, which did not only protect against torture, which was ever-present in case of lower yields, but also meant economic success and a good reputation in society. His father and his mother sacrificed themselves for this better future. His first years in the Catholic school supported the hopes of his parents because his performance could not have been better. However, the more their son, on whom their hopes were pinned grew, the more rebellious he became against the colonial system. After he quarrelled with a teacher, he was dismissed from the school. A world collapsed for his parents. The twelve-year-old found refuge at his auntie's place.

Three months later, he registered in a Protestant school. To get to the school, he had to cope with a long walk of seven kilometres. His aversion to the obligatory worship service and the physical punishment, led to another expulsion from school after two years. He stayed only one year at the next school. This time, he had taken the liberty of correcting the teacher. Finally, he decided to join a training course to become a nursing aid, but received his dismissal however when his past got known. Without having completed any school or training, the fifteen-year-old did not have any other choice than to return to his home village, and to help his parents with the field work. Thanks to his ability to read and write, he found employment with the missionaries. During this time, he read everything he could lay his hands on. The more he read, the less he could accept the failure of his education. He did not see a way out of the oppressing poverty in the village.

That is why he tried again, and moved to the next town. This step marked a turning point in personal, social and political perspective. The young man changed his name for the new beginning to Patrice Eméry Lumumba – *Lumumba: rebellious masses*. He received employment in a mining company, which was glad about any worker who helped to maintain the production of tin in the Second World War, in which Congo was engaged alongside the colonial power. After four months, Lumumba had believed that he had saved enough money for his education. Whilst he was working as an assistant at the post office, he studied privately to obtain his school-leaving qualification in present day Kisangani, at that time Stanleyville, named after the traveller Henry Morton Stanley. His self-confidence grew due to this triumph over the teachers and priests, who fought against him. It was not only the beginning of a social advancement but also the start of a passionate struggle for independence.

After his first employment as a postal worker, and his prompt promotion after having passed the necessary exam, he went to the capital Kinshasa, at that time, Léopoldville, named after the Belgian King Leopold II. The joy over his accomplishment faded quickly when he found out that Belgian colleagues received more than twice as much as what he was earning for the same work. Lumumba decided to connect with different associations to denounce these conditions, and he wrote critical articles for *La Croix du Congo* (The Cross of Congo), and for *La voix du Congolais* (The voice of the Congolese), the only newspapers of the local residents. These articles were about the life of the *Évolués*, literally: the 'developed', which means, the Africans, who live like Europeans - before their adaptation to the European way of life, and their defence of the colonial mission. He also wrote about the inequality between the whites and the *Évolués*. He founnd great resonance by people of this educated class.

The whites lived isolated in Belgian Congo and had every privilege. Limited privileges were promised to the small layer of educated Congolese, for example the possibility to visit public institutions after dark; to take walks at this time; to buy alcoholic beverages; to receive better treatment in hospitals and to access cabins on board of ships. Requirements were a certain level of education, being a Christian, and having the title Évolué (civilised person). For this, the applicants had to undergo complex and degrading suitability test. They would receive unannounced house calls to check different attributes and behaviour such as being in a monogamous relationship; cleanliness in the house; short hairstyle; wearing of ironed clothes; underwear and polished shoes; eating food with cutlery at the table and finally; to always have a handkerchief with them. A final examination follows after the check of their lifestyle, in the course of which the views of the applicant were carefully examined. Lumumba was asked about his reading, when he applied in 1953 to be a part of this so-called 'matriculation', to be able to lead a dignified life.

His information – books about politics, history and the French colonies in Africa – were suspicious, and he passed the test only after a second attempt. In 1956, he challenged the colonial system, appalled by the discriminatory way the Congolese get paid in their own country. He took from the money, which belonged to the post office, what he deserved, in his opinion. When he was charged with embezzlement, his response was "one cannot demand from the Évolués that they live like Belgians, and pay them only half of the salary of what their Belgian colleagues get". This unusual clear criticism of the regime alarmed the colonial masters. Lumumba's detention stirred up a wave of indignation on the side of the Évolués, and initiated a political awareness.

After his release, Lumumba worked as a sales manager of a brewery, and decided to participate in the resistance against the colonial oppression. In 1957, he joined the founding members of *Mouvement National Congolais* (Congolese National Movement), the only party which was represented throughout the country. Lumumba reached many people through his work as sales manager. Due to his charisma, he became a central figure of the Congolese independence movement within a short period of time. He became the red rag for the colonial power, and they reacted with brutal methods to prevent the loss of the cash cow, the Congo. In October 1959, Lumumba was arrested and tortured and in January 1960, he was released.

When his party won the parliamentary elections on 25th May, 1960, the powerful white upper class did everything to prevent Lumumba from becoming the prime minister, but in vain. A hysterical debate sparked off in Europe on the question whether the Congolese were capable at all to rule a country.

The Belgians ridiculed the Congolese on the 'undeniable immaturity of the blacks' and sang a defamatory song, which combined racism with the anti-Soviet propaganda:

And they are dancing Rumba,
Nikita Chruschtschow and Lumumba,
And the UNO must not know,
What they plan for Katanga.

Behind the pretended concern for the future of the Congo, was hidden fear that an inexhaustible source of natural resources and raw materials could be lost. There was the uranium for example, which was needed by the USA for their nuclear programme. Plans were made in secret to rmove the self-confident leader; the more so as he took interest in the unification of African countries, which hopefully would completely break the stranglehold of the former colonial powers and the USA.

On 30th June, 1960, a public confrontation between Lumumba and the representatives of the colonial order materialised. The Belgian King Baudouin arrived with his entourage on the occasion of the 'solemn release of Congo into independence'. The young king gave a speech to the gathered upper class, the foreign guests and the international press, in which he honoured the 'achievements' and the 'civilisational accomplishments' of colonisation. He closed his speech in the pose of the noble Monarch with the following words, "Do not burden your future with premature reformations, and do not replace the structures, which Belgium leaves for you, by others, before you do not know exactly that the new ones are better ... Do not be afraid to turn to us! Even in the future, we will always provide you with advice and support. In this way, we will train together with you the administrators and technicians, whom you will need." He did not mention the million-fold murders, and the inhuman exploitation of the Congolese people at all. Lumumba in the first row was taking notes on a small piece of paper. The Congolese eagerly awaited the speech of their President, Joseph Kasavubu.

He however, gave a speech to please the colonial power. He considered Baudouin well-behaved, and prayed to God to protect the Congolese people and their political leaders. As he finished, Lumumba got up from his seat and walked to the podium. The audience was irritated because there was no more scheduled speeches; the prgramme had ended. The faces of the Belgian settlers darkened; at the same time as the Congolese activists were looking up to Lumumba, full of expectation. The first words of the spontaneous speech already reinforced the feelings of both sides. The uninvited speaker directed his speech only to the Congolese.

He criticised the earlier speakers for their distortion of the historical facts and criticised them for describing the independence as if it was a gift, "No Congolese, who is worthy of the name, will ever forget that it was the struggle, which brought us independence ... A fight, in which we did not fear hardships or suffering, and we did neither spare our strength nor our blood to end the humiliating slavery." The Belgian king was petrified, while a thunderous applause of the Congolese listeners made the hall shake. The representatives of the press squirmed around on their chairs, eager to record the historical scandal word-for-word. "We were ridiculed, insulted and continually beaten, only because we were blacks. Who could ever forget that one addressed a black person naturally, informally, and not because he was regarded as a friend, but because the honourable way of addressing somebody was reserved for the whites. We had our country stolen because of dubious documents which were called law, in reality however, they only certified the right of the strong. ... We will not forget the massacres, in which many died, and neither the cells, in which people were thrown, because they did not want to accept a regime of suppression and exploitation. We will ensure that the riches of our fatherland really benefit its children. We will check all previous acts accordingly, and we will pass laws, which will promote justice and human dignity."

The affronted king looked into the void and decided to depart right away, but was stopped by his advisors with great difficulty. There was an outburst of spontaneous jubilation in the Congolese population. For the first time, someone has had the guts to oppose their abusers, and screamed the injustice to the whole world; the injustice, they had had to endure for generations. In Europe, the reaction to the new man, who had read the colonial powers the riot act, and who resolutely announced a new era, alarmed the authorities. It was an encounter on an equal footing. The following events, which were dubbed the 'Congo crises' in a blurring way, showed what effect Lumumba's appearance had on Belgium, the USA and the western business world.

Two months after the celebration of independence, the rich province of Katanga announced its secession from the new state. This happened with the backing of the colonial powers, Belgium and the USA. The USA pressed for the dismissal of Lumumba by President Kasavubu, whilst the UNO declared itself neutral. When Lumumba retaliated by removing Kasavubu from office, Colonel Joseph Mobutu staged a coup d'état on the 14th of September, declared himself president, and placed Lumumba under house arrest. On the 27th of November, Lumumba was able to flee. He turned to the population in improvised demonstrations in accordance with his conviction that in a sovereign state, the power comes from the people. In this way he wanted to publicly reveal the conspiracy and organise the resistance. After three days, his escape was detected and he was caught and taken to the military camp in Thysville (today Mbanza Ngungu).

On 17th January, 1961, under the impression that Lumumba's followers mobilised themselves, and that soldiers mutinied, the abducted, and severely maltreated head of government was taken away from the prison, which was unsafe by then, and killed by Congolese soldiers, Belgian and CIA agents, together with his combatants Okito and Mpolo. While the rumour was spread,that Lumumba was killed in a village by its inhabitants, the murderers returned to the crime scene three days later, exhumed the dead body, cut it into pieces, and dissolved it in sulfuric acid and burned the remains. The murderers stayed unaffected despite the indictment, which was lodged by his son against twelve parties involved. The news of his assassination was received by many in Europe with joy. Unlike in the West, Lumumba was honoured by the Soviet Union, by the University Lumumba.

In Africa, Lumumba has become the symbolic figure of the fight against the colonial and neo-colonial rule. Like Nkrumah, Cabral and Sankara, he stands for the failed hope for the new construction of the continent, which was destroyed by the dictators and their western allies. Lumumba's last letter to his wife is a legacy for the following generations; "We demand the right of a decent living for this country, the right of an absolute dignity, of an independence without restrictions – our enemies were not willing to grant it to us ... Whether the colonisers kill me or let me stay alive, my person is not so important. What counts is Congo, our poor nation, whose independence turned into a cage. It will regain its dignity, and live under a brilliant sun."

Bibliography
Ludo de Witte: *Government order assassination. The Death of Lumumba and the Congo Crises.* Leipzig 2001;
David von Reybrouck: *Congo. A story.* Berlin 2012;
Thomas Giefer: *Assassination in the colonial style* (movie). 2000.

AMÍLCAR CABRAL Guinea Bissau/Cape Verde

THE SMALL MAN'S HOPE

BY TANDIS

In 1978, Jimmy Cliff gave a concert in Kaolack, which was the second biggest town of Senegal at that time. It was the event of the century for the inhabitants. Thunderous applause and ear-shattering cheers started up, when the reggae star appeared on stage. It took some time to make himself heard. He announced with a serious face that he had to inform the audience about something important ... He would not perform that day, if he would not get his cap back ... For a few seconds, dead silence prevailed ... Excited murmurs could be heard in the station, which fell silent however, as soon as Jimmy Cliff rose to speak again ... Somebody had ripped the cap off his head when he was on his way to the stage ... There was confusion, and amazement as the audience did not understand what was going on. These caps did not cost anything! They were extremely cheap! Each of us would give him ten for free tomorrow ... in every colour ... He could even buy the factory ...

Shortly before the amazement turns to impatience, Jimmy Cliff explained everything to the irritated crowd. ... Cabral had given the cap to him as a present, and he treasured it very much ... The tension released itself in a collective outcry. The idol, who nearly fell from grace for a moment, was supported by his fans again. The loud indignation at the theft however lasted only until the evildoer felt ashamed because of what he had done, and sent the cap back to the owner over many heads and with the help of many hands. Everybody who participated in the improvised relay, was happy and respectfully passed on the relic. The enthusiasm was nearly religious, when the relieved Jimmy Cliff put on his cap, and when the bassist opened the concert with powerful drum beats. It probably turned out to be the best concert the country had ever experienced, and it would go down in the annals of Senegalese history of music, as *Concert with Cabral's Cap*.

The story with the cap is the most outstanding appreciation of a man, who has been widely honoured. Several schools, an airport, an African football tournament as well as a square in Moscow and an avenue in Paris bear his name. It is a story, which speaks of hopes, fights and disappointments of African people at the time, when they established their states.

When Cabral was born on 12th September, 1924 in Bafatá, a village in present day Guinea-Bissau, his father Juvenal Cabral, a primary school teacher from Cape Verde, gave him the name Hamilkar. He was a politically engaged person, and therefore chose a name with a symbolic character: a name, which expresses a deep protest against the massive oppression of the colonial power, Portugal, headed by the fascist Salazar. Maybe Juvenal's secret hope was that his son would take on the personality of his namesake, as one believes in African cultures. His son was supposed to be a proud representative of his people based on the role model of the Carthaginian Hamilkar Barkas, who is considered to be the first resistance fighter against the European predominance in Africa, and whose son Hannibal stood up to the Roman Empire. Cabral's mother, Dona Iva Pinhel Evora, was a seamstress and worked in a fish factory to help make a living for the family. Amilcar Cabral grew up on the Cape Verde islands, which is a Portuguese colony together with Guinea-Bissau.

In 1940, the sixteen-year-old experienced how people die of hunger on Cape Verde, where he is at home with his family since 1932. They die because the Portuguese merchants export all cereals and vegetables produced by the inhabitants of the Cape Verde to Portugal and Europe where the Second World War has caused a price inflation which made great profits possible. Twenty thousand Cape Verdeans fell victim to this exploitation, which meant more than one-tenth of the 180 000 inhabitants. For the first time, the young Cabral questioned the political conditions in his home country. What caused these cruel deaths? Why did the Portuguese have the power in this land? In 1944, the second famine catastrophe followed. This time the 'silent genocide', as it was called later, took thirty thousand lives. These traumas shaped Cabral's thinking and action.

When he received a scholarship to study in a university in Lisbon in 1945, he decided to study agricultural science, one of the few courses of study to which black students were also admitted. Due to this, he belongs to the privileged in the colonial system. Not many people could attend school, let alone receive a scholarship. Cabral however, saw through the perfidious strategy to divide the population in 'natives' and *Assimilados*, 'assimilated people', who were supposed to serve as buffer between the population and the occupying force. He analysed this strategy in his writings. He made it his duty to warn the privileged groups of the colonised people of the estrangement from the majority of the population, and of the collaboration with the colonial power.

The people at the Institute for Agricultural Sciences were quite astonished about the new student because he was black. Though many Africans were living in Lisbon (in the golden period of slavery, they even accounted for ten per cent of the inhabitants), they did not appear at the university. People thought the man had lost his way. Former fellow students described him not only as intelligent but also as sociable and elegant. His political engagement began in Lisbon, by his participation in a demonstration against Salazar, an admirer of Mussolini. Very soon, Cabral was promoted to the position of moderator for student assemblies.

He is being observed by two talent scouts of the well-known football club, Benfica Lissabon during a football match of his institute. After the match, they move up to him and amaze him with the offer of a test-training. One of his friends sees right away the political dimension of this offer. "This would be a sensation!" he exclaims, widely opening his eyes, and seemingly taking an opportunity with the right hand. "It would be of the utmost significance for the whole diaspora," he continues with a haunting voice. "Every goal would be a shot across the bows of the colonial Armada! In the interviews, you could draw the attention towards the scandalous occupation of our countries! And equally importantly, he says confidentially, "every shot through the legs of one of them, would be a triumphant pleasure;.for thousands upon thousands!" he adds with a mischievous smile, "Let alone the tackling, kicking their shins, at best with a nice tackle."

He is not the only one who thinks like this because all blacks are confronted with open racism and glaring discrimination. Cabral does not accept the offer of Benfica. It is not enough for him to become a soccer star.

In 1949, Leopold Sédar Senghor, who later became the president of Senegal, published an anthology of African poetry with the title *Anthologie de la nouvelle poésie nègre* (Anthology of the new Negro poetry). The book marked the beginning of the *Négritude* movement, which became the symbol of the self-assertion of African nations, and it showed Cabral, as he was writing in retrospective, that all blacks in all parts of the world were protesting. In the texts of African writers, which were published by Senghor, he came across the experiences and longings, which he himself tried to work through in his poems since his school years. The awareness that humans everywhere in Africa were pressing for change, strengthened the hope in him that soon they would be freed from colonial oppression. In the same year, for the first time, he spent his summer holidays at home. Full of enthusiasm, he started to talk to the farmers in the surrounding villages, and he showed and taught them new techniques to control soil erosion, and he introduced to them measures to help them increase their yields. He also used these meetings to discuss political issues. After the first conversations with the farmers from the neighbouring villages, he wanted to address a much wider circle with the help of a radio programme, and he plannned to organise an evening course in the Cape Verdean capital, Praia. But the governor prohibits both.

"How long will it take, until we get rid of these monsters?" his father asks him, embittered.

"Not longer than ten years," Cabral replied despite his setback, and told him about the initiatives of the well-educated people, about the hundred thousand forcibly recruited soldiers, which were used as cannon fodder in the Second World War, and who no longer believed in the invincibility of the whites or in other myths. His father died a few months later.

More purposeful than ever, he went back to Lisbon at the end of his vacation, and engaged himself in circles of African students from the colonies. After the completion of his studies, Cabral went to Bissau, the capital of the Portuguese colony, where he had lived up to the age of

261

eight, and where he worked at this time for the agricultural and forestry service. He preferred this employment as 'second-class' engineer to a well-paid position in Portugal. He wanted to revive his old connections in Bissau but had to realise however that he was shunned by most of them. Their fear of PIDE, the Portuguese secret police, who suspiciously observe every activity just as the Gestapo, their role model, was too great; and Cabral was not unknown for the colonial adminstators because he had already been arrested during demonstrations in Lisbon.

Thanks to his work, he could travel throughout the country without obstruction, and he could collect information about each region, about their traditional structures and cultural peculiarities. The highly active engineer however was a thorn in the flesh of the colonial authorities. They denied him the permission to establish a sports club, when he tried to do so in 1954. In the same year, he was forced to see the governor, a naval officer.

"Now, Cabral, are you the leader of the local Mau-Mau movement?" he asked sarcastically.

Cabral answered calmly, "There is no Mau-Mau here, as far as I know. It exists only in Kenya."

"Fine. Listen to me Mr. Engineer, live your life. Be the man of the new era, but do not put your career at risk!"

After this conversation, the governor ordered Cabral's expulsion from Guinea-Bissau and the Cape Verde. He received permission to visit his family once a year. Cabral moved to Angola, where he instituted the grassroots Movement for the Liberation of Angola (MPLA) in December 1956 with the local intellectuals. Three months before he had formed the African Party for the Independence of Guinea-Bissau and Cape Verde. (PAIGC). At that time, he went underground and signed his articles and poems with Abdel Djassi.

In these years, historical events buoyed him up, as well as all other politically conscious Africans: the French colonial troops had suffered a devastating defeat in Dien Bien Phu, at the hands of the Vietnamese freedom fighters; the National Liberation Front (FLN) in Algeria had entered into the armed fight; in 1955, the first Afro-Asian solidarity conference took place in the Indonesian Bandung. The Non-Aligned States, which represented more than half of the population of the world demanded the cancellation of the racist world order, and they agreed upon a co-operation as well as support for all independence movements. The colonial powers were alarmed by the new players on the international stage, and they realised that their time was up. Therefore, they decided to carry out a preventive decolonisation (Eric Hobsbawm). They wanted to rather recognise the independence of the colonies, to still have economic and cultural influence rather than lose potential partners in the Cold War, and release them into independence. This is how it was said complacently. By the end of the 'African year' 1960, only twenty-four (from a total of fifty-three) states had been freed from colonial rule, despite many agitations for independences. It was not until the middle of the 1960s, that nine more followed. The territories occupied by the Portuguese have a long way to go: the Portuguese colonial power keeps the colonies even more in a chokehold.

In1959, Cabral leaves the underground and moves in the neighbouring Guinea-Conakry into the headquarters, which the president of the new state, Sékou Touré, has made available for the PAIGC. The colonised and the colonialists are equally electrified when he addresses the people for the first time on radio, "The moment has come for our people to prepare to take responsibility for a decisive era in their history upon themselves, that is to say, for the fight for national liberation ... It will only be victorious when all children of our fatherland stand up for it without distinction on the grounds of sex, ethnicity or skin colour ... It is the fight of all Guineans and Cape Verdeans, who have committed themselves to search for the happiness of all children of both of these countries. "This voice from the radio seems like redemption for the population of both countries." Finally, there is a perspective out of the oppression! The opposite side on the other hand persists in their claim to power with brutal force.

In August of the same year, the harbour workers of Pidjiguiti go on strike. The colonial authority orders to fire on strikers. Eighty-five workers die. The PAIGC trains the fighters with even greater determination, and they make clear that they do not fight against the Portuguese people as such, despite torture and killing of actual and presumed members carried out by the colonial power, but that they are fighting against the Portuguese colonial rule. That is why it is forbidden to attack colonisers just because they are white, and there are also Portuguese fighting for the PAIGC.

Cabral underlines in his seminars again and again that the decolonisation has to be accompanied by real improvements for the people, otherwise peace and progress will remain empty phrases. The PAIGC not only maintains health care stations accordingly, but also shops for the people, which offer them an alternative to the expensive range of goods of the Portuguese merchants. When the fighters are not engaged in fighting, they work with the farmers on the fields. The secret construction of schools even in remote settlements also belongs to the preparations for the future state. Cabral developed four school books in line with the mental decolonisation.

Cabral gave much thought to Karl Marx, like many intellectuals, who are confronted with imperialism and its inhuman ideology. Differently from the dogmatists, who misused him, he regarded Marxism as a method, which is based on detailed analyses of the social contexts, and which makes insights into necessary changes possible. Out of this understanding, he does not regard people as mere recipients of political decisions, but as conscious players of the societal reorganisation. The principles of solidarity and democracy are supposed to be valid in the PAIGC. No cadres exist, but instead only representatives of the single groups. There are no differences in rank in the army apart from the commanders, who are elected rotationally. Cabral emphasises the autonomy of everybody regarding their thinking and acting as another basic principle because units often have to operate without any contact with other groups or to the party leaders, due to the distances and missing communication possibilities.

After the first successes of the PAIGC, something Frantz Fanon describes in his book, *The Wretched of this Earth* can be felt: The experience of the violent colonial oppression affects the thinking and the behaviour of the oppressed. In this way, the PAIGC-fighters had been confronted with tyranny and humiliation as well as with the privileged status of certain groups at the expense of others. After being isolated in military camps for years, and after brutal fights, the partly young commanders were confronted with the unusual task of establishing the new order in the liberated villages. As such, some of them allowed plundering and mistreatment of the population. Some performed like feudal lords, and again, others declared themselves independent clan chiefs and owned armies, where only personnel from their own ethnic group was accepted.

Considering this misuse of power and the separation, Cabral and the party leaders faced the decision to either take drastic measures in line with the philosophy of the party or to give up the fight because without a uniform approach, the resistance against the Portuguese army and their NATO-allies had to remain unsuccessful. They called for a general meeting, which took place from the 13th to the 17th of February, 1964 in a forest clearing close by the small town Cassaca, which was difficult to access. An aggressive atmosphere prevailed instead of the comradeship of earlier days. Three of the accused commanders did not appear, the others came with their bodyguards. The leadership of the PAIGC and the blameless commanders saw themselves outnumbered, and could only rely on Cabral's reputation and his persuasive power.

On the evening of February the 15th, the decisive confrontation arises. The participants are sitting in a big circle, which is shielded by armed bodyguards, against the background of a colonial counteroffensive in the form of cluster and napalm bombs against the city Como. At first, the delegates of the cities report about the raids, the misuse of power, and even about executions. After that, a hearing of the accused takes place. Many however, refuse to give evidence.

Cabral rises to speak after that. To his mind, the uncontrolled exercise of violence corrupts the vision of a new society and a dignified future of the population. Moreover, it endangers the aims of the anticolonial fight. "Without the support from Guinea, Ghana, Senegal, Morocco, Algeria and other countries, even from Europe, from the Soviet Union and Sweden, our movement would barely have a chance ... Do these reports show that this is what they have to expect from us? ... What is the difference between us and the damned colonisers when everybody takes what they want only because they have weapons? ... Does anybody believe that he or she can do something alone with a village army against the heavily armed colonial army? In addition, does anybody believe that one can establish a future against the people? ... Whoever deviates from the principles of the party or ignores instructions harms the common cause, and has to be excluded as a traitor. It is better, when we are not so numerous, and instead, do not cause any suffering for the population of our country than when we are many, and some of us commit injustices however."

The guards put their hands on their rifles, when they heard these words. One of those persons who felt accused of a betrayal of the common cause, walked into the middle of the circle and challenged Cabral, "If you consider me guilty, then take my weapons away from me and order an investigation!..."

The crowd holds its breath. Cabral says in his matter-of-fact way, "You are right. I command that you be disarmed."

The bodyguards load their rifles and pistols. The commander pulls his weapon and walks up to Cabral. He stops walking one metre in front of him, holds up his pistol ostentatiously … and puts it down in front of Cabral's feet. He orders to disarm all the other accused and this happens.

An examination was carried out. All offenders were degraded and sent to zones far away from their home regions. Those who proved themselves after that got a second chance. Two out of the three commanders, who wanted to boycott the meeting were arrested, sentenced to death and executed. The third of them was killed by a Portuguese bomb.

The PAIGC drew consequences from their experiences with egoism and misuse of power. They elected a civil judgment body of the people to punish any wrongdoing on site; on the other hand they formed a multi-ethnic troupe, which was supposed to prevent ethnocentric tendencies, and they established institutions, which would support the integration of the population groups and the national consciousness in the liberated zones.

Ten years of fighting and an even greater test than the confrontation of Cassaca were still ahead of them. Only in 1972, the PAIGC is officially recognised by the UNO as the legitimate representative of the people of Guinea-Bissau and Cape Verde. Cabral has nearly reached his aim.

On 19th January, 1973 he visits Sékou Touré in Guinea-Conakry. Samora Machel, the first president of the other Portuguese colony, Mozambique, is a guest there at this time. He is one of the most passionate opponents of the apartheid regime in South Africa, who will die in 1986 in unexplained circumstances in a plane crash. His predecessor at the top of the Mozambican liberation movement, Frelimo, Eduardo Mondlane, was murdered in 1965 by a letter bomb by the Portuguese secret police PIDE, who also tried several times to kill Cabral.

A reception at the Polish embassy follows after the meeting with these presidents. After that, Cabral drives with his green VW Beetle to his headquarters. The streets are empty in this night because it is only nineteen degrees. This is cold for West African weather conditions.

Armed men emerged from the darkness, when Cabral and his wife pass the barrier and stop in front of his quarter. His bodyguards flee. Cabral does not understand what is going on because the attackers are comrades. Ironically, a Navy officer, the PAIGC is very proud of, holds his gun up and shoots at him. He collapses, gets up again and says, "We can discuss any problem, if there is something. But what is going on here?" The murderer, by the name Inocêncio, innocence, shoots Cabral several times in the head. This will however turn out to be a Pyrrhic victory for the Portuguese colonial power, who contracted the murder ...

The indignation is limitless in Africa, when the information about the murder spreads. A shock is triggered in Guinea-Bissau and Cape Verde by the report of the assassination. People's assemblies were summoned in the villages. The same unanimous decision is taken everywhere: The insidious murder cannot stay unpunished! Two weeks after the deed, the party leadership issues the slogan for the punitive action. The tenth anniversary of the founding of the OAU (Organization for African Unity) is chosen as the date for the action. On the 25th of May, 1973, the PAIGC-fighters initiated the *Operation Amílcar Cabral*. The punitive action rapidly develops to the final offensive against the colonial regime. It climaxes in the capture of the most important military base in the south, the camp of Guiledje. The colonial army counts hundred and fifty casualties, whereas one PAIGC-fighter is killed and one is injured. The number of dead people on the Portuguese side would have been even higher, if the PAIGC-forces had not left an escape-corridor open, to prevent a massacre.

After the devastating defeat in Guiledje, the governor of Portuguese-Guinea and Cape Verde steps down. On 24th September, 1973, the independent state Guinea-Bissau is proclaimed. Cabral's brother Luiz is elected as president. In 1975 Aristides Pereira another co-founder of the PAIGC, becomes president of the republic of Cape Verde. Cabral's successors could not realise his vision of a common state. The power struggles also prevented a co-operation of both states, and led to a division of the party, and to anti-democratic coups.

What would Cabral say today about the almost total liberation of the continent from the colonial occupation? Maybe these words from the year 1965, which defined the objective of his political struggle, "It is useless to liberate a region, when the people remain without the fundamental means of subsistence after that." His demand for democracy is just as crucial today, "We have to fight no matter the cost so that our citizens can accept that only the people have the power in our country. Up to now, they did not feel that way."

Chapter 36

This declaration of belief in public interest and popular sovereignty constitutes the universality of Cabral's thinking and of his acting as well as the longing, which his name evokes in Africans. Not least, also the cap of the ordinary people that bears his name until today stands for this.

Bibliography

Cabral, Amilcar: *The theory as weapon*. Bremen 1983;
Ziegler, Jean: *Against the order of the world. Liberation movements in Africa and Latin America*. Wuppertal 1985.

THOMAS SANKARA (Burkina Faso)
THE SOLDIER OF THE PEOPLE

BY M. MOUSTAPHA DIALLO

It is 20th May, 1983. There is turmoil in Ouagadougou, the capital of Upper Volta (today Burkina Faso). Grammar school pupils, students, workers, civil servants, unemployed people and hawkers followed the call of the labour unions and the left-wing parties. They have been flocking from the suburbs and the surrounding villages in buses, shared taxis, on mopeds, donkey carts and on foot into the city to confront the ruling military junta. Watched by the furious eyes of the security forces, who were ready for action, and known not to be soft to people, they support a call, which is unusual for a civil society: Captain Thomas Sankara has to be liberated! A strange demand from people, who have lived under a succession of military regimes since 1966. Why did they endure the military governments until now? Moreover, why do they not immediately demand democratic elections, when they are already turning themselves against the rulers? This however is another story ...

On the 16th of May, the captain, for whom they go onto the streets in Ouagadougou on 20th May, had been the Prime Minister of the military government. Therefore, the question arises, what prompts the population to stand up for this man in this way? The answer is both

269

simple and paradoxical: Sankara's democratic attitude. He won the trust of the people and a military regime is per se undemocratic. In addition, he had given their longing for honest politics a concrete form. Because of his charisma he was now a disturbing element for the government and its foreign allies. They arrested him, blinded by their intoxication with power, without taking into account the reaction of the population.

For more than two months, the protesters brought the country to a standstill. On 4th August, a parachute unit from the town Pô arrived in Ouagadougou. Colonel Blaise Compaoré headed it. The message of the arrival of the elite troop got the stuck confrontation moving. Sankara was released, and was appointed president. In a very short time only, he became the icon of the young generation of Africa, at the top of the new military regime, with the National Revolutionary Council as executive authority. Until today, he belongs to the great models of the continent. What is the basis of his popularity?

Whoever wants to answer this question, has to know what encouraged him, which experiences shaped his world of ideas and determined his actions. Thomas Sankara reported from experiences in his childhood, which engraved themselves into his memory.

When he was ten years old, the children of the French school director had been given a bicycle for Christmas. The young Thomas and his friends, who could only dream of a bicycle, did everything to be allowed to ride on it only once. They got the sand for the children of the director when they wanted to build a sandcastle. They got everything for them, whatever they needed. They cajoled them, carried their bags for them. The young French children however did not let anybody touch their bicycle. At some point, he understood that there seemed to be no way against the sadistic egoism of the privileged friends, and he decided to just take the bicycle and make a round with it, "no matter, what would happen afterwards". He was dismissed from school, and his father was put in prison.

The second experience took place one year later in 1969. The country had just become independent. The flag of the new state was hoisted in the schoolyard instead of the French Tricolor. French students took the flag down and burned it. A group of local students, Thomas first, pounced on the colonial offspring, and gave them a sound thrashing. His father was sent to jail again. This way of treating his father was as hurtful as enlightening for the eleven-year-old. Did one show one's gratitude like this to a man, who risked his life for the liberation of France from the Nazis, and who had to go through the hell of German captivity? Moreover, what was the value of the independence, which was celebrated in a big way, when the French still had such power over them?

His political actions were also very much influenced by an event in the post-colonial time. The country was hit by drought once again, and the families in the neighbouring villages put their last savings together, and chose one of them, who had to go to the capital to buy millet. The man rode his bicycle for several hours in the direction of the town which was completely unknown to him. He had to wait for several hours more in a line, feeling totally lost, whilst people, who came later, were attended to because they could speak French. Desperately, the man returned to his bicycle, which was no longer where he had left it. The small bundle of banknotes was also stolen from him. The man killed himself. He was buried provisionally in the town, whilst the starving families waited for his return.

Thomas Sankara's social background shaped his personality. His father who worked as a helper at the post office after he had completed his military service in the colonial army, was a Fulbe. His mother came from a Mossi family. The Mossi were the dominant population group in the former Mossi empire. In the conservative years of the 1950s, neither group accepted a child of such marriages fully. Therefore, in his early years already, Thomas had to deal with negative aspects of his heritage. Despite the material hardship and the fact that Fulbe were not respected at all, he experienced his father as a proud man, who was always helpful to his neighbours. Thomas received a lot of love from his mother, who had great empathy for him and all his siblings, and who tirelessly supported the family. He was the third of ten children, and learned from the cradle to share, and to take responsibility for his younger siblings.

After completing his high school education, the gifted student chose the career of an army officer. It was not known whether this decision was motivated by the conviction that a land had to be capable of defending itself against attackers or by the financial situation of the family. In May 1972, during his training in the military school in Antsirabé in Madagascar, the neo-colonial president of Madagascar, Tsirana, was overthrown by an uprising of the population. In the evening, a discussion arose about whether the coup was justified and how each of them had to react to it.

"The president is our supreme commander," said one of those who were very faithful. "And even civilians know what happens in the case of insubordination."

"And what if the president is the wrong one?" replied his rival. "If he only wants to get rich, and arrests all opponents, what do you do then as a soldier?"

"We must not interfere in politics, or have you ever seen generals as presidential candidates? We are bound to neutrality," said another.

"How is neutrality supposed to look in a confrontation between the people and a tyrant?" asked Sankara. "Do you want to interfere and restore order? The order, which caused the conflict?"

"You will be executed by a firing squad, if you take sides with the people, and the majority of the army however supports the president," pointed the first speaker.

"That is why one has to be prepared," answered Sankara.

He could not explain what he meant by this exactly because the discussion was interrupted.

In the evening, he wrote in his tattered notebook, "A soldier without political consciousness is a trained perpetrator." Since this day, the expression 'Army of the People' meant a great deal to him, and he read everything he could found about social theory.

On his return to the homeland, he joined other young officers, who suffered under the leadership of the old guard from the colonial time, and who longed for a modern army. In 1976, at the age of twenty-seven, Sankara, due to his military abilities and his charisma, received the order to command the newly established command unit in Pô. Despite his meteoric career, he remained true to his ideas about an army of the people and discreetely established contact with labour unions and left -wing oriented parties, although no co-operation took place. A coup in November 1980 demonstrated the urgent need of a democratic renewal, which was the focus of his initiative.

In September 1981, the new military government surprisingly offered him the post of State Secretary for Information. The government expected that it would be more accepted by the people with Sankara in this position, due to his personal charisma and his popularity among the soldiers. The inclusion of the commander of an elite troop in the political leadership was also advantageous for strategic reasons. Sankara, who refused the coup, did not accept the offer at first; only when the new ruling powers stressed their intention to establish democratic conditions, and when they granted him political options for action, were they able to persuade him.

Half a year later, a confrontation between Labour unions and government took place. The regime put a ban on strikes to make the only means of pressure by the civil society inoperative. Sankara stepped down from his position to protest against this onslaught on civil rights. He warned in a TV speech, "Woe to those who want to gag the people!" After that he was transferred for disciplinary reasons. Another half year later, a group of officers overthrew the military government. The new rulers also approached Sankara. This time, they offered him the post of the head of the government. The thirty-two-year-old assumed the office because he believed that he would have a concrete chance to prevent further imminent coups from happening and to develop his political vision. He declared in his first speech following the famous resistance fighter Samory Touré, "Ouagadougou will be the *bolibana* (end) of imperialism".

Two months after his appointment as Prime Minister, he gave a speech during a conference of the non-aligned states in India, which caused the world's public to sit up and notice. His radical statement about the continued domination of the former colonial powers alarmed the Western political leaders. Above all, the French president, Mitterand, who regarded the former colonies as an area of influence for France, was startled. The shrill tones from his African backyard made him position himself right away. Mitterand's advisor for 'African matters' arrived in Ouagadougou on the day after Sankara added another defiant speech against Western imperialism, on 15th May, 1983. Twenty-four hours later, Sankara was arrested with other officers, who were close to him.

It is certain for the people: the only representative of the government, who spoke for them, was supposed to be silenced. The consequence was the protest campaign which ended with the release of Sankara, and with the overthrow of the military regime. It was the beginning of a radical policy of 'cultural renewal'. It was also the start of a fight against three opponents: Sankara stood opposite the sluggish dinosaurs at the top of the neighbouring countries: the Western forces, who aimed to bring the deviant state, at all, back on track, at all cost, as well as the beneficiaries of the old order.

Sankara gave a clear signal right away: Symbolically he put an end to the use of the colonial name Upper Volta and renamed the country Burkina Faso: 'Land of the Righteous People'. The new name stands for the final liberation from the colonial burden; however, also for the overcoming of the negative parts of the tradition that allowed a social hierarchy. The name Burkina Faso was formed from words from the languages of the Mossi and Diula, who are the dominant groups in the country, and it was supposed to underline equality, which was the main aim of the social change. This definition of a new identity was followed by a comprehensive programme, which was based on social justice, direct participation and autonomous development.

Peoples' boards were established for this purpose, where the population was supposed to participate actively in decision making processes. Literacy programmes in the local languages were created to enable the people to participate in political life. The neo-colonial mentality was supposed to be overcome with the help of an information campaigwhich made the principles of the new social and economic policy, the contradiction of imported consumer behaviour and the wasteful use of resources a topic of discussion. The consistent implementation of the political programme revealed soon that the new name of the country was no empty phrase.

Sankara suggested a supervisory committee to prevent the unjust enrichment of individual groups. He was the first to disclose his financial situation and demanded from his ministers to do the same. He replaced the expensive limousines of the government fleet by middleclass cars. A limit of 150 000 Francs CFA (about 230 €) was set as the highest remunerations and the lowest were doubled. Sankara waived his presidential salary and received 138 000 Francs CFA like any captain. He wore clothes like any average citizen and participated in the regular clean-up operations in the city districts.

The situation of villages, which were neglected up to this time, was improved within the framework of their own efforts. For example, new roads were not tarred but built with red earth. Sankara supported the local production with equal consistency to overcome the dependence on imports from abroad. As such, the new government achieved successes nobody had ever thought possible.

Within four years, Burkina Faso, which had previously suffered constant famines, had freed itself from food imports, and it had achieved this without any help from abroad. This food self-sufficiency was all the more impressive as the country does not have any significant mineral resources; and harsh weather and drought cause difficulties. Furthermore, it is one of the countries which have very little infrastructure because the French colonial administration regarded it principally as a workforce pool for the plantations in Ivory Coast. The government even received the praise of the World Health Organization for the standard in health care. Moreover, in four years, Burkina Faso became one of the cleanest countries worldwide. Despite sabotage by Western and some African countries – for example in the case of the export of agricultural products or, the much-needed cement - Thomas Sankara had proved that a complete independence in Africa is no utopian idea.

A special success of the National Revolutionary Council was the support of the women, who experienced an improvement in their situation, as it had never been before. The plan to abolish polygamy and female circumcision however, encountered bitter resistance, and in fact, by women. The government was amazed when it recognised that polygamy meant that it freed them from daily routine work especially in the countryside, and that they felt that circumcision is an essential part of their female identity. The government responded to this unexpected resistance with compromises and relied on a future solution to the problem through education and information. The chosen compromise not only showed pragmatic thinking but also respect for the democratic popular will.

In the field of foreign policy, Sankara was marked by an active solidarity with the victims of oppression and discrimination. Two months after the change of power, he sent a plane fully loaded with meat to Angola, although Burkina Faso itself was suffering from a famine. He justified this apparent paradox relief action by this argument; "We are starving; our comrades in Angola however are in a much worse state. They were attacked by the South African racists." In 1986, he gave the ANC symbolically ten guns as a present to urge them to take actions that are more decisive in view of the atrocities of the white apartheid regime against the black population in South Africa. One year later, he organised a forum, which was supposed to initiate concrete actions against the racist regime. With equal dedication, he was committed to Pan-Africanism and to a co-operation with the African Diaspora in the USA and in the Caribbean.

As one of the few presidents from economically weak countries, Sankara met the dominant Western powers as equals. As such he showed solidarity with countries like Cuba and Nicaragua, which were ostracised by the Western world, and were shunned by the dependent states. Moreover, he condemned the capitalist system, in which the masses were working hard for wealth, but benefited from it the least.

The young generation of Africa celebrated Sankara like a pop star. Somebody finally got up in the stifling atmosphere of insincere policy and neo-colonial dependence and said, "No!" It was "No" to humiliation of a whole people by exploitation and dictation; "No" to cover-up and keeping peace by means of pittance and alms. All of a sudden, the meaningless summit meetings of African presidents became interesting because one of them expressed exactly what the people felt and he awakened the lethargic group. Sankara appeared at meetings in army fatigues with rolled up sleeves to expose the hypocritical army members, who disguised their absolute power with civillian clothes, and said smiling, "I am carrying a gun because I am a soldier. However, I am not the only one: The others are just hiding their weapons." On another occasion he proudly turned to the presidents, who imitated the representatives of the wealthy industrial nations by wearing their expensive designer suits, "Everything I am wearing on my body has its origin in Burkina Faso, from the growing of the raw material to the last seam." With his commitment to the union of the African states, which had been discussed so very often, and his concrete suggestions for joint activities, he became a thorn in the flesh of the predominantly selfish political leaders, who had more and more difficulties in hiding their reactionary stance.

Sankara aroused great enthusiasm amongst the African youth with his self-confident stance towards the arrogant Western forces, especially the lesson he taught the French president Mitterand was retold everywhere. On his first visit to France, a minister received him at the airport, as was usually done in the case of African presidents. When Mitterand made his return visit, Sankara did the same. This demonstration of equality became a political issue because it was considered as an affront to the 'godfather'. During the discussions, he offered his guest a seat on a shaky armchair; with the excuse that the poor economic conditions in the country, could not afford comforts as in France. Moreover, when Mitterand invited the West African presidents to meet him during a stopover in Dakar, Sankara was the only one, who did not turn up.

The powerful in the West were visibly irritated by this "upstart". When Sankara criticised imperialism and the invasion of Grenada by the USA in his first declaration on foreign policy, the US Ambassador appeared right away and delivered a message from President Reagan, his authoritative and worldly president, "Burkina does not understand the issues in Central America. It is too far away. However, should his government continue to interfere with the affairs in Central America, the government of the United States would feel forced to check all agreements on co-operation and all aid programmes for Burkina Faso one more time." Sankara replied to this kind of threat with more recalcitrant response to the 'forbidden countries', and with his first speech at UNO general meeting in 1984. In this speech, he denounced the 'scandal of the veto power', but also the inaction of the world community in the face of the brutal suppression of the Palestinians and the black population in South Africa. As the only African country, Burkina Faso boycotted the Olympic Games of 1984 in the USA because of the worldwide toleration of the apartheid regime.

On 29th July, 1987, Sankara added more to this with a speech, which caused a great sensation. In front of the assembly of the OAU (Organisation for African Unity), he ordered the African governments to jointly refuse the debt repayment. The 'debt crisis' in the developing countries came about due to sinking prices on the world market for raw materials, and due to rising interest burdens. These crises in turn led to the measures of the Structural Adjustment Policy which was imposed on developing countries by the World Bank and the International Monetary Fund, and which perpetuated their dependency on the industrial nations. With this public statement, Sankara blamed everybody who did not want to join him. Even though the problems of debt restructuring and of the viable debt-service-ratio for the developing countries in the international world are subjects of discussion up to today, at that time, Sankara's frontal attack against the neo-colonial system was the last straw that broke the camel's back.

In the afternoon of 15th October, 1987, Thomas Sankara was ambushed on the way to a meeting of the National Revolutionary Council. The ambush was controlled by the armed forces, but also from the outside, and by politicians of the neighbouring countries. The first car was torn up by grenades, when the car convoy of the president reached the fenced area. Sankara and his escort saved themselves in the next building and looked for possibilities to defend themselves. The attackers strafed the building massively so that Sankara said finally, "There is no sense in that. They want me." After that, he got up and went to the door.

Nine other people fell victim to the crime. Under cover of darkness, the attackers buried the murdered in a collective grave.

Compaoré, his companion, who then fought for his release and won, became president. He let 'natural death' be entered in the death certificate. The new ruler disbanded the National Revolutionary Council as his first official act, and invited the population to a rally. The people did not offer him this platform. Instead, thousands of them went to the graveyard to pay tribute to the murdered. For several days, the grief-stricken population said good bye to Thomas Sankara in an endless parade on the scene of the crime. Their mourning was mixed with impotent rage. They had become hostages of a ruthless band.

It was not easy to come to terms with the bitterness. The people in other countries had followed the development of the young man with deep admiration and heartfelt sympathy because they saw in him the embodiment of incorruptibility, courage, pride and long-sought after renewal. Young men secluded themselves to hide their tears, the students scheduled a memorial service instead of lectures, teachers did not teach their subjects, but told the pupils about Sankara and his meaning for Africa. Once again, an unholy alliance had destroyed the dream of a whole generation with the force of arms. On the other hand, Compaoré, who had refused to date to explain the background of the murder, and whose repressive regime has no qualms about killing journalists who crtiticise him, such as Norbert Zongo for example; this Compaoré enjoys worldwide recognition, not least when he visited Germany in 2012.

The killing of Sankara was an attack on the hopes and the aspirations for self-rule for a whole continent because he had shown the way out of the servitude in which the African people are still being kept. Therefore, his name is a legacy, not only for Africans.

At a time of neo-colonial suppression, Sankara took over the torch of self-empowerment, and he ignited the flame. He definitely would have wished that the subsequent generations would have caused the fire to blaze again. When he was once asked, which image he wanted to leave for posterity, he answered, "I only wish that my actions convince the greatest sceptics that there is a power, which is called *the people*, and that one has to fight for the people and with the people. Moreover, I would like to pass on the conviction that we ... will gain a victory."

Bibliography

Thomas Sankara: *Thomas Sankara speaks. The Burkina Faso Revolution 1983-1987.* New York 2007;

Jean Ziegler: *Against the order of the world – liberation movements in Africa and Latin America.* Wuppertal 1985.

LAPIRO DE MBANGA (Cameroon)

MUSIC AS WEAPON

BY FLORENTIN SAHA KAMTA

Icons of African music like Fela Kuti, Lucky Dube and Alpha Blondy made a name for themselves by challenging the leaders with their music. They cast the scream of the masses against the grievances from which they suffer, into songs. The Cameroonian singer Lapiro de Mbanga, who has been living in exile in the USA since September 2012, is following in their footsteps. Since 1985, he has been fighting against the regime of President Paul Biya, and he proves in an impressive way how music can play an important role in social and political controversies. Lapiro is an ambivalent personality in the struggle for a more just allocation of the resources in Cameroonian society. His career is even more interesting because since the 1990s, he is not only exposed to the rage of the power that be, but also the resentment of his own followers.

Lapiro – actually Lambo Sandjo Pierre Roger – was born in 1957 in the Cameroonian small town, Mbanga, as a son of a multi-millionaire but from the beginning he identified himself more with the deprived, because he grew up with his grandmother in poor living conditions. Thus his role models are always people who dedicated their lives to the fight against social injustice and political oppression: Mahatma Ghandi, Malcom X,

Nelson Mandela and the murdered Cameroonian anti-colonialist, Ruben Um Nyobé. Moreover, he declared his sympathy with the ideals of the French revolution.

Very early already, Lapiro stands on the stage as *Ndinga Man*, guitar man; he plays the Makossa-music, which is very popular in Cameroon. From the beginning, he rejects the political leadership in Cameroon without any compromise, and goes into exile in Nigeria when he is only twenty years old. It is there that he gets to know world-famous and committed singers such as Jimmy Cliff and Fela Kuti. As a guitarist in Fela's band, he experiences the fearless government critic at close range, and he lets himself be inspired by his vision of a world without discrimination. Right after his return in 1985, his single *Pas Argent No Love* (No love without money) becomes a hit in Cameroon. His music surely entertains, but it especially expresses exactly what those who feel deprived of their rights think. Soon he became the voice of Cameroonians despite constant censorship. The secret of his success is not least to be found in his statement about a policy which alienates the rulers from the population.

French is considered to be the magic key for social success and power in Cameroon, and English is said to be the 'key to the world'. Pidgin-English on the other hand, which is mostly spoken by local business people, is considered to be a 'key to nowhere'. The well-read Lapiro decides to use 'Camfranglais', a mixture of Cameroonian, French, and English and languages he calls 'Mboko-Talk' and completely ignores the hierarchy of the colonial languages. A sentence like *No Make erreur tara* can serve as an example of that. *No Make* is Pidgin, *erreur* French and *tara* is proper name in Cameroon from the well-known local language Eton. The sentence literally means, "Be careful not to make a mistake, my dear!" and it is ambiguous. Although Lapiro expresses himself in interviews in French as well as in English, he refuses to translate his songs and explains that the simple people, who are called *mboutoukou* (fools) by the elite, can understand him. He proudly proclaims his belonging to the 'small people' and shows this also with his outfit, which matches the visual appearance of a criminal. The youth take the 'Mboko-Talk' up and develops it further, whilst the educated people react by shaking their heads. Today, more and more scientists recognise this creation of language.

In the years of the economic crises, Lapiro becomes a figurehead of the social movements. Under the pressure of the World Bank and the

International Monetary Fund, the government introduced rationalisation measures, which led to collective dismissals and the shutting down of companies. Many young people survived by working as street vendors, car washers, drivers of moped taxis and something similar. The government sent the police off, especially, against these artists of life, who feed their families without any state support. In those days, the single *Mimba wi* (Don't forget about us) gained sensational popularity. In it, Lapiro called on the rulers in the name of the victims of the economic crises:

We no wan kick-oh
We no wan go for ngata
We de daso for ndengwe
A beg mimba wi-oh, yes tara.
We no wan problem para
We no wan go for Ndengui
We di fain daso garri
For heleo we own family-oh!

"We, who were forgotten even in the times of the economic growth, do not want anymore that you give us something from the 'national cake'. We are only begging you to let us live; we will surely find a way. But do not send us to prison; we are no robbers. We are fighting for survival. Help us to survive. Think of us."

At the beginning of 1990, something unbelievable happened. After many conversations between the people affected and the police chief, many of these criminalised activities were officially accepted as professions. Hundreds of thousands are still working in these professions and pay tax.

The role of spokesman became the singer's downfall. The wind of democracy blew over Cameroon like in many other African countries. The young generation, led by students, demanded extensive reformations and transparency. To add emphasis to the demands, they carried out the so-called *opération ville morte* (operation dead city), which paralysed whole towns: markets and shops opened only on Saturdays. Hundreds of students were killed during the confrontations with the police, and many spokesmen – writers and journalists amongst them - had to leave the country.

Lapiro stands up to those mass protests and declares that the rulers do not suffer because of these operations, but only the traders and the consumers, which means the ordinary people. The amazement is boundless on both sides: The sharpest critics of the regime speak against the uprising. The power apparatus does not pass up on such an opportunity. The police chief turns to Lapiro to end the continuing unrest. In a speech read out on the radio and television, the singer begs the striking people to end the general strike. Whilst the population wonders about this appeal, the government leaks the information that the musician had received a converted amount of 35 000 Euros. He denies that he has ever gotten this money. However, the arrangement with the other sides is more than enough. The concert from 20th June, 1991, during which Lapiro plans to put out a statement, becomes a debacle. Before he could say a word, he is beaten up; the angry mob also destroys his business premises and his house. Overnight, the idol has become a hated traitor. Lapido is desperate and feels completely misunderstood. He retreats to his hometown Mbanga. In 1992, the government cancelled the one-party-system, which had existed since 1962.

In the following sixteen years, Lapiro's followers give him a cold shoulder, and consider him an outcast. Despite his isolation, he continues to give his view on the political situation in the country. In his new albums, he denounces the corruption, the manipulation of elections and the mismanagement, and blames the president for ruining the country. At the same time, Cameroon is rated in 1998 and in 1999 as the most 'corrupt country' in the world by Transparency International; until 2004, about forty per cent of the Cameroonian budget was embezzled per year. In 2008, when the 80-year-old president aimed at a constitutional amendment so that he could rule for life, Lapiro answered with the single *Constitution constipé* (Clogged Constitution), and this time he even sings in French because he also turns to the international community. In this song, he describes Paul Biya as an old, tired and completely overburdened man, who allows the enemies of the republic to do what they like. With the expression 'Enemies of the Republic', he accepted a term, which was used for those who wanted to overthrow the president. The singer bluntly invokes all Cameroonians at home and abroad to be ready for an offensive against the incrusted and corrupt regime.

His colleagues Longuè Longuè, Joe La Conscience and Le Général Valsero protested equally vigorously. Some of their songs are: *50 ans au pouvoir* (50 years in power), *Touche pas à ma constitution* (Hands off my

Constitution), *Ce pays tue les jeunes* (This Country Kills the Youth). It comes to a confrontation, which goes down in the history of the country, when the civil society calls for protest marches against increased living costs and the planned constitutional amendment. From the 25th to the 28th of February, 2008, the population fought heavily with the police, the gendarmerie and the armed forces. Approximately a hundred and forty demonstrators were killed. Lapiro was arrested along with countless others for incitement to revolt, call for illegal meeting, destruction of property and looting. The musician's rehabilitation arises from the blow against him. Although his single *Constitution constipée* is forbidden, people listen to it in coaches, bars and residential houses as if Lapiro had never fallen in disgrace.

He was sentenced to three years of imprisonment and a financial penalty in the amount of 472 000 Euros in a kangaroo trial. The draconian punishment develops into an own goal for the government because now Lapiro's fight is internationally recognised. Several organisations such as the PEN and the American lawyers' organisation *Freedom Now* demand his immediate release and the annulment of the monetary fine; the French guitar producer Mondomix and a group of French musicians compose the song *1000 Euros pour la liberté* (1000 Euros for liberty) to mobilise the French general public; the Copenhagen organisation for artistic license gave the *Freemuse Award* to the detainee in 2009. Even the UN-Secretary General personally intervened to secure his freedom. Moreover, in a writing from 8th February, 2012, an UN-Committee demanded the Cameroonian government to restore justice to the musician. Despite everything, Lapiro remained in prison for three years.

But the circumstances of his release from prison reveal that the government is afraid. One day before the termination of his sentence, he is secretly taken home by the prison authorities, because secret agents had been warned of a rush of the masses in front of the prison. Now he also calls himself *Ngata Man* – Ngata means prison in Pidgin-English, the more so as he can be arrested again anytime because of the open claim. Significantly, he is not allowed to be present on stage in the whole of Cameroon. Even for concerts and events which are in connection with his name, he does not get permission from the authorities to attend. On 9th November, 2011, President Paul Biya was confirmed in office, as expected. The world also congratulated him, including the President of the Federal Republic of Germany, Christian Wulff, at the time.

Biya pursues his efforts all the more unembarrassed in his bid to muzzle Lapiro. In 2012, the musician replied with a new single *Démissionnez!!* (Step down!!) In it, he denies him any justification to rule the country, and he demands from him to sign his own arrest warrant, and to join his former accomplices, whom he brought behind bars for fear that they could compete for power. On 27th May, 2012, Canal 2, the biggest private channel in Cameroon, had to temporarily cease showing their Sunday program *Jambo* because *Démissionnez!!* is played. Considering this massive persecution, Lapiro was asked by a journalist whether the whole struggle he was going through was not futile, and whether he was rather not seen as the eternal provocateur. The way into exile, which is chosen by Lapiro surprisingly at the end of the year 2012, confirmed this point of view.

However, the question of the journalist expresses an attitude, which is widespread in many African countries, and which is justified by the motto: *If you cannot beat them, join them.* The emphasis on a supposedly growing sign of fatigue could be found in many observers from the West, who criticise the absence of a way developed by Africa on its own. This is what Celestin Monga, a writer and economic scientist, who is living in exile lets Lapiro know in an open letter addressed to him: Western people say that Africans are lost in fatalism and that they have accepted misery as an unchangeable fact of their life; except for tears, bitterness and a blunt nationalism, they had not shown anything else to the world. In other words, that Paul Biya continues to rule despite his 'unbearable incompetence' (Lapiro), shows how docile the Cameroonian people are as in the so-called Stockholm syndrome, and that they sympathise with government which tortures them daily.

Lappiro, Longuè Longuè, Joe La Conscience and Le Général Valsero demonstrate with their music, how untrue this criticism is. Their music is a place of remembrance for the struggle, which were fought by the Cameroonian population at the risk of their lives. Moreover, by commenting on the political developments, and by pointing out grievances and courses of action, they are keeping up the spirit of change completely in line with the power of the spoken word in the African tradition. In this sense, Lapiro's music is a weapon against the policy of demagogic governments, which take the general public hostage. Not least because of this, he remains one of the most successful Makossa singers of all times.

Chapter 38

Bibliography

Wolfgang Bender: *Sweet Mother. African music.* Wuppertal 2000; Lapiro de Mbangas songs can be found on www.tube.com.

MIRIAM TLALI (South Africa)

NOTICE THE SKIES

BY KAGISO LESEGO MOLOPE

There may be a beautiful rare bird flying over me. There may have been a gorgeous full moon last night, and perhaps behind me a Morula tree in full bloom, but I do not notice, I do not see any of it because we are fighting.

My name is Miriam Tlali. I am a curious young woman. I want to know everything. I wish that I were surrounded by outlets of knowledge, many media that send out information about the world, but I am not. I am a young African woman living in Sophiatown. I am not surrounded by libraries or bookshops. I do not have access to places and things that would teach me about all the many different wonders of the world.

Although I do have many ideas of how my own world works, I don't have much to read about things that are far away because there is a lot that the government will not allow me to reach.

I also realise that there is something wrong with the simple things, like how we children have been playing. I remember that sometimes we would throw stones at the other children across the street even though we had nothing against them. In fact, sometimes we would play very well, it's just that at other times we would be aware of the fighting around us, that we were supposed to be against one another. So even though we didn't feel hostility towards our neighbours, we knew that we were not on the same side of this war.

In Sophiatown I have neighbours of different colours, but we have played together and lived alongside each other for a long time. The shebeen at the corner of this street is owned by a Black woman, and the dry-cleaning shop is owned by an Indian man. I have friends of different races. But this mixing, this living side by side, is about to end because look outside and tell me you see what I see: Bulldozers, dust rising against the houses, the shops, the people. This is where I've grown up and this is the place that I will always remember as my home. Look at the shebeens where people came together, the shops where women would meet and laugh, the houses where we've been brought up. This is all going. This will all be gone and something new will be built here. A new place where I will not be allowed to live, only work.

After high school I will go to the University of Witwatersrand. But this will not always be open to me. I will have to move from there. I will have my learning interrupted so that the University can only be open to people who have a different skin colour from mine. Yes, my skin colour is what matters the most in these times. It is what determines where I am and where I am not allowed to play, eat, work and study. These are the times we are living in, in South Africa. The system of Apartheid, where people are divided and moved from their homes, is tearing the country apart. I lose the home that I grew up in and I will be forced from the university where I choose to study.

Some other things are difficult. There are different needs here that also determine where I go. At a certain time I will have to seek employment as a book-keeper, or what some call a typist. But this skill is important. Being able to type and doing book-keeping means that I can find a job and make a small living. This will serve me well in the future. I can pay for things that are difficult to pay for, perhaps even – and most importantly – my education. Education is the most important thing, especially for women and girls. All over Africa women and girls cannot get an education, they have to leave school and work. They have to provide for their families. They don't have books to read. They don't get the opportunity to study. But we believe that education is what will set us free. We believe that education is what will bring light to our people.

I have always been aware of the inequalities between Black and White people in my country, but I have also always been aware of the inequalities between women and men. I work very hard to liberate myself. I work very hard to educate myself and I work very hard to educate my fellow South Africans. As I grow older I use books to speak of inequalities, to highlight discrimination, to expose the unfairness of what is happening to us. So I write books. You know what happens? I am the very first Black woman to have her book published in English in my country. This means that, because so many people who speak English read in English, they will understand what my life looks like. They will understand how my life feels. My first book is called: *Miriam at Metropolitan*. The second one is *Amandla*, which means 'Power'. Then I wrote *Mihloti* and then *Footprints in the Quag*. These books tell the world about my life and the lives of Black people in my country. They tell the world about the conditions we live under. I hope they bring change to my country, so that every child can someday be able to notice and enjoy the skies.

Bibiography
Miriam Thali; Geteilte Welt, Frankfurt/M 1989; Soweto Stories Erzablungen. Frankfurt/M. 1992.

STEVE BANTU BIKO   (South Africa)

I WRITE WHAT SUITS ME

BY ANDILE M-AFRICA

It is a Monday morning. A small piece of brown cardboard is tied on the rusty gate of the school, confronting us. Inscribed on the cardboard is the writing; "Our Leader Has Been Murdered". The cardboard is fixed perfectly in the centre of the gate, a little below the top bar. Small pieces of wire hold all its corners. No wind or rain will harm this important notice. It is written with a fine ball point by a writer who could be amongst us.

That time has arrived. My heart has been waiting for the time. They could not kill a man who had a car that I liked, who was jolly, who greeted all the time, who helped our Gogo down the street whenever she was sick, who had friends that were always happy, friends that I looked up to; and still hope that it would pass easily. No!

In front of the gate I was part of a hostage that I loved, a hostage that was transforming me into a silent protester. I could see the same in the faces of my fellow scholars. We were all in it. We may not have had a speaker to voice our protest but, our insides understood and spoke in one voice to us all.

The previous day, a Sunday of the 25th of September 1977, Steve Bantu

Biko was laid to rest by thousands of mourners who came from all over the country and from abroad. Building up to this funeral it had been pain and tension. The whole country was in shock and in anger. In a vigil at our school on the day before the funeral, strong versed poetry came from pained hearts and invaded my tiny body; songs that spoke directly to the then white head of state, John Vorster, and to his Minister of Police, Prisons and Justice all-in-one, Jimmy Kruger, were sung spiritedly by all who were there.

As we moved from that classroom and brought the service to the assembly area since more and more buses of mourners were arriving, I looked around. A new picture had been imposed in the assembly space that I knew so well. Our arms were not folded, this time around. We were not standing in queues of boys and girls. We were not listening to the Christian verses of the Catholic catechism. The sky above and the ground around the school were infested with the white military. Yet, we were not scared of them. We were ready to take them on.

Steve Bantu Biko was very important to all of us in that assembly. Our eyes were opened by that man and by the idea that he and his fellow activists had evolved. It was not a new idea. It was an old idea of freedom. What was new was the way it was brought to us. In a very skilful way, those men and women of Biko's generation managed to infiltrate our minds. They had a special effect on our world outlook. They eroded fear from our system. They brought purpose into our lives. For once, we stood with our sober heads held high. Yes, there was still oppression but we were beginning to refuse to participate in our demeaning.

The political being of Steve Bantu Biko may have started earlier but for me the third period in the afternoon of the 6th of March in 1963, at a Christian missionary school called Lovedale College where he was a student, is very critical. Kaya Mathias Biko, his elder brother, had been a student at Lovedale since 1962. He was also a student activist, a defiant branch secretary of the Pan Africanist Congress. Steve Bantu Biko had just entered Lovedale College in the beginning of 1963. On this particular day, the 6th of March, Mr Weeg, the principal of Lovedale College, walked into Kaya's class. He stood by the door and called, "Mathias Biko, come to my office".

Mathias, a so-called Christian name given to Kaya as a mark of European colonialism, walked out of his class, following the instruction of his principal. In the corridor he saw his younger brother, Steve Bantu

Biko. He too had been called to the principal's office. As they walked towards the office, there was a car standing there with a number plate CD 143. They stopped and looked at each other. This car had come from their home town. Something must have happened at their home, they feared.

At the principal's office there was a strange bunch of guests - men who were wearing long army overcoats, who clearly had not had any sleep. The principal bellowed at them; "Gentlemen, here they are". The two brothers were bundled into a vehicle. They were driven to a police station. They were brought into the station one after the other. In the police station Steve Bantu Biko was told by the police, after a few questions, that he had been expelled from Lovedale College. He was instructed to walk back to the school hostel and collect all his belongings and those of his brother, Kaya, who was to be detained, brought to a magistrate and convicted and made to serve a sentence in one of the apartheid prisons called Fort Glamorgan Prison.

Thrown out and on his own, the fatherless Steve Bantu Biko had to spend the whole of 1963 without school. With only his mother who worked as a domestic in a white household, a brother who was serving a sentence in prison, a sister in a nursing school and a younger sister in a lower grade, he sat and contemplated his future. He had not been involved in politics at the time. He was just a Biko in a school where another Biko, his elder brother, happened to be a student leader. His coming to the College was shattered by the weight of a total power of a state that ruled with violence. His dream of making the best of himself through education had to make sense of the hastily erected blockade between him and what he saw as his destiny.

This was an important period for Steve Bantu Biko. In the midst of reflecting on this event he had nature around him. There were rivers and there were seas. There were birds and there were animals. There were hills and there were mountains. He could look at the colours that nature brought to his eye, how these complemented each other. He could hear the sounds of his people, how these represented their being. He could look at the still and flowing waters, how these twisted and turned as they travelled to the seas. He could appreciate the sense that his own people imposed on their surroundings, the names of places and people, his own names and those of others.

It was a time to do an introspect, to reach the self that resided in the deep wells of his body, a self that had been capped under a heavy stone of silence. If the colour of his skin derived from the dark of the night when he was conceived, then it was time to claim the pain and the comfort of that experience. If his blackness came from his parents, and from the parents of his parents; and that the heat in his blood was a statement of a void in that parentage, and the sensitivity in his nervous system was a current of the continent of Africa, then these experiences had to find his undivided attention. If his first journey through the birth passage left the pain and the sweat of the womb on his hands that clenched in fists, it was time to reveal the prize.

In 1964 Steve Bantu Biko enrolled at St Francis College in Marianhill in Natal Province. He matriculated there in 1965. In 1966 he entered the medical school of the University of Natal (Black Section). Both St Francis College and the medical school became the spaces of political experimentation. Whereas at St Francis College he started to involve himself in political discussions and debates; at the medical school his activism was like the works of fire. In the same year he arrived, he ran for elections of the Student Representative Council. He won a seat. He joined an existing student organisation on campus, the National Union of South African Students (NUSAS), which was predominantly white in its membership, character and direction; he led a walk out of NUSAS by black students; he led serious discussions and debate on the position of being black and being a student in a South African university and college; together with others he formed the all-black South African Students Organisation (SASO) and was elected its first President. He helped to form a lot of black political establishments that catered for various sectors of the black community and that were affiliated to the Black Peoples Convention (BPC) that he had helped to form in 1972.

On the development front he led black people to work for other black people. Before, white Christian missionaries were the ones who worked among black people. For once, black people saw the need and the obligation to work for themselves. A string of structures were built to undertake specific tasks in developing the political awareness, while at the same time, enhancing the standard of living of the people. These structures were all co-ordinated by an umbrella organisation called Black Community Programmes (BCP).

In 1972 Steve Bantu Biko was expelled from the university. He had not written an examination because he was always on the road, visiting other universities and colleges and attending conferences. The university mistakenly thought that he was a failure. Three years down the line, the man built from the ground a health centre with outstanding facility and personnel in a village called Zinyoka, the Zanempilo Health Centre. He invited his fellow students who had not been expelled and had qualified as doctors, to work at the centre and help the people for free.

A vociferous reader and a prolific writer, Steve Bantu Biko led the establishment of many publications. Under his Presidency, SASO started a student's bulletin called Saso Newsletter. In it Steve Bantu Biko wrote a column entitled "I Write What I Like" under a pen name Frank Talk. Those pieces that appeared in that column of the Saso Newsletter have been published into a book with the same title, "I Write What I Like".

Working with his colleague Prof. Bennie Khoapa, Steve Bantu Biko established an annual publication that reported and discussed trends in the black community. The publication was called *Black Review* and it profiled all the attempts of liberation nature by all sectors of the black community. *Black Review* also served as a barometer of struggle and it was a space where black advancement could be seen and measured.

Steve Bantu Biko started another publication called *Black Perspective* that published in-depth essays that dealt with a variety of issues by black thinkers. In the history of South African literature it was the first time that writers, poets and artists from across the country rose up as a result of a direct influence of a political ideology and collectively set out on a conscious effort of delegitimising the white government. Black Consciousness, the ideology that Steve Bantu Biko and his generation of activists evolved, spurred the publication of many titles that did not only speak to black discontent but also made qualitative contributions to African literature.

Poet, writer and literary critic, Mafika Gwala met with Steve Bantu Biko in the student circles in Natal Province. Both got to work together in the Saso Newsletter as well as in the BCP publications and in the Black Consciousness Movement conferences, consciously enhancing the total outlook on the struggle.

Poet and writer, Wally Mongane Serote whose titles include *Yakhal'inkomo* (1972), *No Baby Must Weep* (1975), *To Every Birth Its Blood* (1981); met and worked with Steve Bantu Biko. Other luminaries such as Sipho Sephamla, Miriam Tlali, Prof. Mbulelo Mzamane, Prof. Njabulo Ndebele are some of the names that acknowledge the impact of Steve Bantu Biko and Black Consciousness in their works. Steve Bantu Biko was part of the founding of the Black Workers Project which assisted existing trade unions and helped to establish others such as the Union of Black Journalists (UBJ). He led a Black Press Commission that was looking at establishing, amongst other things, a black publishing house.

It was under direct security police pressure that Steve Bantu Biko shone through. When he was banned in March 1973 together with seven other colleagues, who were all leaders of the Black Consciousness Movement, he threw out blocks of cold ice in the face of the white state. He was in Port Elizabeth at the time, a town in the eastern part of South Africa, running a workshop for the youth with Prof. Barney Pityana, Prof. Harry Nengwekhulu and Mr Bokwe Mafuna who were student leaders at the time. Police came to the venue of the workshop, arrested them and led them to a police station. They served them with documents informing of their banning and restrictions which were signed by Jimmy Kruger, the Minister of Police, Prisons and Justice all-in-one. In the words of Bokwe Mafuna;

"My God! Steve was so fearless that day. He was telling those boers (police men) who were trying to assault us, 'you dare try, I will moer (beat) you'. He was unbelievably brave in front of those boers. We were trembling, Nengwekhulu and I, knowing that this is it. I was so scared. Aware that my God, we are in some situation here. Nengwekhulu was worse."

While restricted and under round-the-clock surveillance by the security police at his home, he started projects that made his home town a political capital of the country. In a township where I live and where he grew up, Ginsberg Township, Steve Bantu Biko established a scheme that funded the education of many of us, the children who came from poor families, the Ginsberg Bursary Fund. He had been assisted by a community fund himself when he was younger.

With our parents, he facilitated group buying of groceries to beat the high prices. He re-opened the Ginsberg crèche that he attended as a child and that had closed down. For the first time in the life of that town, an office of politics was opened by Steve Bantu Biko. He operated there openly and fearlessly. A lot of activists came from far areas to volunteer at the programmes of the office. Others settled and married local girls and families were started.

The health centre that was opened in a village outside of King William's Town had a full time doctor in residence, Dr. Mamphele Ramphele, a fellow medical student and a co-founder of the black SASO. Dr. Ramphele is the former head of the World Bank and the former Vice-Chancellor of the University of Cape Town. There were professional nurses that Dr. Ramphele had recruited from a nearby hospital. Dr. Ramphele was assisted by two other activist doctors, Dr. Dubs Msauli and Dr Siyolo Solombela, who came in from time to time.

The health centre provided quality health service to the people for free. When the police state decided to detain Dr. Ramphele, Dr. Msauli and Dr. Solombela, so that the centre could close down, it was Steve Bantu Biko who picked up a telephone and called a friend and a colleague who was practising 1000 km away. That friend, Dr. Chapman Palweni, an activist as well and a founder of the Black SASO, left his paying job at the Kuruman hospital, poured petrol in his own car, and came to volunteer his services at the health centre.

For political counsel, activists travelled from various areas of South Africa as well as Southern Africa to Ginsberg township to consult with Steve Bantu Biko and to draw strength from him. Our township became a destination of ideas. Even when activists were hauled in front of magistrates and judges, facing possible long sentences on Robben Island prison or death in the Pretoria gallows, it was Steve Bantu Biko who ran around to make sure that there was legal representation and access to the detained. When his colleagues were facing sabotage charges in the famous SASO/BPC Trial, he came forward to participate in their defense. His performance in the witness box of that Pretoria Supreme Court did not only strengthen the resolve of those who were on trial, he became the body and the soul of the Black Cause. The entire country was not going to be the same after the things he said there. The Soweto Uprisings broke out and their flame was caught by the entire urban South Africa.

Steve Bantu Biko believed in group work. One of his obsessions was to observe the potential of those he worked with and those he came across. He understood that in the same way that the white power structure operated in its totality, as the expulsion of students who were seen to be undesirable by the state, was done by the police; the execution of the struggle for liberation and the building of the future society had to involve all hands. People had to be encouraged to see themselves as the cause and the course of their own change and development. Terms such as 'ordinary people', 'people on the ground' would not be in the vocabulary of Steve Bantu Biko. People are capable of teaching even the most western schooled a thing or two, he believed.

Under Steve Bantu Biko South Africa gave the world the meaning of resilience and focus in words and in actions. All these were engraved in his person. Whereas today South Africa fashions itself as a place where corruption and greed are rampant, as a country that is insensitive to people's needs and as a state that can unleash violence on its citizens as in the Marikana Massacre; the era of Steve Bantu Biko was different. Black people related totally differently to each other when Steve Bantu Biko was around.

His leadership, and more, his person provoked and attracted talent from all. Ways and means were found to channel all available energies to the service of the people. He was a thinker, a planner, a strategist, an activist and a teacher. He knew his people because he lived with them. He was an excellent communicator and a keen and active listener.

Whereas we stood in silent protest in front of the gate at our primary school in 1977 when Steve Bantu Biko was murdered, the importance of this man which was brought to me by his colleagues who visited Ginsberg Township a few years later, cleared the confused feeling of discomfort that I had about my surrounding. Steve Bantu Biko's importance and that of his generation informed my senses and intellect about a need to identify my role in the collective tasks of my generation. Steve Bantu Biko is a jewel of its own kind that Africa gave to the world.

Bibliography
Steve Bantu Biko; *Ich schreibe was mir passt*; Berlin1079.
Andile M-Africa; *The Eyes that hit our lives; A Tribute to Steve Biko* King Williams Town; 2010.

Chapter 41

OLIVER REGINALD TAMBO (South Africa)

A GREAT SOUTH AFRICAN MIND

BY LULI CALLINICOS

Really great minds have great hearts too. South Africa has been blessed with many such men and women. One was Oliver Reginald Tambo, a quietly brilliant man who had a profound influence on the liberation movement of South Africa. His life story is a fascinating lesson of how his early world and his pursuit of a good education laid strong foundations for his character and vision of a better future, and for the respected and trusted leader that he became.

Oliver Tambo and the African National Congress

Oliver Tambo was a leading figure for 50 years in an African political movement that attracted members who came from different language groups, religions and cultures. His political life began as a founder of the African National Congress Youth League in 1944. From then on, he played a leading role in every key moment in the history of the African National Congress (ANC) until he died in 1993; he was elected its general secretary in 1952, Deputy President in 1959 and was then mandated to lead the ANC's Mission in Exile in 1960 after the movement was banned by the government. The plan was that Nelson Mandela, his partner in politics and in their law practice, would stay inside the country to mobilise people in the underground, while O.R. would alert the international community to the injustices and gross human rights abuses of the apartheid system of the whites-only South African government.

The ANC had been formed in 1912 to unite the African people to resist the laws of white supremacy of a colonial South Africa. The government was a coalition of whites who had fought each other to establish who would dominate and control the wealth of South Africa. Yet even if they were united, the white population constituted only a fifth of the country's population.

The Tambo family in Pondoland

Tambo's family lived in the kingdom of Pondoland. It was one of the last African states to enjoy independence, but in 1893, it was annexed by the British.

It was against this background that Oliver Kaizana Tambo was born in October 1917. It was a time when the Union of South Africa was at war with Germany, and sent black and white troops to protect British colonies. The baby's father pointedly named his son Kaizana (after the German Kaiser), to commemorate his enemy's powerful enemy.

Little Kaizana was born into a large and busy homestead. It consisted of grandparents, uncles, aunts and cousins, ten brothers and sisters, his father and three mothers. His own mother, Julia, was sociable and energetic, a Christian who held large, bustling gatherings of worship in her hut. She eventually converted her husband and the youngest wife to Christianity, and all the children were baptised. O.R. admired his father's skill because his three mothers got on so well with each other!

Kaizana had an active and happy traditional childhood. From as early as three years old, he learned the essential skills of the rural economy. Years later, he vividly recalled how proud the small boys were to tend the calves, ensuring that they were permitted to suckle only after milking. As the boys grew older, they were given the task of herding the cattle and taking them to the best pastures to improve their milk.

The whole family contributed to the homestead economy. Work was not separated from home or community. Herding, like other productive activities, would be done in groups and would include social interaction and co-operation. The community also shared other productive tasks. For example, whole families helped other families with the demanding task of ploughing. During the spring and summer, families would organise a number of work parties, where the whole community would come to help. At the end of the day, steaming pots of food would be ready to be shared by all, served with traditional beer. The get-togethers after a hard day's work would be accompanied by storytelling, songs and dance performances. No one was allowed to go hungry.

Once, O.R. remembered, a small family arrived from faraway with nothing. The community shared their food, gave them a hut and lent them a couple of calves. They were called 'Natinga' – 'Nothing'. Within a couple of years, however, the Natingas were able to return the borrowed cows but were allowed to keep the calves produced by them. And so the Natinga family was able to survive in their new home and community. The value system and day-today lifestyle of the community was therefore one of sharing, and the small child soon learned to share his mother and his father with the bigger family, of which he was a part, and with the community at large.

The Pondo people, like most chiefdoms in South Africa, had a consensus approach to decision-making. At council meetings, everyone had a say; although in those days only men attended these meetings! Opponents to a plan were encouraged to speak up. After a thorough discussion, the chief and his advisors would get the feel of the meeting. Chiefs relied on their councillors to prevent them from acting contrary to the popular will. This practice of decision-making by consensus, and never straying too far from their constituencies of the traditional leaders, was to play a profoundly important role in the ANC style of leadership of Tambo and other leaders, such as Nelson Mandela.

The reluctant school boy

Tambo's father, Mzimela, was a traditionalist, but he also saw the value of western education. Working in the village trading store for many years, he was impressed by the white trader's ability to run an independent business and keep its books. The trader also made money, which gave him relative power and status. O.R. recalled: *'People went to him to buy. He had a car, horses – he was a reference point to the community – and he had servants. In general he was a chief in his own right.'*

Not a literate man himself, Mzimeni was very astute. He decided that his children should be independent when they grew up. He quickly grasped the value of a western education, and insisted that his children go to school, even though the nearest school was 18 kilometres away.

On his first day at school, young Kaizana was asked to come back the next day with a new 'English' name. After his father and mother discussed it at length that evening, the little boy took his new name to the teacher. It was, he said, 'Oliga' – later the name was adjusted to 'Oliver'. The school teacher turned out to be very strict and beat the children for the slightest offences. Oliver began to dread school and would find excuses not to take the long walk to school. Mzimeni was so determined that his children should persevere that he moved them several times to better schools and paid relatives in other districts with bags of maize for his children's upkeep.

As he grew older, Oliver wanted to join other boys his age who left home to find work. He remembers being very embarrassed when an old man reprimanded him as he was walking to school one day, saying he should be ashamed that his father was having to herd the cattle while his child messed around at school. Oliver envied his friends' adventures. They crossed the Umtamvuna River and went to the neighbouring province of Natal, to work in the sugar plantations or in the coal mines. When they came back, recalled Oliver, they were no longer children but young men, and told intriguing stories of the world beyond the village.

'They were young men, and I was still going to this school. So I began to think in terms of leaving, escaping to go and work there as a "garden boy" or even in the sugar plantations. I would work there and bring back money for my parents – that's what everyone else was doing.'

What Oliver did not realise was the cheap black labour system of the farms and mines, and the dangers of contracting tuberculosis or losing one's life in an accident from the bad working conditions. In later years, Oliver lost an uncle and an older brother, who were killed in a mine explosion in a coal mine in Natal. Another brother came home after years of poor living conditions in a hostel on the sugar plantations, coughing his lungs out.

In the meantime, his father insisted that Oliver must stay on at school. One day, when he was about eleven years old, Oliver met a lad who was in the debating society of another school. He was deeply impressed with the ease with which that youngster spoke English. The experience transformed his attitude to education. He discovered in himself a love of discussion and debate. English, he realised, was a key to skills, independence and power.

Not long afterwards, Oliver was given an opportunity through a family friend, to enrol at a missionary school called Holy Cross, about 70 kilometres away. His father could not afford the fees, but the school was able to find two kind English sisters who spared the sum of ten pounds a year for the schooling and boarding fees of himself and his brother Alan. His older brother, working as a migrant labourer in Natal, also sent a small additional amount from his hard-earned wages to make up the shortfall.

From then on, Oliver never looked back. Really motivated to learn now, he worked hard, and starred in class. Five years later, the school found him a place at the highly respected black school of St Peter's in Johannesburg, the city of the gold mines. Many years later, O.R. linked the kind deed of the English sisters to the international support "for those engaged in the struggle for liberation from oppression and the apartheid system in particular" in the years to come.

> 'They had stretched a couple of hands across the lands and oceans to the south of the continent of Africa to give aid and support to two unknown children. Two unknown African children.'

Johannesburg, the city of gold

Oliver's schooling at St Peter's gave him an excellent education. The teachers were dedicated members of the Community of the Resurrection who believed they were educating 'the new leaders of Africa' and taught them about responsibility that came with the privilege of learning. He was exposed for the first time to boys as well as girls from other parts of the country, who spoke other languages, and also got to know street-smart city children. In Johannesburg he was also exposed to race prejudice and segregation. But Johannesburg was also to be his future.

In the meantime, back home his parents fell ill. First his mother passed away suddenly, from a clot in the leg, and then a year later, Mzimeni, who had been ailing, died too. At the age of sixteen, Oliver Tambo was an orphan. He was heartbroken. His parents had not lived to enjoy their son's gaining the highest marks in the matriculation exams written by both white and black students. Just when he was within sight of earning a greater income, Oliver would not be able to repay their foresight, love and sacrifice.

Oliver decided to study science because there were not enough mathematicians or physicists amongst the small number of black professionals. He had first wanted to study medicine to compare indigenous methods of healing with western medical science, but the white university would not allow black medical students to perform autopsies on white cadavers, nor were they allowed to learn by attending to white patients in hospitals. Fortunately, his top marks earned Oliver a bursary to study for a Science degree at the University of Fort Hare in the Eastern Cape.

Three years later Oliver graduated with a B. Sc. degree and then enrolled for a diploma in higher education. His calm disposition and his integrity made an impact on his lecturers and his fellow students. He was deeply religious, though he did not flaunt his beliefs, and he was also an intellectual, excited by, and open to ideas. His life-long friend, Nelson Mandela, who also attended Fort Hare, recalled his first impressions:

> 'From the start, I saw that Oliver's intelligence was diamond-edged; he was a keen debater and did not accept the platitudes that so many of us automatically subscribed to... It was easy to see that he was destined for great things.'

Oliver was elected chairperson of the Students' Representative Council; but before the year was through, he was expelled for upholding a student protest on a point of principle. He left the university without his diploma. The news of his expulsion reached his old school, St Peter's. They immediately raised extra funds and offered him a post as Maths Master.

Back in Johannesburg again, his fame for his top marks and his principles spread in the black community. He also met Walter Sisulu, who, most unusual as a black man in a racist society, was an estate agent in downtown Johannesburg. The huge majority of black men and women by far, were low-paid workers, migrant miners or domestic servants. Sisulu attracted the young elite to his office – teachers, journalists, lawyers and intellectuals who loved a good discussion on politics and life. Sisulu had not had much education, but was seasoned in life experience and had a wealth of wisdom and political insights. Oliver met many interesting people at Sisulu's office.

Getting involved in political activism

The group of young men who visited Sisulu's office also responded to the invitation of Dr Xuma, the medical doctor who was also the President of the African National Congress. They were attracted to the ANC because the organisation aimed at uniting all the black ethnic groups of South Africa, regardless of language. The ANC's weakness, they decided, was that it did not reach out to ordinary people. Its members were chiefs, professionals and elites, like themselves. Yet the ANC had a long tradition and an honourable nationalist vision. They therefore formulated a plan of action to revive the movement by forming a youth league.

Firstly, they all registered as members of the ANC. Then, at the next annual congress in 1944, they proposed the formation of an ANC Youth League, which the mother body accepted, along with a new Women's League. The Youth League proposed a militant plan of action for mobilising the masses of the people. Its manifesto declared:

'We believe that the national liberation of Africans will be achieved by Africans themselves... We believe in the unity of all Africans from the Mediterranean Sea in the North to the Indian and Atlantic Oceans in the South... and that Africans must speak with one voice.'

At school, Oliver was a popular teacher, fair but strict, and exciting and interactive in his teaching methods well ahead of that time. He also recruited a number of his students into the Youth League. Many grew up to become well-known leaders in the liberation movement.

The apartheid state and the black response

In 1948, the whites went to vote in a general election. For the first time, the National Party won with an outright but narrow majority. It was promoted by Afrikaner nationalists who preached the complete separation of whites from other races. They also believed that because of their fewer numbers, whites must ensure that they would always be the rulers of the country.

They went further, by embarking on a vigorous programme of social engineering, that is, over the next few decades, they passed laws that blatantly discriminated against people of colour, forcibly removing millions of black people from their lands and from the cities, moving them to less fertile parts of the country. The aim was to divide up black people into smaller, separate ethnic groups called 'homelands'. Education, health care, residential areas, work, were all legally defined according to race. Only Africans had to carry passes which controlled their movements and where they could apply for jobs. If they could not find work in a so-called white area within 72 hours of arriving, they would be arrested and made to work as convict labourers on white-owned farms.

Skilled work and training was reserved for whites, and black wages, even for teachers, doctors and nurses, were one-fifth of the salaries of their white counterparts. Only the whites had the vote, and only whites could live in the pleasant leafy suburbs, serviced by black domestic workers at a pittance of a wage. Black people had to live in shacks or matchbox houses built far from 'white' areas and had to travel far to get to their places of work.

For black people, going about their daily business in the city could easily land them in prison. Every day they could be insulted, cursed or beaten. Daily, their innate dignity was attacked. Oliver was persuaded to leave his teaching profession and study law. In 1952 he joined Nelson Mandela in starting the first black firm of attorneys. The two men consciously combined the values of sharing and concern for the community where they had grown up with the skills and knowledge of the ruling class, which they used as a weapon to defend their people.

When the Youth League presented its Programme of Action in 1949 to the ANC annual conference, it was accepted by an overwhelming majority. As a result of the campaigns that followed, by the early 1950s the ANC's membership increased from 40 000 a few years earlier, to 100 000.

Creatively borrowing resistance strategies from earlier organisations, the Youth League advocated consumer and bus boycotts, strikes and 'stay-aways' from work, public protests and civil disobedience. By this the ANC stormed into people's consciousness. Oliver, who had such a quiet and respectable demeanour, had an iron will, and fully promoted the militant programme.

Mass protests and the consequences

In the 1950s, tens of thousands of people participated in protests, facing prison, detentions, severe restrictions on their movements in and out of their houses, and being permanently removed from their homes. As time went by, a non-racial labour movement allied itself to the ANC, and other oppressed groups such as the South African Indian Congress and the

Coloured People's Organisation joined the alliance too. A few hundred whites, some of them Communists, as well as other radicals formed a Congress of Democrats and joined the ANC alliance.

During this period of the expansion of the ANC, Oliver and his close comrade Nelson Mandela began to rethink their idea of the nation. They were now more inclusive, and felt that the struggle should include all democrats, regardless of colour, race or creed. Oliver himself chaired a meeting that called on whites to join them in the struggle against apartheid.

In 1955, these ideas were included in a Freedom Charter. Ten thousand Freedom Volunteers went to factories, buses and trains and homes in the townships to ask women and men what would be their demands to guarantee a free and democratic South Africa. The responses were remarkable. Apartheid's crass, racist treatment of black men and women did not stop them from calling for an inclusive, democratic and free society.

The Charter, which was the result of tens of thousands of responses, was summarised by a National Action Council of five people. Oliver Tambo was a member of that Council. They formulated the demands into ten main clauses. The introductory clause began with, 'The Land Belongs to All Who Live in It'. The Freedom Charter was read out to a Congress of the People, seven thousand delegates from all over the country, while police and special police intimidated the audience by taking down the names of everyone there.

The following year, the Freedom Charter was adopted once it had been discussed in all the branches around the country. That was also the year that twenty thousand women marched to the Prime Minister's offices to protest against the extension of the pass system to African women. The event made a deep impression on the country, and delayed the implementation of this shocking law by a few years. In December of that year, 1956, one hundred and fifty six people from all around the country were arrested for High Treason. The state argued that the Freedom Charter was a revolutionary document and its ten clauses amounted to a desire to overthrow the state. Oliver Tambo was one of the accused, along with the President of the ANC, Chief Albert Luthuli, Nelson Mandela and 153 others. December was also the month that Oliver was married to his sweetheart, nurse Adelaide Tambo. Oliver was lucky that by then he had been granted bail and so did not have to get married in jail!

The trial dragged on for years, but in the meantime, bus boycotts against rising fares, strikes by workers against the appallingly low wages, and plans for a strategic series of protests that would gather in strength and numbers were afoot in the ANC.

Into exile

But then a shocking tragedy hit the country. On 21st March 1960, a breakaway movement, the Pan Africanist Party (PAC), organised an anti-pass campaign of their own. In the township of Sharpeville, more than 69 protestors were shot dead. A panicking government immediately banned the ANC and the PAC and thousands were rounded up and jailed. This meant that these movements would now have to operate underground. The President of the ANC, Chief Luthuli, as pre-arranged, instructed Oliver Tambo to leave the country. Oliver, who was planning to be ordained as a minister of the Anglican Church, earnestly discussed this choice with his wife. They concluded that this was the divine calling that was intended as the purpose for his life: to work for his people, in exile; to take the message of the struggle for the liberation of the people of South Africa and indeed for Africa, to the international community; to obtain their support in isolating an unacceptable and uncivilised rule based on hate, instead of universal respect and love for the innate dignity of all human beings.

In the next thirty years, Oliver Tambo learned many lessons and made many difficult decisions. He impressed millions of people with his modesty, his rational fine mind, and his consistency. It was often easy to underestimate him because he was not a showy sort of person. But always, as one began to get to know him, those who preferred to dismiss him as the leader of a 'terrorist organisation', had reason to revise their ideas. His integrity, his clear thinking and intelligent analysis of the dilemma of his people, earned him many friends from across the political spectrum, from left to right, around the world.

It was Oliver Tambo who kept alive the names of Nelson Mandela, Walter Sisulu and the thousands of others who were imprisoned on Robben Island. It was Oliver Tambo who was able to explain that the apartheid system was as wicked as the Nazi system of fascism, and therefore justified the armed struggle, just as Europe in the 1940s had to fight to destroy an evil system.

Oliver Tambo faced many challenges, including the need to sustain the many people who had fled into exile; the frustration amongst the young soldiers in the military training camps, waiting to go home to fight for their people; divisions over the best strategy to get back home to liberate South Africa, and the constant danger of infiltration of a ruthless apartheid state. But amongst the many fine cadres who joined him in exile, it was Oliver Tambo that the members trusted and loved, and on whose judgment and character they relied.

Tambo worked incessantly until his health gave in. Adelaide Tambo, once recalled how she reprimanded him for driving himself too hard, he gave her one of his piercing looks.

'I had other plans for my life', he said. 'I wanted to be a minister of the Anglican Church... But God had other plans for me. God's plan was for me to fight in the political liberation for my people.'

Bringing home the ANC
Just a few months before Nelson Mandela was released from prison, Oliver Tambo returned from a carefully worked consultative process with heads of African states to discuss with them the terms that the ANC was preparing to conduct negotiations with the apartheid government. The process was exhausting, and the very next day, Tambo suffered from a severe stroke. After months of treatment, he was finally able to fly home. Although he could not speak publicly to express his delight at being home at last, the crowd deliriously welcomed him back. During his years of exile, they secretly listened to his broadcasts on Radio Freedom, and sang songs about him. He symbolised the consistent and unchanging commitment to the freedom of his people. It cost him his life, as it had cost the lives of thousands of others. And when at last he addressed the first ANC conference in South Africa in 32 years, he said he was delivering the ANC; bigger, stronger, intact. Many challenges still lay ahead. Political democracy still had to be matched by economic liberation and much more work was needed to mend the destructiveness of racism:

'It is our responsibility to break down barriers of division and create a country where there will be neither whites nor blacks, just South Africans, free and united in diversity.'

Oliver Tambo passed away on 23rd April, 1993, one of South Africa's most deserving sons.

CHEIKH AHMADOU BAMBA (Senegal)

THE QUIET REVOLUTION OF AN ISLAMIC SCHOLAR

BY MOUSSA DIALLO

Once every year, Senegal is in a state of emergency. Crowds of people stream from all parts of the world to Touba. The city of about 500 000 inhabitants, these days increased in population enormously for three days in 2011, three million people stayed there. People of all skin colour and delegations from all continents trooped to Touba to celebrate the holiday, which is dedicated to the memory of Cheikh Ahmadou Bamba. Nothing happened in his life-time to make anybody expect that such a tribute would be accorded him. People did not only fight against Cheikh Ahmadou Bamba, who is now celebrated, but he was also considered mad by others. This mark, which was left on him by his fellow human beings, was an expression of their perplexity when faced with behaviour which is out of the ordinary and with strong self-will.

Cheikh Ahmadou Bamba was born in 1853 in a village called Mbacké. His father Momar Antassali was a *Serigne*, an Islamic priest. His mother, Diara Busso also came from a deeply religious family. The way of the eldest son seemed to be mapped out in this pious, conservative family. He would also become an Islamic priest, head the Koran school, which his father had taken over from his grandfather. He would lead a quiet

309

life, completely in line with the commandments of the Prophet. Actually, the small boy liked to learn, and to the joy of his parents, he stood out because he quickly grasped what he was taught. The attention of his teachers was attracted by his quiet unconventional ways and by his loud and critical questions. He wanted to know why the alphabet start like this and not in another way? Why were people, who did not work, the richest? Why were kings more powerful than the *Serigne,* and why did they still ask them for advice? And since a certain childhood experience, the question, whether a jihad could be just, did not give him any rest.

When he was a small child, he had felt the consequences of the "holy war" on his very own body. When in the middle of the 19th century, El Hadsch Omar Tall brought the jihad to the whole country, the *Ceddo.* The followers of African religions became so suspicious that they only saw the followers of this conqueror in their Muslim neighbours, who wanted to force their belief on them. Bamba's father preferred to go into exile in this poisoned atmosphere. During his father's time in exile, which made him hate the arbitrariness of the rulers, as well as exclusion and disadvantage, Bamba suffered the hardest blow of destiny. When he was fourteen years of age, his thirty-three year old mother, with whom he had had an especially close relationship, died.

After he had completed his Islamic studies in Senegal, he went to Mauritania for further studies. He had to listen to the Arabic scholars, who taught at universities there, if he wanted his religious education to be recognised beyond domestic borders. He experienced how much black Africans were despised in the Mauritanian society where slavery existed unofficially. The Arabian racism was even more shocking for the religious adolescent, because black Africans in Saudi-Arabia were among the first to acknowledge the Prophet Mohammed. Therefore, he planned to stand up against this inhuman attitude.

When he turned thirty-one, his father, who had become Kadi or Islamic judge at the court of Lat Dior Diop, King of Cayor in Senegal, died. After the funeral, the elders moved up to him, and pointed out that by custom, he had to pay a visit to the king so that he could express his condolences to him. He refused to carry out this gesture of subordination. The elders were shocked by his decision and could not believe their ears. They tried to avoid any provocation, in particular, from the ill-tempered Lat Dior, because they were Muslims at the court of a Ceddo-King. They anxiously awaited the reaction of the king. Shortly thereafter, he sent a messenger with the surprising wish that Bamba should be the successor of his father, and become his Kadi. The elders heaved a sigh of relief. The dreaded wrath of the rulers was stemmed, and they would be avoided and they would have an important representative in the inner circle of power in Senegal. The chosen one however, rejected the offer outright. Worse still, his reason for his shocking 'No', was that the king's palace corrupted the soul. The whole community was taken aback. Lat Dior accepted this majestically, probably because the obstinate scholar was his nephew. However, this matter could have also ended differently for Bamba. The people anyway considered him to be mad because he turned the offer of such an honourable, lucrative post down for life.

Soon after this event, he called everybody together and told them about his plan, which amounted to a revolution, namely a revolution in a religious as well as in social, cultural and political sense. He told them that he wanted to be more than just a Koran teacher, and he asked, who else had the wish like him to belong to the new community of the *Muridullahi*, the community of those 'who are longing for god'. The people assembled could not believe their ears. A young African planned to go his own way without any Arabic backing in the strictly structured Islamic world! "Now he had even became megalomaniac!" was the prevailing opinion. One of the elders was startled and wanted to know how this would be. "There have always been fraternities, and they all come from Arabian countries ... How can you establish a new one, and besides, an African one?"

"It is not forbidden. Islam is not owned by any particular people." was the Cheikh's answer.

First, this sounded plausible, however not all insecurities had been removed.

"Will the Arabian scholars accept an African fraternity?" someone asked.

The question was on everybody's mind. Bamba had expected this question because his experience with the Arabian scholars in Mauretania was that they did not see African scholars as equals. He felt sad when he realised that his fellow citzens thought so little of themselves. However, he did not let his feelings show and answered calmly, "I do not intend to ask them for permission." Incredible amazement could be seen on their faces. Somebody asked carefully after a moment of astonished silence, "But ... Ahmadou, do you not have teachers yourself in Mauretania?"

He replied calmly, "I do not know, what they can still teach me."

Even though they were impressed by the self-confidence of the young man, they still thought that his plans were daring. In the end, they were looking for a new teacher, one who was following the well-tried tradition.

Only thirty among them joined Cheikh Ahmadou Bamba on his new way. He moved with them to the border between the kingdoms of Bawol and Cayor and founded a new settlement. He baptised them in the name of *Daaru Salam* (House of Peace). The name did not only have its origin in the pious nature of a believer, but it was also to be understood as a statement on the colonial wars that shook the country. Bamba chose a name for himself that was just as problematic: *Khadimu Rassul* (Servant of the Prophet). He indicated his independence from any worldly power with this name as well as his independence from any Islamic doctrine. It was the beginning of a revolutionary project which was going to bring him a lot of hostilities.

If he wanted to realise his vision of a new society, first of all he had to overcome the intellectual domination of the Arabic world because nearly all available books came from the Arab countries. He also wrote texts about a wide variety of topics from theology, law, literature, morality, education and others. His essays were characterised by an un-dogmatic attitude: Everything was supposed to be checked and modernised and adapted to a changed time. In his main work *Masaalikal Jinaan* (Ways to Paradise), he explicitly requested that one should have a progressive understanding of theology, "Do not leave all advantages of god to the elders, because in doing so you would fall victim to aberration."

The writing of his own textbooks had a second function that was as important: the abolition of the monopoly of knowledge that consolidated the social hierarchy. He had always seen his task in, "Writing books that could be understood by anybody, a prophet or no prophet".

The majority of the population remained excluded from education, because the imported writings were written in Arabic and therefore only accessible by a small upper class. This condition contradicted his idea of equality as well as his understanding of knowledge that was an essential prerequisite for him for the creation of awareness and autonomy. He liked to illustrate the meaning of knowledge with images such as 'targeted approach' versus 'fidgeting' or with the African initiation rites as prerequisite for the transition into adulthood. He also aimed at the power structures with his opinion that religious knowledge and education should be accessible to everyone. As such he dissociated himself clearly from the existing conditions: He criticized other scholars, who served the interests of the ruling classes or who said nothing to grievances as privileged persons in the colonial system. Moreover, he questioned the legitimacy of the local rulers, who came to power with the help of the colonial administration.

The news about the young and fearless intellectual, who championed the rights of the disadvantaged groups in society, spread quickly and had tremendous attraction. At first, impoverished waivers from the North and griots, the singers and guardians of history, who lived on the generosity of their patrons, followed the Murid-brotherhood. They extended their settlements through community work. They carried the message of the Cheikh in the surrounding villages with great enthusiasm. They talked about the dignity of men, about justice and fraternity that concerned their spiritual leader; about modesty and honesty, which separated him from the rulers. Within a short period of time, the community grew by great increase in members in the six surrounding kingdoms; in some places whole villages professed Murid the 'Initiate'. Even followers of African religions, followers of the aristocracy and other intellectuals became members of the brotherhood. For a long time already, Islam fulfilled the function of a silent protest under the French occupying power which threatened people with arrest, when they had the smallest reason to suspect a revolt. Soon, the Murid-movement became the bulwark against the foreign rule.

The growing influence of the rebellious scholar attracted the attention of the beneficiaries of the existing conditions. *Serigne* and local rulers quickly realised that more and more farmers and craftsmen were turning away from them. Worse still: They did not comply with their tax obligations; instead they contributed to the fraternity that strove for a just distribution to people in need. The local rulers, who had been let down by their subjects, turned to the colonial administration with their complaints. They listened to them attentively.

One also became aware of the Cheikh in the circles of the resistance, and the leaders repeatedly tried to motivate him to declare Jihad. He appealed to them to lay down the arms and to 'take up the fight for the mind and the heart'. His followers also urged him to start an armed fight against the French occupying forces. Cheikh Ahmadou Bamba answered to their wish in a discussion group by asking the war supporters, "Where is El Hadsch Omar? Where is Lat Dior? Where is Albury Ndiaye, the last King of the Wolof?" He listed all the kings, one after the other, who went to the anticolonial war, and every time, his conversation partners mention the places where they had died in this war or where they have gone into exile. Then he replied, "No drop of blood will be shed in the war I will fight," and he reminded them of the prophet, who had said after a decisive war that they will now turn to the *Great Jihad*: the Jihad against the enemy inside, which meant against the temptation, the individualism, the arrogance and all weaknesses a person is supposed to overcome. This answer was one of the most well-known passages in the oral transmissions about him. Cheikh justified his attitude in a treatise about peace, *Ihamu Salaam*. In this writing he commented that the colonial power will leave the occupied country someday, but "beware, if we lose the fight for the mind and the hearts, then, we will carry for them on a silver tray the riches of our countries."

What the Cheikh meant with 'fight for the mind and the hearts', one of his most important concern, is that their own cultures and the humanistic values that also exist in Islam, have to be embedded in the consciousness. Like this, he planned to counteract the mental colonisation, which turned Africans to thankful subjects, who were convinced of their inferiority. He not only opposed the aggressive assimilation policy of the colonial power with an autonomous African identity he also developed a strategy against the 'charm offensives' of the Catholic Church, a pillar of strength of the assimilation policy: Cheikh organised popular counter events on the occasion of the celebrations, which were organised by the missionaries to come into contact with the people, and as such, he kept the inhabitants away from the church. In this way he was doing something, which was half a century later called 'non-violent resistance'. Because he attached great importance to knowledge, he made the compromise that the children attend the French school on the condition that they come to his school in the afternoon.

The second direction or thrust of the 'fight for the mind and the hearts' was the fight against the social hierarchy in the societies. He elevated work to the most sincere way of living against the aristocracy that disrespected the working population and abused them. In this context he formulated the guideline, "Work as if you would live forever, and pray as if you would die tomorrow". This shaking of their conception of the world should not remain the only imposition on the aristocrats: In the *Daaray tarbiya* – schools for practical education, the aristocratic children received a training to enable them to work as shoe makers or blackmiths. These professions were previously reserved for children of the lower caste ñeeñg; contrarily ñeeño received a training to become teachers. This profession had been reserved for aristocrats and girls were involved which was also against the prevailing praxis. He declared the local language, Wolof, to the teaching language, and in doing so he created an egalitarian, supportive community that could cope with the colonial everyday life with their heads held high. This was part of the groundbreaking action of the Cheikh. He, together with his representatives, who were sent to different locations after their training, became the greatest opponent of the French colonial power. In the summer of 1895, the District commanding officer reported his suspicion to the commander Leclerc, his superior. He was already alarmed by the situation in the settlement of the brotherhood close to the English colony Gambia and ended his writing with the assessment, "We have to get rid of the man".

On this 5th of September, 1895, Cheikh Ahmadou Bamba was accused of 'preparation of a Jihad'. The indictment alleged that camels that transported weapons, and women, who were preparing couscous to supply the warriors had been seen. The indictment was based on a plot between the local leaders, who feared to lose their influence, and the commander Leclerc, for whom the rebellious scholar was a thorn in the flesh. In the trial records it was noted that no proof could be produced for the accusations. However, the 'activities of the followers were highly suspicious'. Therefore it decided to expel the accused to Gabon, until the unrest, which was caused by his teachings, would subside. Sending him into exile was similar to a death sentence at that time. Nobody had ever returned from banishment to the tropical rainforest. On the 21st of September, 1895, Bamba was escorted to the harbour of Dakar. Hundreds of supporters, sympathisers and onlookers watched, when he boarded a ship. It was the day, on which one celebrates every year now in Touba - the memory of Cheikh Ahmadou Bamba.

His supporters converted their rage with determination and religious discipline into a persistent commitment to the continuation of their community. The colonial power was definitely not supposed to triumph over the master! The suffered injustice brought many new members to the fraternity and strengthened the solidarity. Their steadfastness against the colonial chicaneries and attempts to intimidate became a demonstration of cultural self-confidence; and despite all obstacles, they succeeded in sending a brother of the Cheikh on the journey to Gabon. This dealt a painful blow to the colonial administration.

The administration did not have any other choice than to plan the next move faced with the persistency of the followers and their growing number. Four years after the banishment, the message was spread that the Cheikh was dead, but the Murid-brotherhood remained steadfast and unwavering in loyalty to their leader.. Three years later, what had been deemed impossible happened: On 8th November, 1902, Bamba returned on a ship to Dakar. That he had survived the banishment seemed so unbelievable that some people claim, even today, that the colonial administration had sent someone else to pacify his supporters; and therefore only this photo with Bamba, whose face is covered by the turban existed.

How victory over nepotism became possible is more interesting than the conspiracy theory. His followers had found the only gap in the unjustice system; they could beat the unfair opponent through the elections for the French parliament, in which part of the Senegalese population was allowed to participate. The brotherhood offered to the Franko-Senegalese candidate François Carpot to help him win the elections if he would advocate for the annulment of the banishment sentence. Carpot was elected in April and Cheikh returned in November.

When he showed himself in the harbour of Dakar on the ship's deck, there was jubilationr, as never before. The joy was because of the long-awaited return of the spiritual leader and it was also a liberating expression of the triumph over the all-powerful opponent. This mutual experience was felt as the proof of strength, which further reinforced the solidarity amongst the supporters. Cheikh declared to the enthusiastic crowd that he had forgiven everyone who had done him wrong, and that he invited everybody to his hometown Touba on the anniversary of his being sent into exile.

The colonial administration had no intention of letting sleeping dogs lie, on the contrary, he once again received court summons half a year after his return from Gabon. He sent word to the authority that he did not have time to attend to the summons. The colonial administration found this sufficient excuse to deal with the problem by armed violence. On 13th July, a troupe of two hundred armed soldiers marched to Touba with the order to take away the cleric and to show no mercy in case he refused to come along with them. The fraternity was ready to resist in any way, when they heard about it. They would not stand back and watch once again, the colonial power sending the innocent master into exile but the Cheikh, who rejected any form of violence, shouted indignantly, "I do not ask anybody to defend me!"

This time, the colonial administration sent him into exile in Mauretania. They expected that the man would be 'disenchanted', when he had to stay where his teachers were at home. He would be a tiny light in Mauretania. But the plan failed. The people set out from all parts of Senegal. They defied the desert on camels, donkeys, horse carriages or on foot to support him at his place of exile. The colonial administration was annoyed that they had to watch the way to Mauretania being turned into a pilgrim trail. It got even worse: distinguished Arabic families joined the brotherhood. In the year 1907 after four years of exile, in order to limit further damage, the 'eternal enemy' was brought back to Senegal.

However, this action still did not mean that this was the end of the chase. He was put under house arrest in Touba, the place he had called 'blessing'. In 1912, he was sent into exile in Diourbel, which was a few kilometres away, only to make him leave the 'blessed place' Touba. On 19th July, 1927, he died in Diourbal. His opponents did not want to leave him alone even after his death: After his family had buried him secretly in Touba, as he had wished for, the colonial administration planned an exhumation and the return of the corpse to Diourbel. The fear of unrest seemed to have prevented them from doing so.

What was Cheikh Ahmadou's attitude towards people of other faiths? That is what one would ask today. Several stories are known concerning this topic; the following story might be the most impressive: a local Christian lived in the area of Daaru Salam. He had a particular affinity for alcohol and this characteristic made him an outcast. Every day – sometimes more and sometimes less drunk, he passed by a settlement and saw the Cheikh seated under the big mango tree. The Cheikh was always writing or reading something. Every time he said to him, "My hardworking friend! Are you moving forward?" "My friend! Do you also take a break once in a while?" "Good day my friend! One day, you will have to tell me, what you are always writing and reading, ok?"... Every time, Bamba looked up with a smile and nodded to him in order to greet him. One day at the usual time, the daily distraction failed to appear;

until sunset nobody staggered past him. The Cheikh said in passing that the funny man had missed his daily round.

Somebody said, "Oh, him! He was found dead this morning".

The Cheikh jumped up abruptly. The hasty movement that did not match at all with his rational manner, irritated his students, and they asked themselves what had been wrong in what they had said. He however did not mind them anymore and prayed for the man, as if he were one of his followers. This would have been a violation for an ordinary Muslim. The gathered people reminded him of the fact that the man had been a Christian and not a good one at that. The Cheikh replied only, "He called me his friend."

They were ashamed, lowered their gaze and remembered the lesson.

The Congolese scientist Jean Pierre Mulago writes about the independent interpretation of Islam with which the Cheikh Ahmadou Bamba founded the most dynamic and in the meantime, most influential community in Senegal, "For everybody who thinks about the means for the development of the African continent, it is necessary to discover the richness of the teaching and the work of Cheikh Ahmadou Bamba." It is also important for the US-American Michelle R. Kimball to "highlight the life of a Muslim saint, who led a successful and entirely non-violent fight for peace in the past century". He would have been glad about such appreciation and every Murid would respond to this with the recognition call, "Akassaa!"

Bibliography
Oumar Ba: *Ahmadou Bamba face aux autorités coloniales (1889-1927)*. Abbaville 1982.
Cheikhouna M'Backé A. Wadoud: *Cheikh Amadou Bamba – un modèle de progressisme et de renovation*. www.marjalis.org.
Michelle R. Kimball: *A Muslim Peacemaker of the 20th Century – Shaykh Ahmadou Bamba*. 2005. www.intlpeace.org/lit-Bamba.htm.